Art & Language International

Robert Bailey

Art & Language International

Conceptual Art between Art Worlds

Duke University Press Durham and London 2016

Text designed by Mindy Basinger Hill
Cover designed by Amy Ruth Buchanan
Typeset in Garamond Premier Pro by Tseng Information Systems, Inc.

Library of Congress Cataloging-in-Publication Data
Names: Bailey, Robert, [date]
Title: Art & language international : conceptual art between art worlds / Robert Bailey.
Other titles: Art and language international
Description: Durham : Duke University Press, 2016. |
Includes bibliographical references and index.
Identifiers: LCCN 2015044900|
ISBN 9780822361497 (hardcover : alk. paper) |
ISBN 9780822361688 (pbk. : alk. paper) |
ISBN 9780822374121 (e-book)
Subjects: LCSH: Art & Language (Group)—History. | Conceptual art—England—History.
Classification: LCC N6768.5.C63 B355 2016 | DDC 700.942—dc23
LC record available at http://lccn.loc.gov/2015044900

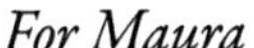

For Maura

Contents

Illustrations

Acknowledgments

Researching and writing about an art collective provides constant reminders that production is always social. With this in mind, I want to acknowledge several people without whom I could not have completed this book. First, I must thank a number of people involved with Art & Language. For archival materials, images, conversations, correspondence, hospitality, or some combination of these things, I thank Mel Ramsden and Michael Baldwin; Avril, Dan, and Rebecca Burn; the Smith family; Mayo Thompson; Carole Condé and Karl Beveridge; Joseph Kosuth; Michael Corris; the late Sarah Charlesworth; Nigel Lendon; and Zoran Popović. Circumstances did not allow me to meet or correspond with Charles Harrison before his passing, but I would still like to recognize here the singular example he provides for all scholars of Art & Language.

This project began during my time as a student in the Department of History of Art and Architecture at the University of Pittsburgh. While I was studying there, Terry Smith encouraged my interest in conceptual art, and he remains a most valued mentor, colleague, and friend. Special thanks are also due to Josh Ellenbogen and Kirk Savage for challenging me to think about conceptual art in unfamiliar ways that proved essential to the directions that my research and writing took. Douglas Fogle, Gao Minglu, and Giuseppina Mecchia were attentive readers of my work in progress, and each provided important guidance and advice.

A number of other people gave me sustaining reassurance, flashes of insight, or both, and each deserves my heartfelt thanks: Alexander Alberro, Cristina Albu, Drew Armstrong, Bruce Barber, Gretchen Bender, Tony Bond, Dan Byers, Luis Camnitzer, Kathleen Christian, Brianne Cohen,

Thomas Crow, Goran Djordevic, Okwui Enwezor, Hal Foster, Charles Green, Boris Groys, David Joselit, Branden Joseph, Grant Kester, Sandy Kirby, Alison Langmead, Katheryn Linduff, Lucy Lippard, Chips Mackinolty, Chris McAuliffe, Barbara McCloskey, Ian Milliss, Melissa Ragona, Bennett Simpson, Henry Skerritt, Ann Stephen, Reiko Tomii, Zhiliang Wang, Paul Wood, and Komozi Woodard. I also thank for their valuable feedback those of my students in Pittsburgh and Norman with whom I have discussed Art & Language as well as the audiences at the many venues where I presented my ideas in the course of their development. My colleagues in the School of Art and Art History at the University of Oklahoma created a welcoming environment in which I could complete work on this book, and I thank them for that. Near the end of the writing process, two anonymous readers for Duke University Press provided invaluable feedback on a draft manuscript, and their suggestions proved especially helpful as I finished writing.

The staff at a number of institutions facilitated my research and deserve my sincere gratitude. Among them are Getty Research Institute, Los Angeles; Museum of Modern Art, New York; Archives of American Art, Smithsonian Institute, Washington; Frick Fine Arts Library, University of Pittsburgh; Hillman Library, University of Pittsburgh; Barco Law Library, University of Pittsburgh; Fine Arts Library, University of Oklahoma; Bizzell Memorial Library, University of Oklahoma; The Esther Raushenbush Library, Sarah Lawrence College; Lisson Gallery, London; British Library, London; Wadsworth Atheneum, Hartford; Schaeffer Library, Power Institute, University of Sydney; Museum of Contemporary Art, Sydney; National Gallery of Victoria, Melbourne; National Gallery of Australia, Canberra; Art Gallery of New South Wales, Sydney; Galerie Daniel Templon, Paris; castillo/corrales, Paris; Blackwood Gallery, University of Toronto; and Museu d'Art Contemporani de Barcelona, Barcelona. Trevor Fuller at Place Gallery in Melbourne kindly made the archives of Pinecotheca Gallery available. In Pittsburgh, Veronica Gazdik helped with digitizing images. Brent Goddard did the same in Norman.

For monetary support, I gratefully acknowledge the generosity of the Mellon Foundation; the Luce Foundation; the vice president for research of the University of Oklahoma; the School of Art and Art History at the University of Oklahoma; and, at the University of Pittsburgh, the College of Arts and Sciences, the Friends of Frick Fine Arts, and a Wilkinson Travel Grant.

My editor, Ken Wissoker, showed an early and abiding interest in my work, and for that I am deeply grateful. I must also thank Jade Brooks and the rest of the staff at Duke University Press for all that they did to make this book a reality.

The dependable support of my parents, Bob and Gwyn, and my brother David is a tremendous source of comfort to me, and it played an essential role throughout my research and writing process. Last, Maura McAndrew, I dedicate this book to you with love.

Introduction

Not quite an art movement, not quite a research institute, not quite an activist group, and not quite a rock-and-roll band, Art & Language is an internally contested and outwardly perplexing entity that has drastically reconfigured itself numerous times since its inception in the mid-1960s. Constant throughout its existence, however, is an intensely intellectualized and deliberately contrarian collaboration involving its two namesakes: art and language. The specifics of these changes and continuities have led the collective to produce some of the most unorthodox, complex, difficult, misunderstood, and important art of the twentieth and twenty-first centuries. This art has not one but many histories that intersect and diverge in dizzying ways. While this book examines several of them, it focuses on one in particular depth: the history of Art & Language's international collaborations, which spanned the years 1969 to 1977 and involved dozens of artists, art critics, and others living and working in the United States, England, Australia, Yugoslavia, and elsewhere. At a time when established modernist and avant-garde approaches to radicalizing art became inadequate to a globalizing world then and still rapidly transforming itself and art along with it, those who participated in these collaborations found in their internationality opportunities to strengthen their intellectual grip on the world and to reorganize their capacities for acting within it by rethinking together what art is and does. The pedagogically and politically oriented work that emerged from those collaborations shaped Art & Language's substantive contributions to the development of the conceptual art movement and the wider conceptualist tendency in art, both of which remain crucial for how contemporary art's history continues to unfold, especially where the theory and practice of artistic radicalism are concerned.

At the center of Art & Language's international collaborations was a section of the larger collective based in New York City. This is not Art & Language's better-known English cohort, which founded the group, persists today, and has been the subject of much more commentary and interest from art historians, art critics, curators, and collectors. The lesser-known New York group was, from its inception in 1969 until its dissolution in 1977, a multinational association that gathered in or near the SoHo neighborhood from which some of the most celebrated art of its time emerged. Meetings took place at Joseph Kosuth's studio, Ian Burn and Mel Ramsden's loft, and Karl Beveridge and Carole Condé's apartment. Those who assembled conversed about art; the making, display, and viewing of art; the attitudes, discourses, markets, and institutions that accrue around art; and the cultural and societal functions of art worlds. Through seminars in Melbourne, Adelaide, Auckland, and Belgrade conducted by other participants, including Terry Smith, Michael Corris, Andrew Menard, and Jill Breakstone, the collective's sociality extended further afield. The work that these people did together and, on occasion, apart from one another found in conceptual art a set of strategies for making art by negotiating its entanglements with language and an incredible range of other things, including philosophy, education, politics, capitalism, socialism, science, technology, communication, music, travel, culture, identity, anthropology, society, government, nations, states, institutions, and history. The group's practice was as interdisciplinary as it was international.

Talking to one another, always including the messiness of arguments, digressions, and lapses into nonsense alongside the highlights of insight and breakthrough, became this group's distinctive mode of collectively directed autodidacticism, and what Art & Language's New York section said to itself during its meetings literally formed the basis for what it sent out into the world as art. The artworks, writings, journals, films, videos, and musical projects forged in this crucible of talk had a few important champions in New York. John Coplans, editor in chief of *Artforum*, published writings by Burn, Smith, Menard, and Preston Heller. Jaap Reitman, owner of an important art bookshop in SoHo, distributed *Art-Language* and *The Fox*, journals that were the most widely available vehicles for Art & Language's work. And John Weber, a dealer sympathetic to the collective's artistic and political radicalisms, showed its work at his gallery, which occupied part of a building at 420 Broadway in SoHo that also housed the galleries of other major dealers including Leo Castelli, André Emmerich, and Ileana Sonnabend. Such opportunities were, however, the exception rather than the rule for the New York section of Art & Language, and much of its work first appeared overseas, usually in exhibitions and publications partially or totally facilitated by its English counterparts or in the places where it conducted its international seminars. As a consequence of this scattered reception, the response to its work has been patchy and correspondingly lackluster.

Despite declaring an interest in Art & Language's various manifestations, the art historian Charles Harrison, who is the collective's most subtle, engaged, and sustained commentator, openly states that he is "avowedly partial and Anglocentric" in his approach to writing its history due to his close personal and professional association with the section of the group based in England.[1] Harrison's focus on certain parts of Art & Language's total body of work yields an incomplete view of its overall contribution, even as his accounts of the collective remain the best available. This bias also characterizes Art & Language scholarship more generally, and with so much attention directed at work that it did in England, what happened in New York—to say nothing of the further international links forged by the section of the group based there—has slipped by nearly unnoticed, leaving untallied the vital role that Art & Language's international collaborations played in the history of conceptual art. Omitting this fuller scope of the collective's work has further distorted its overall reception by preventing recognition of the collective's multifaceted response to art's growing entanglements with the cultural, economic, and geographical aspects of globalization. The small amount of scholarship on work that Art & Language did outside England has not sufficiently rectified these distortions, as those who have written on the collective's New York section, however well, have done so in summary or piecemeal fashion, and no comprehensive art historical attention has been paid to the work it did outside of both England and New York.[2]

The geographical confines of his account notwithstanding, Harrison is entirely correct throughout his work on Art & Language that the collective's achievements (and, it is worth adding, its shortcomings too) have much to do with its relationship to its main historical predecessor and major antagonist: modernism. Indeed, "the practice of Art and Language," as T. J. Clark also recognized, is "directed to the problems of modernism."[3] The legacy of modernism, specifically as it was formulated in the United States after World War II, provided Art & Language with a crucial point of departure for thinking about what art might become when it becomes conceptual. Gradually recoiling at art's corruption by the very forces of modernity that it helped to visualize and so to usher into being, the modernism to which Art & Language responded sought refuge in an autonomy that proved unable to sever at least one of its tethers to the world. Clement Greenberg, one of its great critical advocates, called this insistent connection "an umbilical cord of gold" that linked avant-garde artists to bourgeois patronage.[4] While this tie may have compromised art's ability to contest the reorganization of world power following the war, it also meant that artists could know art as irrefutably one worldly thing among others, no more capable of being disentangled from them than of reaching a dialectical synthesis with them, as those avant-garde artists who were more committed to reconciling art and life sought. Art & Language, like many other artists, recognized that art's insistent worldliness needed a substantially more elaborated politics if the radical impulse in modernist and avant-garde art was to persist. It wagered that conceptual art could provide this politics if it was made to confront the concepts that art worlds impose on art—including the very concept of art itself—and counteract their mediating power by mediating them in turn. What Ramsden at one point called "a community practice (language . . . sociality . . .) which does not just embody a commodity mode of existence" was, in these circumstances, both a transnational gathering of disparate groups linked internationally by mutual interest in talking to one another and a means for conceptual artists to position themselves relative to modernism's complicated bequest by organizing opposition to art worlds in New York and elsewhere.[5] Reconstructing the history of this community practice not only restores a lost trajectory in the historical evolution of conceptual art, it also opens new lines for thinking about what conceptual art did amid the transition from modern art to what is now called contemporary art.[6]

Conceptual art's earliest critics and its first historians tended, in the face of art that so demonstratively refused to behave according to the conventions governing modern art for decades or even centuries prior, to emphasize its capacity to negate. They placed priority upon what conceptual art, when compared to seemingly all previous art, modern art included, was decidedly not. Lucy R. Lippard, the first art critic to champion conceptual art, located its importance in a dematerialization of the art object and hypothesized the possibility that, in the near future, art might no longer have a use for objects at all and could, thereby, jettison the commodity form definitively.[7] Two decades later, when art historians and curators first devoted substantial energies to reassessing conceptual art and locating it within art's broader histories, Benjamin H. D. Buchloh identified its "elimination of visuality," and Harrison invoked its "suppression of the beholder" in staking claims for the movement's significance as a deep challenge to the supposedly essential visuality of the visual arts, theretofore always assumed to be perceived by a beholder.[8] Conceptual art was as likely as not to be textual and to assume a readership. For Buchloh in particular, conceptual art's negativity had political consequences by ushering into artistic practice an institutional critique that has since been widely adopted by artists and extensively commented upon by art historians.[9]

Antecedent to these initial efforts, scholarship on conceptual art proliferated beginning in the late 1990s, with several waves of scholars developing previous accounts of the movement in a variety of directions. One of the first waves provided a revised understanding of conceptual art as art that, in addition to negating much that has conventionally been associated with art, also possesses its own distinctive properties. These thinkers began to assert the qualities in conceptual art that are properly conceptual.[10] "In the broadest possible definition," writes Alexander Alberro, "the conceptual in art means an expanded critique of the cohesiveness and materiality of the art object, a growing wariness toward definitions of artistic practice as purely visual, a fusion of the work with its site and context of display, and an increased emphasis on the possibilities of publicness and distribution."[11] This definition bears traces of earlier thinking but is beginning to articulate a more comprehensive profile of what conceptual art, in its own right, is. Similar to Alberro's interest in "the conceptual in art," Peter Osborne considers "the generic Conceptuality or post-Conceptual status of art since the mid-1970s" as a broad feature of recent art first broached by the conceptual artists of the 1960s and 1970s.[12] This "Conceptuality," which lies at the center of Osborne's account of conceptual art and contemporary art more generally, resulted, he proposes, from the former's effort (and especially from Art & Language's effort) to displace traditional aesthetic concerns with conceptual ones. He further suggests that this replacement attempt fails—or, rather, half fails by not displacing aesthetics but all the same asserting conceptuality alongside it as an equally crucial factor for contemporary art.[13]

More recent accounts of conceptual art tend either to specify the multiplicity of ways that concepts or conceptual thinking come to factor in conceptual art or to call attention to those aspects of conceptual art that are not conceptual at all but may buttress, build upon, qualify, or even undermine its conceptuality.[14] Some scholars examine specific disciplines or intellectual movements, such as philosophy, psychoanalysis, structuralism, and post-structuralism, which either parallel or intersect with conceptual art.[15] Others consider the materiality, mediums, and media of conceptual art as sites where concepts come to reside alongside much else besides.[16] Labor, work, technique, and technology have also been recurring concerns for their roles in shaping conceptual artists' works and the relations of those works to a changing world economy.[17] The aims of scholars working on these topics, however diverse they may be, converge in a shared effort to specify better than before the intelligible and tangible manifestations of the conceptual and the nonconceptual alike in works of conceptual art. Each answers questions about what conceptual art is and is not, and this helps to define the movement with greater clarity. However, the enormously wide range of conceptual art's impact, which Peter Wollen identifies as "the single greatest shift in art since the Renaissance," can get lost in the very specificities of such specifying endeavors.[18]

Broader in scope, then, is the work of those scholars interested in recent art's geographies. They have become increasingly aware of a conceptualist "attitudinal expression" that transcends the Euro-American context in which the conceptual art movement largely occurred.[19] Conceptualism is, indeed, evident globally, expressing itself as a tendency that pervades the art of the world after the collapse of modernism, socialist realism, and other modes of modern art. While conceptual art has continued to undergo reevaluation, other scholarly efforts have been made to comprehend better the conceptualisms that arose, sometimes before conceptual art and sometimes after it, in places ranging from the Soviet Union to Africa and from

Latin America to East Asia, usually in response to local artistic traditions and historical conditions distinct from those prevailing in the West.[20] At the same time, the role that internationality played within the Euro-American conceptual art movement has become a topic of nascent attention.[21] Additionally, the complexities of identity politics in conceptual art, particularly where the politics of race and gender are concerned, have been examined with greater facility than ever before.[22] While scholars working in these areas should be celebrated for introducing greater attentiveness to difference and diversity in conceptual art and conceptualism, "today's golf-size umbrella of Conceptual art," to use Desa Philippi's memorable phrase, is perhaps growing so large as to provide a sort of vague and generic shelter to nearly all art made after modern art the world over.[23] The conceptual specificities of conceptual art and conceptualism are, in turn, at risk of being lost.

Turning to Art & Language, especially to its international collaborations, shows that these two scholarly projects—one that has located conceptual art prominently within narratives of art after modernism and another that has made a compelling case for the worldwide emergence of contemporary art following from a global conceptualist episode—need one another. In other words, both specificity and scope inhere together in these collaborations in ways that exceed their particularities to illuminate much that lies outside of whatever intrinsic interest they may have. Nevertheless, Art & Language does not supply the key to unlocking conceptual art's essence any more than it is the crux of a conceptualist transition from modern to contemporary art. All the same, though, when conceptuality travels, as it does to a unique extent in Art & Language's work, it reveals significant things about itself: its ubiquity, even for art that is not, properly speaking, conceptual; its differences from itself, which exist at individual, collective, local, regional, national, and global levels; its capacity to mediate those differences; and, perhaps most importantly, its transformability, which is where Art & Language raised afresh questions about art's worldly role. How the collective's international collaborations staged the mental and material aspects of art's conceptuality between the various art worlds through which it moved during the 1960s and 1970s is, moreover, a matter of more than historical interest because the way it drew on geography to relate theory and practice articulates a politics of art's worldliness adequate to societal and cultural transformations that are still being brought about by the historical force of globalization and look set to continue unabated into the future.

Conceptual art—whether the kind of conceptual art particular to Art & Language or the many other kinds of conceptual art and conceptualism particular to its peers—is worldly in several senses of the term: it is insistently of its world and not caught up with longing for past or future worlds; it thoughtfully evidences judicious understanding of how its world works and how it cannot be made to work; and it is made around the world and travels well from place to place. For Art & Language, a politics of this worldliness could encompass in its full potentiality the entire range of whatever art and its concept are and do in the world. Its great challenge, one that the collective endeavored to meet in different ways at different times, is how to act in the knowledge that none of its actual iterations can encompass this range in its entirety because each must struggle with the specificities of its situation and other limitations on its breadth of relevance. Worldliness, however vast it may seem, is always partial and contingent. At the same time, the great strength that Art & Language found in a worldly politics is, paradoxically, its wide extent, which can involve, for instance, features of institutional critique or identity politics without ever becoming reducible to them. This is something that Art & Language demonstrated, often through recourse to its internationality, by thinking and acting beyond the limitations and particularities that any specific situation or approach might impose on its work. The worldly, however restricted by circumstance, is also always capable of reaching out beyond its partiality and contingency. By drawing upon this generative and volatile mix of narrow constraint and great capacity, Art & Language transformed the intellectual circumstances in which its participants worked in ways that enabled them to forge alliances across considerable geographical and cultural distances that fed back into its work by heightening or broadening the insight into art and the world that it gained from working in this way. This is not the only way that artists can be worldly, of course, but it is an especially sophisticated, effective, and resonant way.

What this book sets out to do, then, is to better understand what this intellectual and social dynamic was in Art & Language's case, what sorts of art, education, and politics were generated out of it, and what ramifications these results have beyond their own particularity. It sets out to do these things at least in part to redeem conceptual art from accounts that treat its inability to realize the revolutionary ambitions of the New Left as an unmitigated failure.[24] Conceptual art proffers, I hope to show, an enduringly relevant politics that acknowledges the unlikelihood of art's changing the world in the ways that many, Art & Language among them, wanted in the 1960s and 1970s but also recognizes that the pursuit is worth it all the same because in the very search itself can be found a crucial mitigation: what was learned and can still be learned, especially where questions about what art is and does in the world are concerned. This then raises the question of method or of how best to build an argument for the worldly politics of conceptual art to which Art & Language contributed between 1969 and 1977 with international collaborations that examined and contested art worlds. The first part of an answer concerns the book's overarching structure, which is historical. History writing contrasts with the dominant trend in the literature on Art & Language, much of it by the collective's current and former participants and associates, which is to reproduce its manner—that is, to do the type of work that Art & Language does and to do it about Art & Language.[25] While this approach is valid, even valuable, more historicizing of the collective is necessary, not least because of the distance it creates from Art & Language's own modes of thinking and discoursing, distance that provides a vantage from which to specify in other ways the artistic, pedagogical, and political dimensions of its work. From an angle external to Art & Language, then, this book aims to show why the collective's project remains so pressing to those who desire and pursue its continuation in one or another form. Moreover, the story of Art & Language's cohort in New York and the international collaborations it undertook has been told only in fragments originally published on multiple continents, sometimes in considerable obscurity, and never before collected in a single place. To be comprehended at all, it needs to be situated within a more comprehensive historical framework, something that this study provides for the first time.

In accordance with this plan, what follows is not a survey of Art & Language's body of work but rather a selective account that privileges the collective's efforts to think art communally, especially during the extreme, highly conflicted, yet very productive period when international collaboration was a priority for the group. To tell that story is to face the challenge of thinking about works of art that insist upon being taken seriously not only as produced images, objects, texts, or performances but also as residue of a theoretical practice. Art history finds itself on unfamiliar ground here. Its disciplinary reliance on describing and evaluating works of art through visual analysis is not always so helpful for talking about art that aspires to do things with ideas, concepts, and theories other than illustrate, picture, or otherwise visualize them. Art & Language is thoughtful in ways that are comparable to, coincide with, or even compete with art history itself. Moreover, when one of the thoughts that this art thinks is that all art can and indeed should be considered as thoughtful in ways that are not essentially different from the thoughtfulness that attends to art, the unfamiliar ground on which art history finds itself turns out, in an uncanny twist, to have been its own home. And when artistic thinking of this sort also yields substantive reflections on some of art history's most central and heavily contested concepts—modernism, for instance—that are significantly different from those that art historians had previously articulated, the source of the discipline's disorientation becomes even clearer: Its purported object of study has come down off the walls, so to speak, and rearranged the contents of its house to bewildering effect.[26]

Here, it is well worth recalling and reiterating Thomas Crow's proposal that "the inheritance of Conceptualism, ignored if not derided by the majority of art historians, provides the field of art history with its best current resources of theoretical understanding."[27] In this instance, such a suggestion might entail that conceptual art, the very art that can be so inassimilable for art history because it emphasizes art's intellectual properties that exceed its visuality, supplies what the discipline needs to resolve certain of its difficulties treating thoughtful art—and all art is thoughtful—on the terms that it demands.[28] In line with this proposition, the work of Art & Language, a group of artists who prioritize the conceptual in art to an extreme degree, can be studied to better understand how art discloses (and conceals) ways of thinking. Approaching its work with care provides reminders that like images, thoughts are materialized in art; that, like objects, ideas and theories get formed artistically; that, like motifs or iconography, concepts become subject matter for works of art; and that, like art's visuality, its intellectuality needs to be squared with its own historical development as well as with the historical contexts that inform it and that it informs. When art, conceptual or otherwise, is treated with these things in mind, much knowledge stands to be gained, particularly concerning the possibilities for thoughtful action that art makes possible.

In this regard, Art & Language's efforts to rethink through international collaborations what the concept of art is and entails are an especially good place to turn, since, like the discipline of art history when faced with conceptual art, the collective found itself to be not at home in those places that ought to have been proper to it. Its work from this especially mobile and unruly period can be understood as an instance of what Burn dubbed "*Homeless* criticism" in one of the many notebooks he filled with thoughts, plans, and reflections during his tenure in the group.[29] Burn's phrase is modeled after one Greenberg coined to name the "homeless representation" he found in artists such as Willem de Kooning, who incorporated noticeably incongruent figurative elements into the otherwise nonobjective style of abstract expressionism.[30] However, the relevance of Burn's phrase, which appears alone on a notebook page without any immediate context and is, therefore, itself a homeless remark, implies much more than its reconfiguration of a modernist critic's concept into a statement about the fate of his critical enterprise would suggest. Indeed, something very much like homeless criticism characterizes Art & Language's international collaborations from their beginnings to their end.

The word "homeless" implies dispossession, and Art & Language's turn to the critical and art historical medium of language necessitated a concession of visual appeal that stripped its work both of the aesthetics demanded by those who expect art to give itself over fully to the eye and of the possibility that such people would serve as its audience. This often left Art & Language adrift, alone together, and, rather surprisingly, the task it repeatedly pursued in this state was to dispossess itself further by jettisoning its beliefs, ideas, and concepts as part of an ongoing criticism of its own intellectual prerogatives. Even within itself it was not at home, preferring instead a state of perpetual rancor among its constituency for the intellectual and social possibilities to which this could give rise. "Homeless" also implies displacement. Burn, an Australian living in New York, experienced this condition himself, and a similar uprooted mobility marks a large portion of Art & Language's sociality and work, particularly work made in or in relation to New York, a city famously inhabited by immigrants and transients. Many in the group there were expatriates, and many were students who came to the city from elsewhere to learn about art. Finally, "homeless" simply means being without a home. For art, a home might best be characterized as an art world that can recognize, legitimate, and celebrate it. The work that emerged from Art & Language's international collaborations received little close or sustained attention from any art world at the time of its making, and it moved around too much to settle down in any one of them anyway. It was also too critical of the art worlds through which it passed to receive their full embrace. Because Art & Language had no place to call its home, because it was always between art worlds, it had to use its wits to become worldly.

One

A Model of a Possible Art World

Initially, Art & Language turned to conceptual art for opportunities that it provided to develop the theoretical and practical dimensions of its work through linguistic rather than visual means. In time, the work it did with language afforded further opportunities, particularly those of a social kind, which expanded the group's constituency into a large and at times unwieldy transnational association and enabled, through the learning that went on among those who participated in its work, new approaches both to art and to the art worlds where that work was made, shared, and received. Some version of this reciprocation, whether of the linguistic and the social, the pedagogical and the political, or the conceptual and the international, fueled Art & Language's work throughout the period of conceptual art's florescence, recognition, and decline as an art movement from the late 1960s through the mid-1970s. It also proved central to Art & Language's efforts to define its own distinctive approach to working conceptually within an international milieu of conceptual artists that pursued a variety of different and often competing directions in their work.

The collective's internationality begins in earnest in May 1969, when its founders, all based at Coventry College of Art in England, first announce international aspirations for their work by publishing the inaugural issue of a nearly eponymous journal called *Art-Language* (figure 1.1). Not only did this periodical circulate internationally, appearing in art galleries and on bookstore shelves in the United States and on the European continent, the editorial introduction to its first issue, in which Art & Language lays out its initial program, also explicitly makes clear the collective's interest in conceptual art on the other side of the Atlantic Ocean. Terry Atkinson, the main author behind this unattributed missive, makes plans for the future

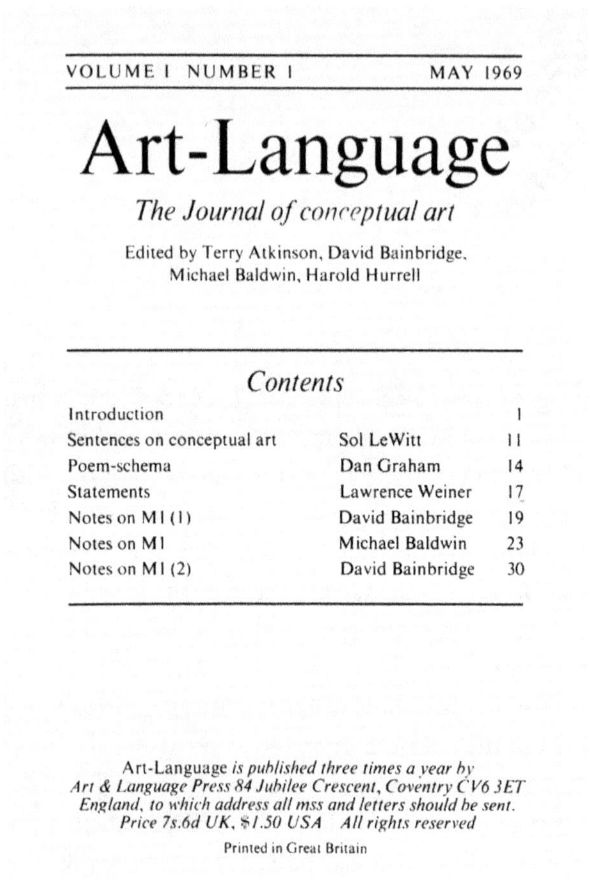

VOLUME I NUMBER I MAY 1969

Art-Language

The Journal of conceptual art

Edited by Terry Atkinson, David Bainbridge, Michael Baldwin, Harold Hurrell

Contents

Art-Language *is published three times a year by Art & Language Press 84 Jubilee Crescent, Coventry CV6 3ET England, to which address all mss and letters should be sent. Price 7s.6d UK, $1.50 USA*

Printed in Great Britain

Figure 1.1 Art & Language, *Art-Language* 1, no. 1 (1969), front cover.

by courting "contributions from American artists," identifying an intention "to furnish a comprehensive report of conceptual art in the U.S.A.," and announcing aspirations to "point out some differences . . . between American and British conceptual art."[1]

Art & Language had already begun to make good on these promises by including in this very issue of *Art-Language* three texts by prominent conceptual artists then living in New York: Sol LeWitt, Dan Graham, and Lawrence Weiner.[2] Atkinson had connected with a number of American artists during his visit to New York in 1967, and these transatlantic submissions to the journal came via his contacts overseas. However, the collective quickly realized that its understanding of conceptual art was not compatible with what these American artists were doing, and it dropped *Art-Language*'s ambitious subtitle, *The Journal of conceptual art*, beginning with the very next issue. The term "conceptual art," Art & Language later told the French art critic Catherine Millet, "was associated with too varied a spectrum of artistic activity."[3] In the journal's second issue, Atkinson complained openly about the "many artists and writers who have gathered beneath the Conceptual Flag."[4] During the summer of 1969, he returned to New York in part to locate other, more compatible contributors to *Art-Language* who might share the collective's primary concern with what "an art form can evolve by taking as a point of initial enquiry the language-use of the art society."[5] This time, Atkinson found lasting allies in Joseph Kosuth, Ian Burn, and Mel Ramsden, each of whom became an important contributor, first to *Art-Language* and, through that vehicle, to Art & Language.[6] With this alliance in place, a lasting New York section of Art & Language began to coalesce, and the collective would maintain this internationality, rather tumultuously at times, until 1977.

Kosuth, Burn, and Ramsden made art that shared a close rapport with what Atkinson had been doing in Coventry along with David Bainbridge, Michael Baldwin, and Harold Hurrell. These four founders of Art & Language were, at this point, teachers and students at Coventry College of Art, and since the mid-1960s they had been making some of the first examples of recognizably conceptual art by writing theoretical texts in a tone that oscillates between academic philosophy in the analytic or Anglophone tradition and a parody thereof. This writing often postulated hypothetical artworks or imagined situations involving art and then speculated about them in detail to arrive at a variety of provisional conclusions.[7] Fairly quickly, it ceased to be a discourse subsidiary to art objects and art situations real or fictive and became itself the main thrust of Art & Language's practice when *Art-Language* took over for a number of years as the collective's main outlet. This was not yet the case when, in 1966, Baldwin conceived of an exhibition titled *The Air-Conditioning Show*, in which a flow of air current generated by an air-conditioning unit is held out for consideration as a work of art.[8] Though an actualization of *The Air-Conditioning Show* would not occur for several years, Baldwin published a short essay about it in the November 1967 issue of *Arts Magazine*, having been facilitated in this respect by Robert Smithson, whom Atkinson met in New York during his 1967 visit.[9] With this brief text's appearance in an American magazine, Art & Language made its first public foray across the Atlantic, though the essay is credited to Baldwin rather than Art & Language, as the group's collective identity was not yet formalized. "Remarks on Air-Conditioning: An Extravaganza of Blandness" speaks of the air-conditioning proposal as a challenge to then-current ideas about the phenomenological experience of a work of art preceding and having priority over other approaches to it such as those afforded by linguistic description.[10] By nominating a current of air as a work of art, Baldwin revealed the extent to which a "viewer" of this phenomenon would need the linguistic dimension of a text (such as the very essay in which he proposed the work) explaining what the work of art is in order to perceive it as art in the first instance—and even then, its crucial component would remain invisible. Language and everything associated with it, Baldwin showed, is as capable of preceding the experience of art as of following after it in the usual modes of reception to which language is conventionally relegated where art is concerned.

This process of working through artistic problems using language rather than visual means lies at the base of the name Art & Language, under which Atkinson, Bainbridge, Baldwin, and Hurrell began officially to collaborate around the time that they launched *Art-Language*. In the first issue of the journal, Bainbridge and Baldwin pursue further the sort of speculative activity developed around *The Air-Conditioning Show* by pondering what sort of art "an alien being from another galaxy" would produce if it had no prior experience of art apart from what could be ascertained by observing the behavior of people in art museums.[11] The alien's hypothetical work is a metal disc connected to a motion detector that rotates almost imperceptibly when in the presence of a viewer, thereby providing just enough stimulation to elicit the momentary cessation of the rather aimless wandering that tends to characterize the outward appearance of the museum-going experience. There are surface-level jokes in all of this about the attention span of the average museum visitor and about minimalist sculpture, but the real target of rebuke is any discourse about art that would assert the sufficiency of the sensory experience of an art object (or the outward appearance of such experience) over a fuller consideration of the more broadly cognitive dimensions that conceptual artists such as Art & Language wanted to emphasize. The American contributors to the inaugural issue of *Art-Language* did not quite share this concern as Baldwin and Bainbridge formulated it. In contrast to Art & Language's work, what Graham and Weiner submitted for publication was not as intensely speculative in character. Both of their contributions can be read like scripts or scores for generating works of art, poems in Graham's case and sculptures in Weiner's.[12] Discursive thinking like Bainbridge's and Baldwin's is not emphasized; instead, the work is largely programmatic and concerned with the role that ideas and concepts can play in the production of artworks rather than in the artistic shaping of theories, though Graham's text does include a theoretical section in which he reflects on the implications that his work has for authorship, production, and other related matters.

Of the three Americans to publish in the first *Art-Language*, LeWitt was doing theoretical work most similar to Art & Language's, but he denied his text, the famous "Sentences on Conceptual Art," the status of itself being art by concluding it with a statement announcing, "These sentences comment on art, but are not art."[13] By contrast, in Art & Language's editorial introduction, Atkinson claims the obverse, "that this editorial, in itself an attempt to evince some outlines as to what 'conceptual art' is, is held out as a 'conceptual art' work."[14] Though the collective would later revise its position about the capacity of an artist to nominate something as a work of art in favor of a more contextual approach to deciding what counts as art, in 1969 its decision that its writing might itself be art was sufficient to provide the collective with a strong sense that what it was doing was not conceptual art if what Graham, LeWitt, and Weiner were doing was.

This sense of difference led Art & Language to New York again in search of new collaborators. On the recommendation of the English critic, curator, and art historian Charles Harrison, who had made initial contact with the collective in early 1969, Atkinson visited with Joseph Kosuth, whom Harrison had previously met during his own trip to New York.[15] Kosuth was, at the time, one of a group of artists affiliated with the dealer Seth Siegelaub that is often regarded as foundational for conceptual art in New York.[16] He too was seeking new colleagues, as he had begun to feel and would state later that year in "Art after Philosophy," his first major position statement on conceptual art, "artists often associated with me (through

Seth Siegelaub's projects) — Douglas Huebler, Robert Barry, and Lawrence Weiner — are not concerned with, I do not think, 'Conceptual Art.'"[17] If Art & Language was putting distance between itself and what was being called conceptual art, then Kosuth was doing the same thing in an obverse way by insisting that the term "conceptual art" referred to a smaller set of artists whose work was, to his thinking, sufficiently conceptual in character. When Atkinson invited Kosuth to become involved with Art & Language, he evidently saw a chance to work with like minds and accepted. Kosuth appears as "American Editor" on the masthead of the second and third issues of *Art-Language*, both published in 1970, and his initial role in this capacity was to oversee stateside distribution of the journal and forward texts by artists working in the United States for publication in it.

Over time, the relationship between Art & Language and Kosuth, who continued to pursue his own work independently of his involvement in the collective, would gradually sour. Regardless of the points of contention that eventually came between them, throughout his tenure with the group, Kosuth made significant and varied contributions to its work as an artist, writer, and editor. His prominence in the art world also brought considerable attention to the collective's activities and afforded many opportunities for it to exhibit and publish. Initially, however, it was his interest in philosophically informed art that made him an ideal collaborator. From an early point, Kosuth was, like Art & Language, practicing art in an investigative mode as a question-posing and theory-positing activity. This approach manifests in a powerfully condensed form in Kosuth's best-known work, *One and Three Chairs* of 1965 (figure 1.2), which uses a ready-made chair to unpack and juxtapose the multiple senses of "chairness" that inhere in representational images, material objects, and, of course, words, concepts, and mental representations.[18]

Burn, an Australian, and Ramsden, who is English, had already been working together since 1964, when both were students at the National Gallery of Victoria Art School in Melbourne. They arrived in New York in 1967, having spent the previous three years in London. Burn and Ramsden were, like Art & Language and Kosuth, inclined to understand art's turn to language as a way to challenge conventions, pose questions, and speculate about answers to them. In a short text of 1969 titled "Dialogue," Burn writes, in a manner that shares much with what both Art & Language and

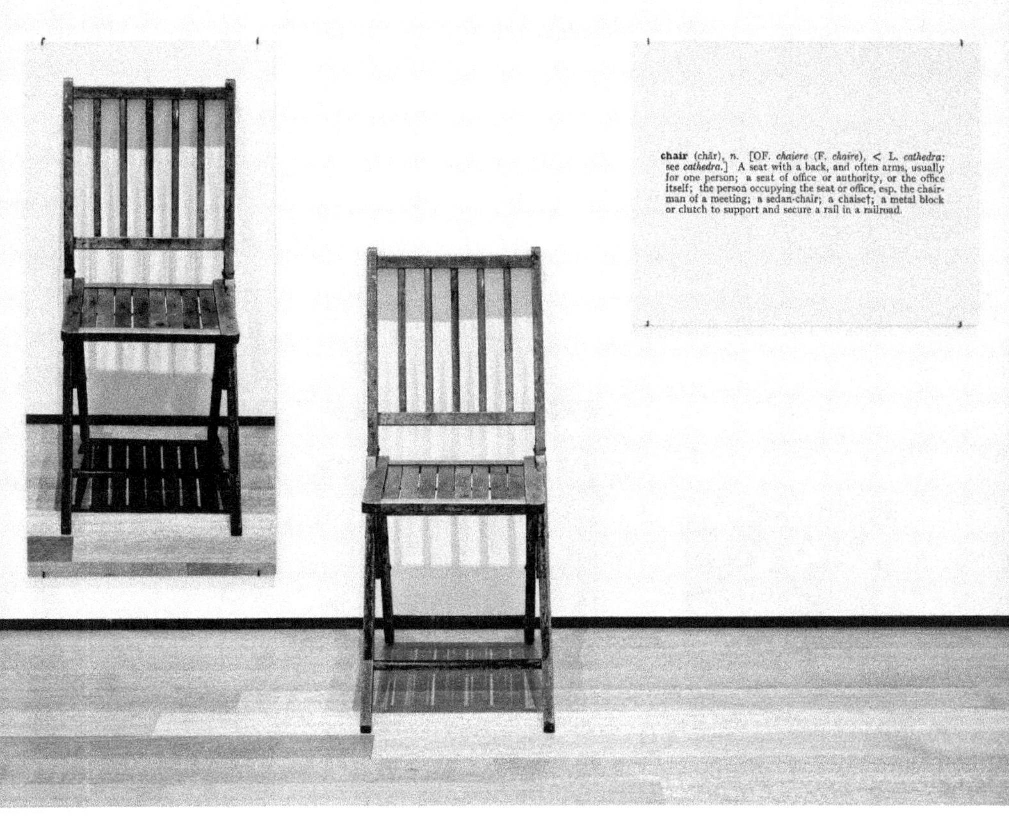

Figure 1.2 Joseph Kosuth, *One and Three Chairs*, 1965. Collection of the Museum of Modern Art, New York (Larry Aldrich Fund). Image courtesy of the artist and Sean Kelly Gallery.

Kosuth were doing at the time, twelve declarative but enigmatic sentences about language and art. One of them reads almost like an explanation of what is at stake in *The Air-Conditioning Show*: "Perception is no longer a direct and unified act; through language it has become fragmented and dispersed."[19] On top of this writing, in the years immediately preceding Burn's union with Art & Language, he too had been troubling sensory perceptions by making works involving mirrors, which were usually framed behind sheets of glass to create subtle perceptual distortions that elicit reflec-

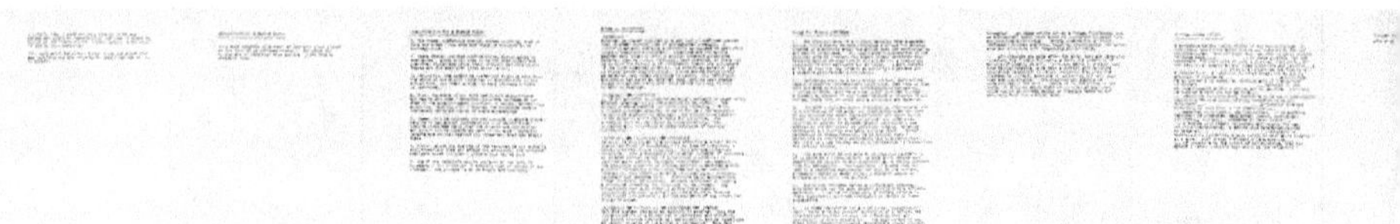

Figure 1.3 Ian Burn, *Mirror Piece*, 1967. Image courtesy National Gallery of Australia, Canberra.

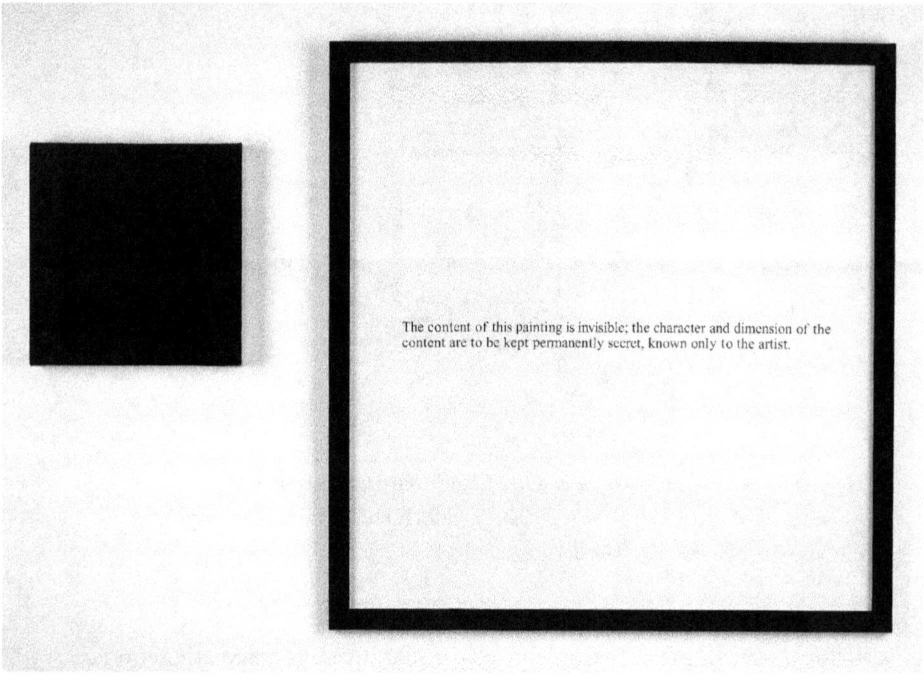

The content of this painting is invisible; the character and dimension of the content are to be kept permanently secret, known only to the artist.

Figure 1.4 Mel Ramsden, *Secret Painting*, 1967.

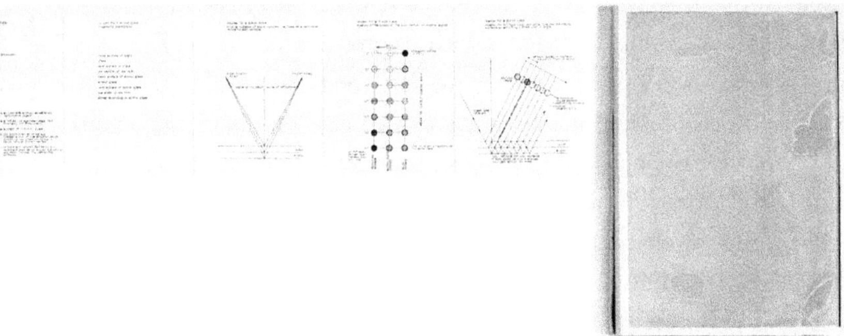

tion on reflection itself in both its literal and figurative senses. One of these mirror works, *Mirror Piece* of 1967 (figure 1.3), was accompanied by thirteen pages of text and diagrams that both explicate how images reflected in the mirror are refracted through layers of mediating glass and theorize about visual perception reaching certain limits.

Ramsden was likewise exploring the limits of the visible and the possibilities of the cognitive more broadly construed in a series of works from this period titled *Secret Painting* (figure 1.4), each of which involves a monochromatically painted black canvas accompanied by a short text explaining that the content of the painting is secret and known only by certain informed parties. Again, the core idea is that visual perception alone is unable to fully access art and that language is bound up with it in fundamental ways. At roughly the same time, Art & Language's English group had, like Kosuth, Burn, and Ramsden, turned to the perceptual and mental paradoxes of ready-made objects, mirrors, and monochromes, so there were direct parallels in their work involving preferred techniques, materials, and forms. In finding these three New Yorkers with such similar concerns, Art & Language finally identified other artists who were, like its original constituents, producing objects that contested artistic conventions concerning visual experience, thereby opening up the ontologies and epistemologies of art, particularly where language was able to lead the way toward an artistic practice based upon writing as much as or more than upon the production of said objects. Owing to these mutual interests, Kosuth, Burn, and Ramsden formed a multinational cohort in New York and Art & Language's first lasting transatlantic interlocutors. Almost immediately, this new section of the collective would begin writing for *Art-Language* and working on projects with its predecessors in England, but it would also develop its own lines of inquiry. The latter would, as this New York group consolidated itself and developed its own distinctive identity, lead it, and not the collective's English founders, to pursue further international collaborations aimed, as this one initially was, at expanding the working group's social size and intellectual range.

It has become common for scholars of conceptual art to separate its practitioners into different camps, and many have identified the alliance that resulted from Art & Language's transatlantic expansion during the summer of 1969 as one such camp. Perhaps the first to do so in print is Ursula Meyer, who in 1972 named Art & Language as copractitioners of what she called, in reference to its predilection for reading analytic philosophy and writing like analytic philosophers, "Analytic Conceptual Art."[20] Of those who have taken up the idea that Art & Language represents a distinct category of conceptual art, Peter Osborne, for instance, distinguishes the work of Kosuth and Art & Language as an "exclusive" or "strong" variety of conceptual art because of its deep commitment to philosophical thinking.[21] Alexander Alberro groups Kosuth, Art & Language, and Christine Kozlov, herself an occasional participant in the collective, together under the heading of "linguistic conceptualism" because their work relies so heavily on language.[22] This pairing of Kosuth and Art & Language, including the work of Burn and Ramsden, is not, however, entirely a retrospective invention of art historians but also the result of strategic self-positioning by the artists themselves during the late 1960s and early 1970s as they endeavored to stake their own claims to the term "conceptual art." Already in the introductory editorial that Kosuth wrote in his role as American editor of *Art-Language*, he contended, "it is here at the 'strict and radical extreme' where agreement is reached between American and British conceptual artists."[23] Uniting around shared preoccupations, Art & Language actively made a case that it differed in crucial ways from its contemporaries, especially other conceptual artists. If the group's English section abandoned the term "conceptual art" when its meaning became, to its thinking, too loose, then the New York section argued polemically for narrowing its application to refer exclusively to Art & Language's activities.

In 1970, Kosuth and Burn seized an important opportunity to express this thinking when they became ghost curators—officially, and in name, the curator of record was Donald Karshan—of *Conceptual Art and Conceptual Aspects* at the New York Cultural Center. The first large-scale museum exhibition of conceptual art in the United States, it featured one of the more international rosters of conceptual artists assembled to that point. Iain Baxter, Daniel Buren, Jan Dibbets, Bernar Venet, and others from outside the United States joined a familiar cast of New Yorkers and a pair of West Coast artists in Bruce Nauman and Ed Ruscha. *Conceptual Art and Conceptual Aspects* is also, importantly, the first exhibition of conceptual art to use the word "conceptual" in its title.[24] That this word appears twice is a loaded decision by the ghost curators, who divided the exhibition into two sections. In the "conceptual art" section, Kosuth and Burn included work by Art & Language's founders among their own and that of the Society for Theoretical Art and Analysis, to which Burn and Ramsden, as well as Roger Cutforth, belonged at the time they became involved with Art & Language.[25] Only three other artists were included in this part of the show, and all had prior connections to Kosuth: Kozlov, who participated in shows at his short-lived Lannis Gallery; Frederick Barthelme, who exhibited at Kosuth's equally short-lived Museum of Normal Art in 1967 and whose text "Three from May 23rd, 1969" appears in the second issue of *Art-Language*; and On Kawara, whose studio Kosuth frequented at the time and whose work he designated "highly conceptualized."[26]

The remainder of the artists included in *Conceptual Art and Conceptual Aspects* appeared in the "conceptual aspects" section of the exhibition because their work, according to the ghost curators, was similar in appearance to what was shown in the "conceptual art" portion but did not partake of the same fundamental inquiries. It had at most certain conceptual aspects but was not, as Kosuth and Burn wanted to frame the category, conceptual art. This distinction is reinforced in the exhibition catalog, which is divided into three sections: "Information 1," "Information 2," and "Information 3." The first section features full-length texts by artists included in the "conceptual art" portion of the exhibition, and the second is composed of quotations from artists shown in the "conceptual aspects" portion alongside what are called, in the table of contents, "reference quotes" from selected historical predecessors to conceptual art, as though only aspects of what these artists said merited inclusion as properly conceptual. The third part contains standard biographies and bibliographies for all the participating artists in alphabetical order. Bound in a gray cover featuring the exhibition title in small sans serif block capital letters and nothing else, the catalog contains no visual images whatsoever. This polemical decision to emphasize text reduces conceptual art to the use of language, and the work of artists such as Nauman and Ruscha is represented not by the images for which they are better known but by a limited amount of quoted verbiage that gives only a partial sense of their activities.

The roots of this distinction between conceptual art and conceptual aspects appear in Kosuth's essay "Art after Philosophy"—the first part of which is the lead item in the *Conceptual Art and Conceptual Aspects* catalog—in which he aligns conceptual art with "inquiry into the foundations of the concept 'art,' as it has come to mean."[27] "Art after Philosophy" includes, particularly in its second part, some of the first attempts to historicize the nascent conceptual art movement and to position Kosuth's account of it relative to his understanding of its forebears. In this regard, he identifies precursors including Marcel Duchamp, Robert Morris, and Donald Judd; early practitioners such as himself and Art & Language as representatives of a "*purely* conceptual art"; a larger group of artists working in a more generally conceptual way; and an emerging second generation of conceptual artists, including Burn and Ramsden as well as Cutforth, who are singled out for developing "a *purer* form of 'conceptual' art."[28] Burn echoes Kosuth's distinctions in his own major essay on conceptual art from this period, "Conceptual Art as Art" of 1970, in which he speaks of a "stricter definition of Conceptual Art" that aims to "devise a functional change in art" and is less concerned with what he denigrates as "conceptual appearance."[29]

When Kosuth and Burn applied this distinction to the curatorial framework for *Conceptual Art and Conceptual Aspects*, a number of the artists participating in the show, including Weiner, Hans Haacke, and Mel Bochner, who had been Kosuth's teacher at the School of Visual Arts in New York during the mid-1960s, voiced discontent about being sequestered in the "conceptual aspects" section rather than the purportedly more authentic "conceptual art" section. Huebler wrote Karshan an angry letter expressing his concerns about Kosuth and Burn's approach, though the exhibition opened as its ghost curators planned it.[30] Kosuth in particular continued to maintain this distinction between two kinds of art bearing the descriptor "conceptual," which he insisted on as late as 1975, when he championed Art & Language as an exponent of "Theoretical Conceptual Art" and disparaged what he called the "Stylistic Conceptual Art" of its peers.[31]

Perhaps the most stalwart critic of the restricted genus of conceptual art that Kosuth and Burn constructed in *Conceptual Art and Conceptual Aspects* is Benjamin H. D. Buchloh, for whom the work of Kosuth as an individual and Art & Language as a collective (he seems to have the English section foremost in mind) is "based on the rather limited understanding of the readymade as an act of willful artistic declaration" in contrast to certain other conceptual artists, for whom precedence is given to "the institutional determination of the object's status" by galleries, museums, markets, magazines, and so on.[32] Even if such an account of conceptual art overlooks some of the subtler ways that what, in "Art after Philosophy," Kosuth calls "the context of art" was already operating in his and Art & Language's work, the actuality is that the collective anticipated Buchloh's very line of criticism and, in the early 1970s, modified its approach accordingly.[33] A shift away from the ready-made is already happening in Kosuth's next major statement of position, his introduction to the second issue of *Art-Language*, in which he identifies conceptual art with "not just the activity of constructing art propositions, but a working out, a thinking out, of all implications of all aspects of the concept 'art.'"[34] Precisely this sort of "thinking out" led Art & Language away from its early interest in the ready-made toward more and more contextual investigations. As Terry Atkinson wrote in a major position statement titled "From an Art & Language Point of View," also published in the second issue of *Art-Language*, "There is an attempt in Art and Language Press work to go for the contextual questions not the object questions."[35]

On September 7, 1971, Art & Language's first solo exhibition in New York opened on Madison Avenue between Seventy-Eighth and Seventy-Ninth Streets at Dain Gallery, the owner of which, Robert Dain, employed Burn in his framing shop and allowed him to organize the show in his adjacent gallery. Art & Language seized this opportunity to redefine its position on conceptual art and insist afresh on its fundamental difference from what other conceptual artists were doing. On display were taped lectures about artistic and philosophical topics written and spoken by Art & Language and made available to visitors as continuously playing audio loops.

A statement accompanying the exhibition and written in the third person but clearly presented in a voice that speaks on behalf of the collective frames the exhibition by lamenting "considerable confusion . . . regarding 'Conceptual Art.'"[36] To rectify this confusion, the statement proposes the taped lecture, which is "as different from other Conceptual Art as it is from painting and sculpture." Conceptual art, it is claimed, "relied heavily on a ready-made technique for its identification as art," while the taped lecture offers "an alternative to asserting in the ready-made context." Unlike their earlier essays in *Art-Language*, which were sometimes put forward as works of art, the participants in Art & Language now emphasize "the fact that their work constitutes knowledge" and their desire "to regard as irrelevant such questions as . . . 'But is it still artwork?'" The lecture "seems to have adequacy simply 'as knowledge.'"

As if to remove any doubt about this definitive turn away from the ready-made, Burn and Ramsden penned an essay for *Art-Language* that withdraws the collective's earlier hypothesis about declaring an article in a journal to be an artwork: "But if one were to hold (e.g.) this article within the standard denotive constraints (as, of course, **anything** may be held if one goes along with the kind of contention that if someone says it's art, it's art) then one would simply infuse it with a status superfluous (and, in fact, misleading) to its understanding."[37] Their new interest in knowledge, particularly insofar as it could enable theoretical work on art that would possess "epistemic adequacy" not reliant upon its being asserted as art and recognized as such, had by this point already found an outlet in a little-known work that Burn and Ramsden made in New York during 1970.[38] Titled *(INDEX (MODEL (. . .)))*, the piece consists of an essayistic text not dissimilar to those exhibited at Dain Gallery (figure 1.5). However, rather than being presented as a taped lecture, it was divided into individually and idiosyncratically numbered passages that were then typed out on a typewriter. Next, the resulting snippets of text were pasted, along with copious accompanying bibliographic entries referring to recent publications in the philosophy of language and linguistics, onto over one hundred index cards, all of which were, finally, housed in a Rolodex. A banal package containing an at times convoluted text, this work nevertheless introduces into Art & Language's lexicon a term that subsequently becomes a major focus of its epistemologically oriented conceptual art: "art world." The crucial impor-

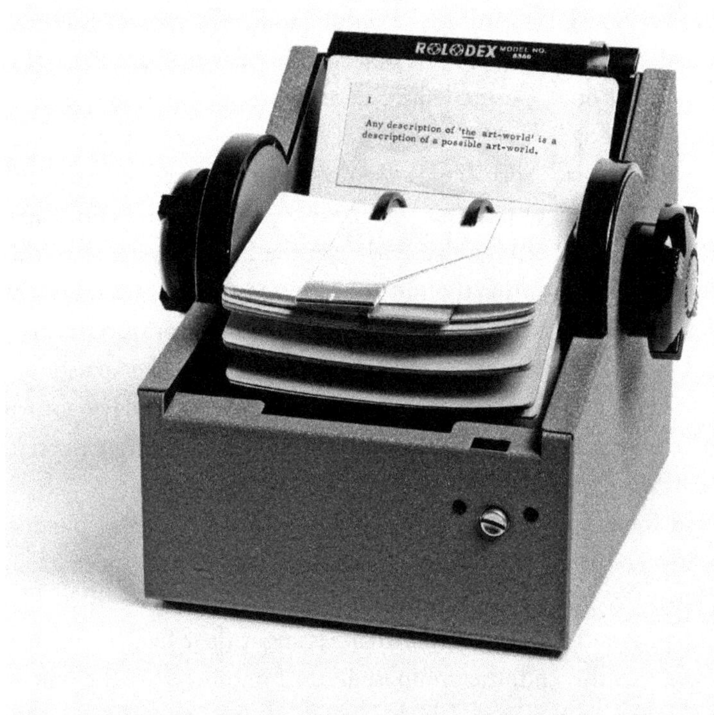

Figure 1.5 Ian Burn and Mel Ramsden, *(INDEX (MODEL (. . .)))*, 1970.
Image courtesy National Gallery of Australia, Canberra.

tance of this term is explained rather enigmatically and enticingly on the card numbered 62, which reads, "One doesn't deal with art-works but art-worlds."

The term "art world" has accrued journalistic overtones that conceal aspects of its more substantive philosophical history. When Burn and Ramsden adopted and adapted it in 1970, it was not yet in wide use, though it began to become more common after 1964, the year in which the philosopher Arthur Danto published an essay titled "The Artworld." In it, Danto deploys the term to explain why Andy Warhol's recently exhibited sculptures of Brillo boxes, which are visually almost indistinguishable from their source material, are art when the ordinary Brillo boxes from which they derive are not. Disregarding the ontological sufficiency of physical, material, and visual attributes of art objects as well as the idea that art is whatever an artist does, Danto defines an art world as "an atmosphere of artistic theory, a knowledge of the history of art" that enables certain things to be recognized as art.[39] Surprisingly, Danto's essay is not referenced in the bibliographical portion of *(INDEX (MODEL (. . .)))*, and Burn and Ramsden seem not to have been familiar with it at the time. Nevertheless, this keyword was in the air during the 1960s and 1970s—it was, Danto might have said, becoming part of its own atmosphere—and his prioritization of theory and knowledge over the visual qualities of art and over artistic intention would have been attractive to Burn and Ramsden, who had grown disdainful of emphases on appearance and volition excluding more conceptual facets of art.

Burn and Ramsden's invocation of the art world in the essay portion of *(INDEX (MODEL (. . .)))* differs, however, in two key respects from Danto's. First, they seek to provide grounding for art theory and art historical knowledge in language rather than letting it float freely in an airy "atmosphere." To this end, they propose in card number 73, "The official language that we employ to speak about 'art' contains an implicit ontological commitment." Second, Burn and Ramsden are as likely to speak of "art-worlds" in the plural as of the singular "the artworld" to which Danto refers. (That Burn and Ramsden were both expatriates who had experienced multiple art worlds at first hand likely played a role in their emphasis on this plurality.) These two differences from Danto's thinking, which form the core of Burn and Ramsden's own initial theory of the art world, posit that an art world is, essentially, a way of talking about art that shapes how it gets seen and made. There are, then, as many art worlds as there are ways of talking about art that have currency with a large enough community to possess some binding power. Tying language and the plurality of art worlds together in this manner provides Burn and Ramsden with a direction in which to continue developing conceptual art into a method for contending with the commitments of art worlds and their entailments for art. If, as card number 1 states, "Any description of '*the* art-world' is a description of a possible art-world,'" then examinations of art worlds might lead to positing them and even supporting them with collective sociality, all things that Art & Language's work took under consideration as it developed.

These tasks would not prove easy, and Burn and Ramsden were aware of this from the outset. Presented as it is inside a device that exists to facilitate communication in the tertiary sector of the postwar economy, *(INDEX (MODEL (. . .)))* exemplifies the "aesthetics of administration" that Buchloh finds typical of both conceptual art and late capitalism.[40] However, Burn and Ramsden's decision to use a Rolodex is hardly an unthinking acquiescence to the apparatuses of the contemporary economy. Neither does it exactly follow the two tacks that Buchloh identifies as conceptual art's most critical deployments of this aesthetic: on the one hand, those practices that "analyze and expose" capitalist institutions and, on the other hand, those practices that "travesty" conceptual art by making a "farce" of it.[41] Instead, *(INDEX (MODEL (. . .)))* manifests Burn and Ramsden's effort to transform what their world provides them toward ends for which such things were not intended. With its promise of easing communication and facilitating business, the Rolodex is far from an appropriate container for a text that is as willfully difficult to understand as the essay that Burn and Ramsden wrote, which does not follow conventional lines of argumentation and assumes familiarity with recent developments in philosophy, science, mathematics, linguistics, and a number of other scholarly disciplines. Moreover, the "contacts" listed in the essay's bibliographical section lead not to a telephone but to a library. If a Rolodex is an object designed to lubricate the sociality of late capitalism, then Burn and Ramsden put a halt to that sociality and detain the user of this particular Rolodex with statements that manifest and solicit a more thoughtful use of language. How to stage such a gesture in the larger arena of an art world—in other words, how to develop languages in which to think and talk about art other than those that art worlds already offer—would be the major challenge that Art & Language faced as its work evolved in the coming years.

The essay "Some Questions on the Characterization of Questions," which appeared in *Art-Language* in the summer of 1972, considers the gauntlet thrown down in work such as *(INDEX (MODEL (. . .)))*. In it, Burn and Ramsden engage in more specific terms with "that system of (public) operations which make up our 'Art-world'" in New York.[42] The word "Modernist" recurs throughout this essay as the name of a central term in this art world's lexicon and a core concept organizing its dealings with the rest of the world. Burn and Ramsden often couple this modernism with an individualism that manifests in the art world's tendency to appear "causally dependent upon the individualistic cognitions of the art-worker and not the other way around."[43] Skeptical of the function that such an understanding serves, Burn and Ramsden posit that the individualism on offer "has become estranged from the epistemological conditions which made it possible in the first place."[44] Indeed, Burn and Ramsden assert that their art world's particular conceptual priorities blind it to its own prioritization of modernist narratives about individual accomplishments. This has, they claim, made it beholden to "the recently manufactured revival of painterly abstraction and stylist mutations of Minimalism," two categories of art that, since the mid-1960s, have usually been discussed as drastically different.[45] However, Burn and Ramsden view them both as developments that extend in modernist fashion from earlier individual artists' work, and they even lump art "characterized as 'conceptual'" into this account as "coarsely 'post-minimal'" because all of it reiterates the art world's commitment to a developmental logic that can, despite drastic differences of form and approach, still be understood as modernist as long as it emphasizes a mounting progression of novel individual styles endeavoring to lay claim to being the latest and most necessary point of departure for future developments.[46] Burn and Ramsden close the essay by suggesting that a capacity to contest concepts such as modernism and individualism will not come easily, as "for Western man, many of these foundations lie in the nature of society itself."[47]

Near the end of "Some Questions on the Characterization of Questions," Burn and Ramsden announce a cautious proviso that "it is obvious that much more needs to be said about all this."[48] Saying what needed to be said, particularly as it concerned the relationship of art world concepts to society, would preoccupy Art & Language's New York section through two iterations of a project titled *Comparative Models* that become increasingly specific about the conceptual proclivities of the art world then centered in New York and provide the section of Art & Language working there with a clearer sense of purpose and direction for its future work. The works that resulted from this initiative are sometimes called *The Annotations* because they utilize a format that is novel for the group, namely anno-

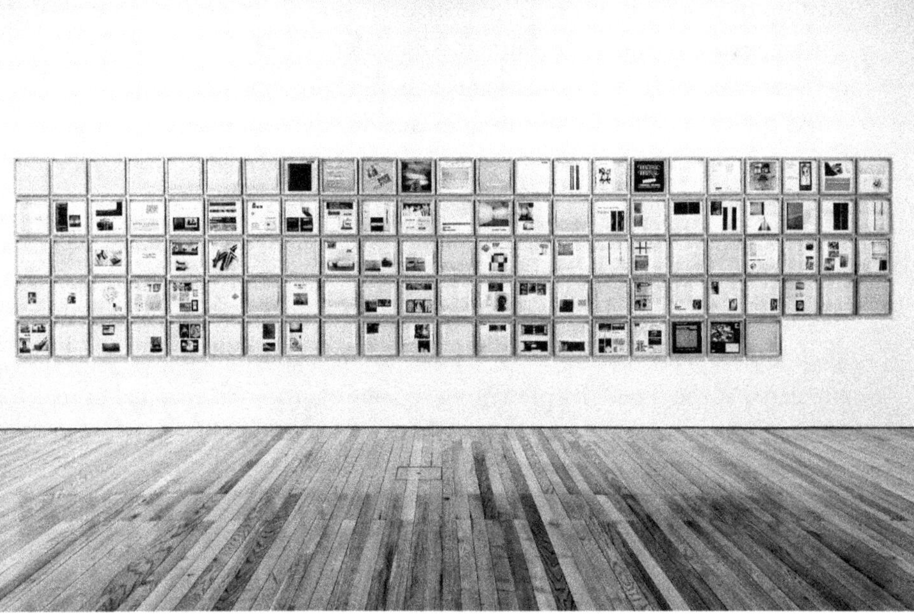

Figure 1.6 Art & Language, *Comparative Models*, first version, 1971–1972.

tating texts authored by others, those others in this case being the contributors to *Artforum* magazine. This methodological move away from writing essays for *Art-Language* and toward a new, annotating mode represents a key shift for the New York section of Art & Language and one that begins to distance it from its English counterparts, though at this point their working relations were still strong. Rather than using language to generalize about art worlds as such, as Burn and Ramsden did in the essayistic text of *(INDEX (MODEL (. . .)))*, or to talk generally about the particular art world with its center in New York, as they did in *Art-Language* essays like "Some Questions on the Characterization of Questions," Burn and Ramsden are now engaging directly with the particularities of an art world's language by subjecting it to annotations that parse its minutiae in sometimes excruciating detail to reveal just how ingrained certain ways of thinking have become and what the consequences of that thinking are. A first version of *Comparative Models* (figure 1.6), which Burn and Ramsden created without input from Kosuth, came together by January 1972. It is an installation designed to occupy the walls of a gallery, and it juxtaposes in a coarse mixture the contents of the December 1971 issue of *Artforum* with typewritten texts coauthored by Burn and Ramsden. These texts comment on passages selected from the magazine, and, in many copies or drafts of the work, sheets of colored translucent plastic or fluorescently colored highlighter indicate which passages from *Artforum* are subjected to Art & Language's annotations.[49]

In 1972, *Artforum* was both the leading contemporary art magazine and, for such a popular publication, possessed of uncommon intellectual rigor, so criticism of its contents effectively doubles as criticism of the highest level of discourse available in the art worlds through which the magazine circulated at the time.[50] By presenting an issue of *Artforum* stripped of its binding and hung on the wall page after page in sequence from cover to cover, as some presentations of the work do, Burn and Ramsden transform the ordinary process of leafing through its pages one at a time into a confrontation with all of its contents simultaneously. This spatial reorganization emphasizes the magazine as a whole and frames *Artforum* as an assemblage of visually dynamic and lush articles, advertisements, texts, and images—a panorama of the art world as of December 1971. The art world here envisioned then becomes the subject of Burn and Ramsden's conceptual scrutiny, which they present in comparatively modest typewritten texts that posit alternatives to ideas espoused or couched in *Artforum*.

In their introductory text, Burn and Ramsden announce their reasons for creating *Comparative Models*:

> The intention is to consider:
>
> (1) ARTFORUM as a model of an established art-world, and
> (2) the present text as a model of a possible art-world.
>
> The possible model is intent on revealing a change in paradigms. As a consequence of this it will introduce the concept of a paradigm shift and not necessarily characterize the form of a new paradigm.[51]

From the outset, Burn and Ramsden draw connections between art worlds and what the philosopher of science Thomas S. Kuhn calls paradigms.[52]

Their understanding of paradigms and also of paradigm shifts derives from Kuhn's 1962 book *The Structure of Scientific Revolutions*, which presents comprehensive theories of both concepts.[53] Kuhn defines paradigms as simultaneously two things: they are "the constellation of group commitments" or shared traits (advanced degrees, professional societies, readership of journals, and so on) that unite a scientific community across geographically scattered institutions, and they are also the "exemplars" or specific fundamental beliefs that such a community shares to orient it in a consistent intellectual direction.[54] Occasionally, research within a paradigm generates results that seem to contradict its basic assumptions, and, should these results continue to prove anomalous, then what Kuhn calls "normal science" — the process of "puzzle-solving" that improves "the scope and precision with which the paradigm can be applied" — can no longer be done in good faith.[55] In the wake of such anomalies, a discipline enters a revolutionary period, the purpose of which is to develop a new paradigm capable of accounting both for what the old paradigm could explain well and for the anomalous results that it could not. Once the scientific community settles on a new paradigm through a complex process of achieving consensus, then what Kuhn calls a paradigm shift has taken place and normal science resumes again within the newly adopted paradigm.

Burn and Ramsden's decision to account for art worlds along the lines of Kuhn's conception of paradigms makes sense given that all three share a belief in knowledge's interdependence on sociality. Consequently, they picture artists and critics as engaged, for the most part, in what might be called normal art. Those adhering to the "ARTFORUM Model" are, therefore, "satisfied with the 'specialized' elaboration of the existing model and are ignorant of any need to create alternate 'possible' models."[56] Moreover, they "agree to perpetuate the established model *as it is*. Their criterion of 'value' is *internalized*: i.e., to 'succeed' within the known model — they thereby lose sight of *externalized* realms of value."[57] Burn and Ramsden resist specialization and internalization because a model or paradigm comprising concepts that orient activity to exemplify them in actual works of art has cultural and societal consequences that deeply trouble them. In their words, "The network of relations, constructs, work, objects, etc., which may be said to constitute the ARTFORUM Model can be seen to be the consequence of the passive acceptance of *reification*. This 'spell' enraptures most forms of public life in our society."[58] Not wanting to be entranced by the reifying charm of capitalism, Burn and Ramsden seek an alternative to the "ARTFORUM Model." The immediate obstacle that they identify is that, unlike scientific paradigms, art worlds are under no obligation to abandon their prerogatives in the face of anomalies. Indeed, because they are not scientific, art worlds possesses a "capacity to 'automatically' characterize all related activities as 'high' art or 'low' art," which enables the dismissal of anomalies and protects presuppositions from being questioned.[59] The scientific equivalent would be a concerted effort by the scientific community to dismiss any science that reached anomalous conclusions as pseudo-science. In Burn and Ramsden's reckoning, the art world persists in bad faith, ignoring the anomalies—such as their own work as conceptual artists—that ought to precipitate a paradigm shift in the way that art worlds talk about art.

Having reached this impasse, Burn and Ramsden leave Kuhn behind by developing an alternative approach to the paradigm shift that would not follow from the appearance of an anomaly but would precipitate the same kind of historically transformative consequences that scientific revolutions do. Against the "ARTFORUM Model," they propose a "Possible Model," which "presupposes the questioning of presuppositions, i.e., it enquires into theoretical frameworks *per se*."[60] Without entirely dismissing the possibility that this model might provide "a basis for sorting out the questions involved in engendering a new paradigm," Burn and Ramsden nevertheless situate the very notion of paradigms—"theoretical frameworks *per se*"—on the side of the "ARTFORUM Model" and envision their alternative model less as a replacement paradigm than as a continuous interrogation of any and all paradigms, *Artforum*'s included.[61] They characterize the difference between the "ARTFORUM Model" and the "Possible Model" not as a contest between two paradigms but rather through reference to the distinction that linguists such as Noam Chomsky often make between performance and competence.[62] The most common example of this distinction, invoked by both Burn and Ramsden as well as Chomsky himself, involves a person who is learning a foreign language coming to master it not by repeating back sentences he has already heard but by learning the grammar and vocabulary of the language to such an extent that he is capable of constructing and understanding sentences he has never before encountered. Accordingly, to repeat back the expectations of the art world, for instance by making a work that fits within its preconceived notions of what art is supposed to be, is to enact a performance, but to have competence in its language is to understand its grammar and vocabulary well enough to defy its expectations in ways that cannot be dismissed as anomalous or "low" and may therefore open its presuppositions to questioning. By doing this, art can partake of something like a paradigm shift but without the return to normalcy that Kuhn would expect. Instead, the "Possible Model" is permanently revolutionary because it "replaces debate *within* the art-practice by debate about the whole practice or enterprise and the ontological/axiological/epistemic status of the practice of art."[63]

Importantly for Burn and Ramsden, this reorientation from performance to competence opens onto the social consequences that art inevitably has because it "seeks out value relations between the art-activity and the socio-cultural background at large," but what is missing from this first version of *Comparative Models* is a more substantive account of the current state of this "status" and "background" that would fulfill the work's promise and reconfigure art's points of contact with the world by facilitating competence.[64] Assisting with the task of better accounting for these things in a second version of *Comparative Models* were two new recruits to Art & Language: Michael Corris, an art student at Brooklyn College, whose involvement began in late 1971, and Terry Smith, an Australian graduate student and art critic residing in New York on a Harkness Fellowship while studying art history at New York University and Columbia University, who joined in mid-1972. With these new participants, Art & Language set about annotating *Artforum* again, only now it was using the September 1972 issue. Like the first version of *Comparative Models*, the second consists of all the pages of the magazine along with typewritten annotations authored by Art & Language (figures 1.7 and 1.8). The key difference between the two versions is that the issue of *Artforum* annotated in the second version is the magazine's tenth anniversary issue, which contains a special section of essays written by several leading art critics of the time, including Lawrence Alloway, David Antin, Max Kozloff, Rosalind Krauss, and Francis V. O'Connor. These essays assess aspects of art practice and criticism over the preceding decade and, as instances of the art world considering itself, are especially useful for Art & Language's effort to think through the language being propagated around art. In terms that resemble

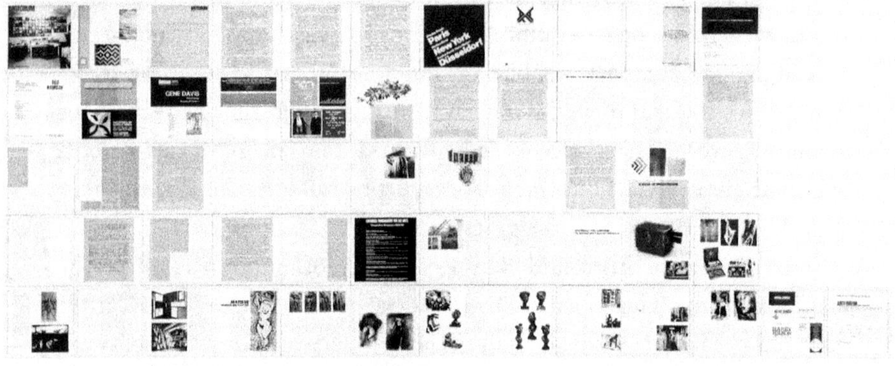

Figure 1.7 Art & Language, *Comparative Models*, second version, 1972.

Danto's definition of the art world as an "atmosphere," a brief blurb atop the issue's table of contents introduces this special section as precisely what Art & Language was looking to disentangle: "a synoptic overview of the art ambience during the past decade."[65]

Though visually and procedurally similar to its predecessor, the second version of *Comparative Models* approaches *Artforum* differently. Where the first version concerned itself with articulating a distinction between what Art & Language wanted and what the art world does by distinguishing a "Possible Model" from the "ARTFORUM Model," the second version focuses almost entirely on detailed analysis of art world language, and Art & Language provides specific explanations of the limitations of that language and what it finds so troubling about them. This analysis enacts, in its own rhetorical strategies, which are sometimes scientific, sometimes philosophical, sometimes casual or amateurish, sometimes jargon loaded, sometimes blunt, sometimes incisive, and always cacophonic, pluralistic, and antago-

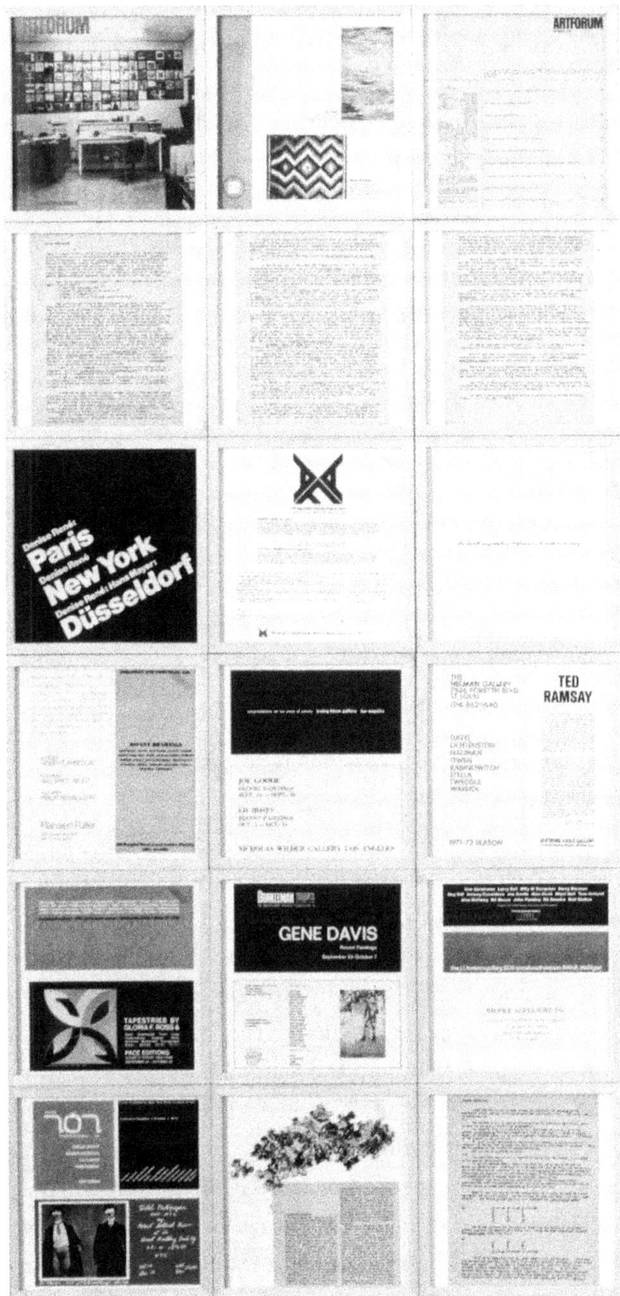

Figure 1.8 Art & Language, *Comparative Models*, second version, 1972, detail.

nizing, the alternative previously relegated to a "Possible Model" in the first version of *Comparative Models*. In other words, the possible, in this second version, is now being actualized, as Art & Language's competence in the languages it has been borrowing from other disciplines equips it with a wider set of ways to talk meaningfully about art.

All of this happens across eight total annotations, seven of which comment on four of the special anniversary issue essays (Antin's is not annotated). The first annotation is the lone exception; it appears near *Artforum*'s front matter and introduces *Comparative Models* in a manner similar to the first version of the work:

> What is the relation between T and T^1 (where T^1 competes with T as the result of criticism)?
>
> T cannot be subsumed under T^1
>
> T cannot be explained on the basis of T^1
>
> T cannot be reduced to T^1
>
> T^1 being critical of T is also inconsistent with T
>
> The intentions of Artforum may, provisionally at least, be taken as T and [these Annotations as] T^1.[66]

Like the first version, the second presents itself as a critical comparison of incompatible approaches to art. However, the relationship between T^1, the alternative that Art & Language juxtaposes to *Artforum*'s T, and T itself is presented as more ambiguous than a strict opposition: "T and T^1 are not isomorphic. The 'concern' however is not whether they are comparable but in the *structure of incommensurability* and the maintenance of incommensurable alternatives."[67]

Art & Language's new interest in incommensurability, which also helps to distinguish the second version of *Comparative Models* from the first, stems from its having read and discussed the work of Paul Feyerabend, whose book *Against Method* belongs to a line of inquiry in the philosophy of science that both elaborates and revises Kuhn's work on the historical development of science.[68] In this book, Feyerabend attacks rigid adherence to scientific method as incompatible with the growth of knowledge, which, he argues, proceeds through the unpredictability that arises when juggling different kinds of thought. Accordingly, he advocates in favor of epistemological anarchy, an idea that held great appeal for Art & Language as it deepened its interdisciplinary interests in pursuit of ways to think and to work that would be unconfined by paradigms, art worlds, or even disciplines such as art. In a particularly concentrated summary of his thinking, Feyerabend writes,

> A scientist who is interested in maximal empirical content, and who wants to understand as many aspects of his theory as possible, will adopt a pluralistic methodology, he will compare theories with other theories rather than with "experience," "data," or "facts" and he will try to improve rather than discard the views that appear to lose in the competition. For the alternatives, which he needs to keep the contest going, may be taken from the past as well. As a matter of fact, they may be taken from wherever he is able to find them—from ancient myths and modern prejudices; from the lucubrations of experts and from the fantasies of cranks. The whole history of a subject is utilized in the attempt to improve its most recent and most "advanced" stage.[69]

Art & Language absorbed these ideas from Feyerabend and incorporated them into its own work. For instance, in the essay "Frameworks and Phantoms," written as the group created the second version of *Comparative Models*, Corris and Ramsden critique modernism in Feyerabendian terms for its assumption that art functions like a "chronological step-ladder starting from Tiepolo" and suggest instead that "'Tiepolo-like art may still be possible" if this modernist teleology is abandoned.[70]

If Burn and Ramsden conceived the first version of *Comparative Models* by appropriating Kuhn's conception of paradigms and paradigm shifts and revising them to help account for the workings of art worlds, then there is no question that reading Feyerabend significantly affected their aims, as the second version no longer relies so overwhelmingly on Kuhn's terminology. Instead, Art & Language foregrounds ideas resembling Feyerabend's: "There is a need to proliferate viewpoints," it writes, "*if only* to combat the tyranny of unexamined systems, our own inhibitions, psychological dogma, and institutional rigidity."[71] Moreover, "we wouldn't like to replace one set of monolithic paradigms with another set of the same kind. We ought to try and address the monolithic system *by competition*."[72] In the first version of *Comparative Models*, the art world appears unsatisfactory because the "ARTFORUM Model" is, as a paradigm, too restrictive and results in commodity artworks that tacitly sanction their conceptual foundations; in the second, paradigms are not as suspect as single-minded adherence to them comes to be. A proliferating multiplicity of incommensurable paradigms sustained in their irresolution now appears to be the ideal situation for Art & Language because it keeps more options in play for theoretical development and practical activity, and these are what Art & Language endeavor to foster by annotating *Artforum* again.

In the second version of *Comparative Models*, Art & Language proposes that *Artforum* is bound by "two or three central paradigms" that, whatever their benefits, conceal the art world's constitutive sociality.[73] Echoing earlier complaints about modernism and individualism first raised in *Art-Language* essays, the collective also identifies empiricist biases in *Artforum* that, when brought together with these other concepts, result in an art world that requires artists to produce commodities presented in the guise of experientially self-sufficient, stylistically distinctive, and historically novel artworks. In practice, making a case that this is so means writing annotations that quickly model an art critic's position, provide an alternative model, and then, by comparing these two models, reveal the social insufficiencies of the original position. For example, Art & Language quotes from Alloway's essay: "'The first exhibition of a newly made work of art is in the studio' is *followed by* this work 'acquiring a record, not simply in terms of places shown and changing hands, but an aura of aesthetic interpretation as well. It belongs to the context of the art-world.'"[74] Art & Language then juxtaposes Alloway's claim, which it refers to interchangeably as "the individualist paradigm of the individual artist" and "Seventeenth Century Individualism," to what it calls both "the social paradigm of the individual artist" and "Historical Materialism."[75] By comparing these two approaches, even in this rough, schematic way, Art & Language shows that Alloway's representation of an individual artist creating art in a studio unfettered by external social factors is structurally limited by its inability to account for the ways that these very social factors shape the studio in which production occurs—even if "Historical Materialism," invoked solely for the purpose of making this criticism, is also potentially, even necessarily, just as flawed as an explanation of how art comes to be.

To make the next move and show how, in addition to being theoretically limited in their power to account for art, individualist approaches to it can also obfuscate the sociality of art and artist, Art & Language turns to O'Connor's essay. It dismisses one passage in particular as

> a caricature of the individual artist as possessor of his or her own person and capacities, owing nothing to society for them. All the features are present: the hostile environment (i.e. fighting the "successes of the 'art-world', the materialistic society" and so on) is efficacious in allowing for both (a) economic and popular success and (b) a rationale for those individuals who justify the fact that they haven't "made it" by laying claim to moral integrity. Under a claim of moral superiority the "purity" of the individual posture is maintained. However, rather than generating a group of morally superior individuals, it generates an individual increasingly ignorant of the dynamics of the very community within which he is enmeshed.[76]

Not only does individualism fail to account for social factors, it also perpetuates those factors as they are by fueling the art world economically and making those individuals who lack a share of its wealth feel morally superior rather than exploited. In other annotations, modernism and empiricism are taken to task in a similarly harsh manner.

The rather hostile language in which Art & Language delivers these pronouncements is a consciously pitched rhetorical strategy. It contrasts with the calmer tone of authority that pervades *Artforum*, which relies on formality and conformity to rigid discursive and linguistic expectations in order to create a sense of legitimacy for itself. This may explain why, of the critics who contributed to the special section of *Artforum*'s tenth-anniversary issue, only Antin, a poet with a distinctively unconventional manner of writing, is not subjected to one of Art & Language's annotations. Indeed, unconventional language, specifically ways of talking about art that are less dogmatic than those on offer in the art world for which *Artforum* speaks, is what Art & Language uses to open up thought about art in *Comparative Models* and thereby stake a claim for the value of its approach to doing conceptual art. While it seems to adhere to the opposite of *Artforum*'s positions — collectivism not individualism, theory not experience, and historical pluralism not modernist teleology — its actual position is carefully and perpetually deferred by its subtle use of language. Close scrutiny of Art & Language's annotations reveals how it distances itself from all of the paradigms it juxtaposes in the second version of *Comparative Models*, even those that seem to resemble what it, as a group, is doing at any particular moment. Reading the text of the annotations with care, very few statements of position are attributable to Art & Language's collective authorial voice. The writing contains many rhetorical moves that separate author from text and deliberately violate the rules of good prose writing: frequent gender-neutral third-person pronouns ("it," "one," "some," "them"), heavy doses of the passive voice, the occasional shifter to introduce ambiguity, and words, such as "provisionally," "perhaps," "may," and "might," that weaken claims by separating them from the beliefs of a locatable speaker. Rather than commit to a position, Art & Language prefers to manipulate and juxtapose positions — to compare models rather than adhere to paradigms. At one point, it makes refusal to commit explicit: "It is to be emphasized that one model doesn't rule out the other. There may also be half-way theories; also, there is no logical necessity at stake in choosing one model over the other."[77]

Henceforth, abstention from paradigm choice becomes a logic — or illogic — for thinking about art, and the question of what sort of practice would best suit this theoretical position orients the next works that Art & Language's New York section would produce. Its theoretical commitment to a lack of theoretical commitment provided much that would guide it toward an answer to this question by supplying an approach to conceptual art that would be abetted by operating in between things, whether in the interstices separating different disciplines or across national borders. Pursuing both of these approaches could, if done in the right ways, provide a wider social base for Art & Language's work that would help to develop further its working methods. By continuing to practice in precisely this manner, Art & Language's New York section embarks on further investigations of art worlds as well as investigations of how its own collectivity does and does not relate to them. When it thinks, whether as a group or with others, social potentiality is recovered from art in the very act of coming together, and the beginnings of a politics appropriate to an anarchistic and perpetually revolutionary art start to emerge. However, this politics had not—not yet, at least—found all of the international collaborators with which to articulate fully the worldliness that, over time, came to characterize it. Quickly, it would become clear that the English section of Art & Language, which had found so much common cause with a few conceptual artists in New York that it brought them into its fold, would not exactly share the interests that those artists were coming to possess.

Two
A Research Program

Midway through 1972, Joseph Kosuth returned to New York from Kassel, Germany, where he assisted with the installation of work by Art & Language at *Documenta 5*, the exhibition that, perhaps more than any other event, announced conceptual art's definitive arrival as the art of the times. What could have been cause for celebration was, for Art & Language, anything but. The collective was in crisis—or, rather, its normative state of crisis was itself in crisis. The work that Kosuth had helped to install, *A Survey by the Art & Language Institute* (now more commonly known as *Index 01* or the *Documenta Index*), had aimed to sort out Art & Language's work to date, to present that work to the important art world audiences that attend *Documenta*, and, in so doing, to provide the collective, still at this point operating successfully through transatlantic collaboration, with a strong and mutually shared direction forward for its work.[1] Unfortunately, *Index 01* accomplished precisely none of this. Following its exhibition, Art & Language's future, even its very existence, still remained up in the air; the audiences it had hoped would engage with its work refused the exhaustive and rigorous terms demanded of them; and the collective had little clear sense of what it had, to this point, accomplished.

An installation that consists of eight filing cabinets and forty-eight photostats, *Index 01* incorporates and rearranges the discussions ongoing since the mid-1960s in and around *Art-Language* (figure 2.1). The filing cabinets contain texts written or published by Art & Language—many, though not all, in the pages of its journal—while the photostats present charts that trace relations of compatibility, incompatibility, and non-relation between the texts to provide those consulting the index with a means to identify a consistent intellectual platform within the cabinets

Figure 2.1 Art & Language, *Index 01*, 1972.

(figure 2.2). The latter component, the photostats, show how the texts are "concatenated"—a favorite term of Art & Language's taken from computer science—to provide both the collective and its audiences with an ordered approach to reading and reflecting on its various and varied writings. (In Kassel, the collective also circulated a simplified version of the concatenations on a poster published by Paul Maenz, who had begun exhibiting and selling its work at his gallery in Cologne [figure 2.3]). As Charles Harrison and Fred Orton describe it, the group gathered together its published and unpublished written work, which was then "subdivided into discrete and coherent sections, totaling around 350 separate items. . . . Each numbered section was then read in relation to each of the others. The relation between each of the resulting pairs—some 122,500 in number—was expressed on a matrix in terms of one of three possible categories: (logical or ideological) compatibility (+), or incompatibility (−), and transformation of logical space (T) which rendered decision of compatibility or incompatibility

(−) B(ii)e 2 3 U(i)b 3-7 M(i)a 1-4 F(ii) M A* E* F* G* H* I* K*
L* N* O* Q* R* S* T* V* X* Y* Z* A(i)* D(i)* E(i)* F(i)*
G(i)* H(i)*

(T) M(i)b 1-8 G(ii) I(ii) J(ii) O(ii) U(ii) H(ii)c

8 (+) P(i) R(i) M(i)a7 B(iii)a 1 2 4 9 B(iii)b1 B(ii)a V(ii)1 X(ii) Y(ii)
K(ii) B(ii)f3 F(iii)1 L(i) 1 2 5 6 A* E* F* G* H* K* L* M* N*
O* Q* R* S* T* U* V* X* Y* Z* A(i)* B(i)* C(i)* D(i)* E(i)*
F(i)* G(i)* H(i)*

(−) B(ii)e 2 3 U(i)b 3-7 M(i)a1-4 F(ii) A* E* F* G* H* K* L* M* N*
O* Q* R* S* T* U* V* X* Y* Z* A(i)* B(i)* C(i)* D(i)* E(i)*
F(i)* G(i)* H(i)*

(T) M(i)b 1-8 G(ii) I(ii) J(ii) O(ii) Z(i) H(ii)c U(ii) I

9 (+) P(i) K(i) M(i)a7 B(iii)a 1 2 4-9 B(iii)b1 B(ii)a V(ii)1 X(ii)
Y(ii) K(ii) B(ii)f3 F(iii)1 L(i)1 2 5 6 H K L N B(i) C(i) D(i)
A* E* F* G* I*O* Q* R* S* T* U* V* X* Y* Z* A(i)* E(i)*
F(i)* G(i)* H(i)*

(−) B(ii)c2 3 U(i)b3-7 M(i)a 1-4 F(ii) J A* E* F* G* I* O* Q* R* S*
T* U* V* X* Y* Z* A(i)* E(i)* F(i)* G(i)* H(i)*

(T) M(i)b1-8 G(ii) I(ii) J(ii) O(ii) Z(i) H(ii)c U(ii) M

10 (+) P(i) R(i) M(i)a7 B(iii)a 1 2 4-9 B(iii)b1 B(ii)a V(ii)1 X(ii) Y(ii)
K(ii) B(ii)f3 F(iii)1 L(i) 1 2 5 6 N D(i) A* E* F* G* H* I* K*
L* O* P* Q* R* S* T* U* V* X* Y* Z* A(i)* B(i)* C(i)* E(i)*
F(i)* G(i)* H(i)*

(−) B(ii)c 2 3 U(i)b 3-7 M(i)a 1-4 F(ii) J A* E* F* G* H* I* K* L*
O* P* Q* R* S* T* U* V* X* Y* Z* A(i)* B(i)* C(i)* E(i)*
F(i)* G(i)* H(i)*

(T) M(i)b 1-8 G(ii) I(ii) J(ii) O(ii) Z(i) U(ii) D(iii) 10

11 (+) P(i) R(i) M(i)a7 B(iii)a 1 2 4-9 B(iii)b1 B(ii)a V(ii)1 X(ii) Y(ii)
K(ii) B(ii)f3 F(iii)1 L(i) 1 2 5 6 A* E* F* G* H* I* K* L* M*
N* O* P* Q* R* S* T* U* X* Y* Z* A(i)* B(i)* C(i)* D(i)*
E(i)* F(i)* G(i)* H(i)*

(−) B(ii)e 2 3 U(i)b 3-7 M(i)a 1-4 J A* E* F* G* H* I* K* L* M*
N* O* P* Q* R* S* T* U* X* Y* Z* A(i)* B(i)* C(i)* D(i)*
E(i)* F(i)* G(i)* H(i)*

(T) M(i)b 1-8 G(ii) I(ii) J (ii) O(ii) Z(i) D(iii)10 V

12 (+) P(i) R(i) M(i)a7 B(iii)a 1 2 4-9 B(iii)b1 B(ii)a V(ii)1 X(ii) Y(ii)
K(ii) B(ii)f3 F(iii)1 L(i)1 2 5 6 A* E* F* G* H* I* K* L* M* N*
O* P* Q* R* S* T* U* X* Y* Z* A(i)* B(i)* C(i)* D(i)* E(i)*
F(i)* G(i)* H(i)*

(−) B(ii)e 2 3 U(i)b 3-7 M(i)a 1-4 J A* E* F* G* H* I* K* L* M*
N* O* P* Q* R* S* T* U* X* Y* Z* A(i)* B(i)* C(i)* D(i)* E(i)*
F(i)* G(i)* H(i)*

(T) M(i)b 1-8 G(ii) I(ii) J(ii) O(ii) Z(i) D(iii) 10 V

13, 14 (+) P(i) R(i) M(i)a7 B(iii)a 1 2 4-9 B(iii)b1 B(ii)a V(ii) X(ii) Y(ii)
K(ii) B(ii)f3 F(iii)1 L(i) 1 2 5 6 A* E* F* G* H* I* K* L* M*
N* O* P* Q* R* S* T* U* X* Y* Z* A(i)* B(i)* C(i)* D(i)*
E(i)* F(i)* G(i)* H(i)*

(−) B(ii)e 2 3 U(i)b 3-7 M(i)a 1-4 J F(ii) A* E* F* G* H* I* K* L*
M* N* O* P* Q* R* S* T* U* X* Y* Z* A(i)* B(i)* C(i)* D(i)*
E(i)* F(i)* G(i)* H(i)*

(T) M(i)b 1-8 G(ii) I(ii) J(ii) O(ii) Z(i) D(iii) 10 V H(ii)c U(ii)

Figure 2.2 Art & Language, *Index 01*, 1972,
detail of wall-mounted text.

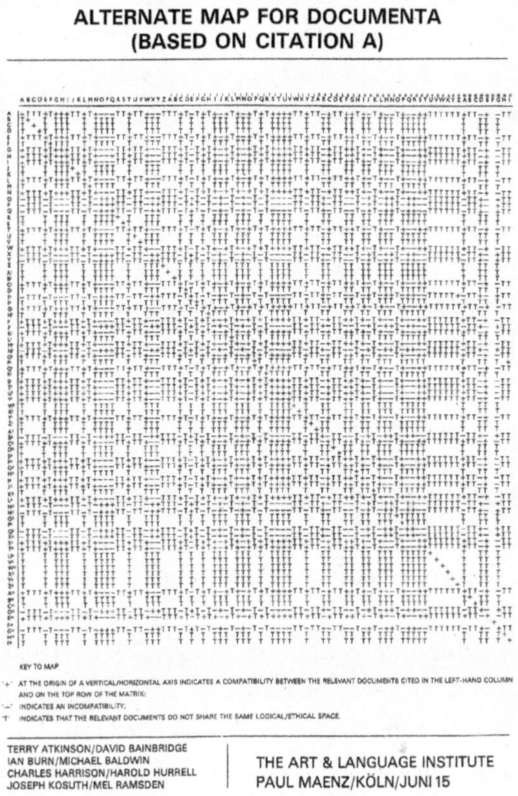

Figure 2.3 Art & Language, *Alternate Map for Documenta (Based on Citation A)*, 1972.

arbitrary or irrelevant."[2] The result of this rather tedious process was not exactly a critical smash. Reviewing *Documenta 5* in the pages of *Artforum*, Carter Ratcliff dismisses *Index 01* as "an unusable demonstration of 'good office design.'"[3]

The name under which Art & Language presented the *Documenta Index*, "Art & Language Institute," was not used again, but its significance for Art & Language is key. In 1971, Mel Ramsden, having returned briefly to his native England from New York, as he regularly did, participated in a series of Art & Language meetings at which it was decided that, in the future, all work by participants in the collective would appear under the collective's name rather than the individual names of its producers, as for instance, essays published in *Art-Language* had previously appeared. In a sense, this shift necessitated yoking past work together to better understand what Art & Language as a collective rather than Art & Language as an affiliation between individuals had done, hence *Index 01*. For *Documenta* and all future exhibitions, it was decided that only the Art & Language name would be used, and the Art & Language Institute was the first form of this name under which a stricter approach to collective authorship was henceforward to be enforced. The individual names of all the collective's participants were, however, also indicated in the entryway to the gallery in which *Index 01* was shown as well as in the exhibition catalog, even though not all of them necessarily made substantive contributions to the piece. Those names were Terry Atkinson, David Bainbridge, Michael Baldwin, Ian Burn, Charles Harrison, Harold Hurrell, Joseph Kosuth, Philip Pilkington, Mel Ramsden, and David Rushton. Oddly, given this new and apparently steadfast commitment to collectivity, the initial invitation to exhibit at *Documenta* was extended not to Art & Language as a group but to Kosuth as an individual. While he continued to make and exhibit work under his own name, in this case he instead maneuvered to provide his collaborators with an important occasion to show what they had done.

In most accounts of Art & Language's history, *Index 01* figures as a summary of the collective's work to date and even a summary of conceptual art as such—it is "the work which put a period to the moment of Conceptual Art in the minds of those engaged in its production," in Harrison's memorable phrasing—but this is not exactly a sufficient accounting.[4] Indeed, *Index 01*'s failure to identify either a foundation for Art & Language's future work or to connect with an audience capable of helping the collective to build a future for itself makes it as much a point of departure as a summary, as its inability to complete the tasks set for it left those tasks to be resolved in other ways. In a somewhat literal turn, indexing itself would be the means by which Art & Language moved forward after *Index 01*, and essay writing for *Art-Language* temporarily took a backseat to a number of other indexing projects that, like the *Documenta Index*, sought to provide Art & Language with greater clarity of project and to provide that project with a sympathetic audience outside of its own growing ranks.

Indeed, a major impetus for doubling down both on indexing itself and on performing the tasks that indexing was to have performed for the group was the gradual expansion of its size, which now included a number of people beyond the initial four English and subsequent three New York–based participants. This growth, among other exigencies on both sides of the Atlantic, also necessitated a collectively worked-out program to orient the work of more than a dozen people who were not always able to gather together and meet in the ways that they once had when the collective was smaller. Additionally, much had happened for Art & Language in England since enlisting its American cohort that made the *Documenta Index*'s project feel urgent. In 1971, Lanchester Polytechnic (formerly Coventry College of Art) canceled the art theory course that Atkinson, Bainbridge, and Baldwin developed and dismissed the latter two from the faculty. Despite this shakeup in the group's material well-being, three students from the art theory course, Graham Howard, Pilkington, and Rushton, began participating in Art & Language as regular contributors. Also joining the group on a permanent basis was Harrison, who as a critic, curator, and editor of the magazine *Studio International*, had for some time been an avid champion of conceptual art in general and Art & Language in particular. He assumed a role as general editor of *Art-Language* in 1971, and joined Art & Language as its in-house art historian. (Kosuth's "American Editor" title ceased to appear on the masthead around this time.) These changes in personnel occurred amid a power struggle within the English group, with Baldwin asserting himself as its leader by taking the initiative in developing *Index 01*, and this alienated Atkinson, who would soon depart to pursue a solo career—the first exit from Art & Language. Meanwhile, Bainbridge and Hurrell also became less evidently involved and slowly contributed less and less to the group as others, especially Pilkington, became more central to its practice for several years.

In New York, Art & Language was also undergoing personnel changes, and by 1973, the group there began to take on a properly communal size and shape to match the group in England and model a more robust alternative to the art world in which it found itself. Eight people in New York participated in the collective's projects that year: Ian Burn, Michael Corris, Preston Heller, Joseph Kosuth, Michael Krugman, Andrew Menard, Mel Ramsden, and Terry Smith. Krugman's involvement would prove brief. Heller and Menard, however, were heavily involved immediately upon joining and continued to participate until the dissolution of the group in New York. Both were students at the Pratt Institute in Brooklyn, and they came to Art & Language's attention after defending its work in the pages of *Artforum*.[5] Titled "Kozloff: Criticism in Absentia," their article condemns Max Kozloff's dismissal of conceptual art in his essay "The Trouble with Art as Idea" by accusing him of deploying a naive understanding of empiricism—the same criticism Art & Language leveled against him in the second version of its work *Comparative Models*.

Though Baldwin provided the impetus for the shift toward indexing in Art & Language's practice and continued to lead indexing efforts in England, Ramsden returned to New York from the 1971 meetings at which *Index 01* was planned, intent on pursuing indexing work there too. From this point forward, he, rather than Kosuth, became the main New York–based interlocutor between Art & Language's English and New York sections. Despite this mutual interest in indexing, two divergent approaches to organizing the group's activities emerged and, eventually, clashed. In England, the formal and logical aspects of concatenating material took precedence and became increasingly elaborate, as in the printouts from the partially computer-generated *Index 04* (figure 2.4), but in New York, an entirely distinct method developed: relatively simplistic and intuitive indexing techniques held sway, and priority was given to addressing the necessarily social process of generating new content to subject to concatenation. The English direction, which Baldwin led over the next several years, resulted in a sequence of numbered indexing projects that bring conceptual art into closer proximity to logic, information theory, and computer science. The work grows removed from art worlds both conceptually and socially, as it turns increasingly inward toward its own formidable and forbidding formal intricacy. In New York, however, a sense of Art & Language's inextricability from art worlds moves the group there to continue its inquiry into art's worldliness. Absent from the filing cabinets of *Index 01* are the textual components of such projects as *(INDEX (MODEL (...)))* and *Comparative Models* that dealt with art worlds. To pursue further the lines of thinking those works inaugurated, the group in New York began to undertake indexing projects outside of Baldwin's numbered sequence. These transformed Art & Language's New York section into what Corris, drawing on the sociologist Diana Crane's research into the methods

Figure 2.4 Art & Language, *Index 04*, 1973.

and mechanisms by which scientists share results, calls an "invisible college."[6] For a time, the group functioned as "a community organization based heavily on (a) the activity of collaboration and (b) the existence of an infrastructural network termed the 'information exchange group,'" but by the time the indexing project came to an end the following year, it had become a looser sociality that blurred distinctions between its inside and outside and between its collectivity and the art worlds relative to which it was situated.[7] The internal contradictions of the indexing project itself would effect this further transformation and open the group in New York to the world in new ways that came to include drastic reconfigurations of its internationality.

The approach adopted in New York also developed further Art & Language's interdisciplinary interests, especially in the philosophy of science, and continued its previous efforts to model its practice on the ways that scientists conduct research while remaining cognizant of the differences between artistic and scientific work. The writings of Imre Lakatos proved particularly influential on the indexing projects that Art & Language undertook in New York, and already in a mockup of the second version of *Comparative Models*, the last work Art & Language made there prior to its turn to indexing, reference is made to an "Art & Language 'programme,'" invoking Lakatos's concept of the scientific research program.[8] By his definition, a research program "consists of methodological rules: some tell us what paths of research to avoid (*negative heuristics*), and others what paths to pursue (*positive heuristics*)."[9] Negative heuristics protect the "hard core" of a research program, which is composed of methodological rules that are not to be challenged through experimentation.[10] These rules are axiomatic and their correctness is assumed even though they are, of course, potentially misguided and misguiding. They simply are not challenged in the interest of devoting research to better understanding what their application can do. Accompanying them, then, is a positive heuristic, a "protective belt of auxiliary hypotheses which has to bear the brunt of tests and get adjusted and re-adjusted, or even completely replaced, to defend the thus-hardened core."[11] Testing the positive heuristic through experimentation suggests avenues for continued research, and it is through challenges to the positive heuristic that scientific discovery occurs and knowledge grows. The success of a research program is judged, according to Lakatos, not by the irrefutability or consistency of its negative and positive heuristics but rather by whether or not it occasions a "progressive problemshift" more regularly than it does a "degenerating problemshift."[12]

Though Art & Language's New York section never explicitly formulated a research program along the precise lines that Lakatos describes, it nevertheless picked up several features of his theory and incorporated them into its working process during the course of the indexing project. In particular, the trial-and-error methodology and corresponding comfort with error that Lakatos identifies as essential to scientific discovery found artistic applications in Art & Language's work, which began to take on a more intensely research-like character. With its expanded numbers, the New York section of Art & Language set off in this direction with a new project that provided raw material for an index that would, in the course of time, come to be called *Blurting in A&L*. Each week for several months, the participants in this project met, usually at Kosuth's studio, to circulate among themselves short texts they had written. The texts concerned a wide range of topics, though Art & Language's own working direction and its relationship to the art world were never far from consideration, and these topics generally oriented the writing. Each text commented on one or more of the preceding texts to form an elaborate web of interconnected annotations in which Art & Language's standing interest in annotation as a literary technique was turned inward on its own discourse, which became the positive heuristic that it subjected to testing. Rather than becoming noisy feedback, the group's annotating brought those doing it into discussions with one another so that their individual assumptions and ideological baggage came to the surface for examination, transformation, exchange, or rejection in favor of other beliefs and ideas that could then be subjected to similar challenges, an outcome akin to Lakatos's conception of progressive problemshifts. This collectively directed pedagogical endeavor began to identify a mode of sociality in conceptual art's capacity to stimulate learning. In other words, Art & Language's New York section began to organize—or disorganize—itself in a manner that differed from the hermetic retreat of its English section and from the art world around it.

Sometimes referred to as "the annotations," though it was never given a formal name or title and is not to be confused with the somewhat more formalized title *The Annotations* that is sometimes given to *Comparative Models*, this project came to a rather abrupt halt after about six months of steady work. The result was a typescript of several hundred pages, of which there is no definitive or authoritative version, as each participant kept a personal copy that might be incomplete and also might include his own marginal reading notes, which would not necessarily be shared with the rest of the group (figure 2.5). Each of the roughly 120 individual annotations (most participants contributed between fifteen and twenty-five) is a page or two in length and bears an identifier consisting of the initials of its author followed by a unique number as well as an indication of the other annotations to which it is itself an annotation. For example, the manuscript page headed "MR 10 see PH 1" may be read as "Mel Ramsden's tenth annotation, referring to Preston Heller's first annotation." In this way, the annotations form interlinked and overlapping chains and clusters of varying length and

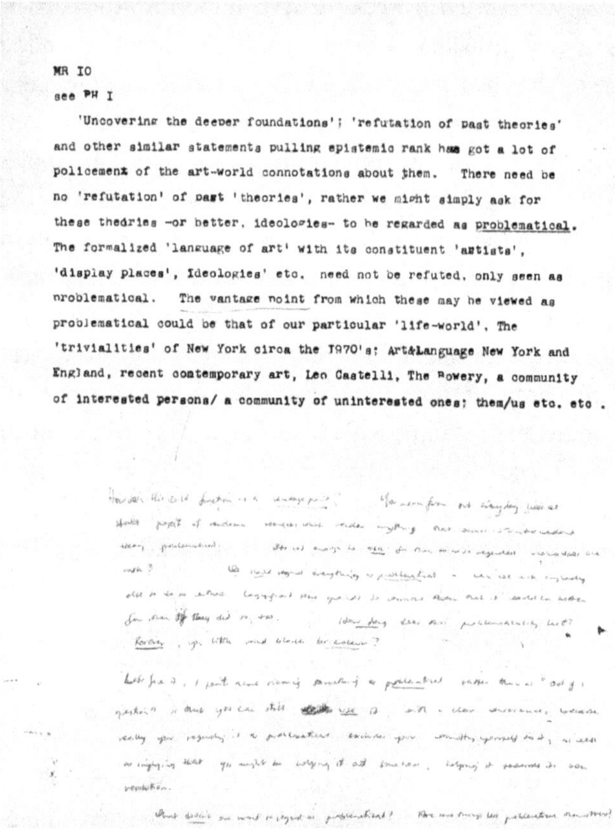

MR IO

see PH I

'Uncovering the deeper foundations'; 'refutation of past theories' and other similar statements pulling epistemic rank has got a lot of policement of the art-world connotations about them. There need be no 'refutation' of past 'theories', rather we might simply ask for these thedries –or better, ideologies– to be regarded as <u>problematical</u>. The formalized 'language of art' with its constituent 'artists', 'display places', Ideologies' etc. need not be refuted, only seen as problematical. The vantage point from which these may be viewed as problematical could be that of our particular 'life-world'. The 'trivialities' of New York circa the 1970's; Art&Language New York and England, recent contemporary art, Leo Castelli, The Bowery, a community of interested persons/ a community of uninterested ones; them/us etc. etc .

Figure 2.5 Art & Language, manuscript page with an annotation by Mel Ramsden and handwritten notes by Terry Smith, 1973.

density. Together, they become an ad hoc index in process and a sui generis web connecting ideas, proposals, and counterproposals that criticize and develop one another as they accumulate.

In a document circulated internally within the group in the aftermath of the annotation project, Ramsden invokes two terms that had emerged from Art & Language's work — "pandemonium" and "going-on" — to characterize the significance of this project as a means to move beyond limitations in its earlier practice of writing essays for *Art-Language* as well as the approach to indexing being taken at that time in England. "In the Annotations," he writes, "the pandemonium, replacing the earlier analytic 'insights,' was most important because it was constituted through conduct. It wasn't existentially alien to the NYAL situation, which is what I felt by this time the essay writing had become. We replaced refinement, improvement, the warding off [of] anomalies, with praxis, the strong possibility of confusion, contradiction, living with the difficulties, it became a 'classroom situation'—we directed our activities toward a community of enquirers in which all share and all participate. We constitute going-on through praxis (the Annotations)."[13] Pandemonium (the word itself originates as the name of hell's capital in John Milton's *Paradise Lost*, which gives an indication of how fiery Art & Language's proceedings were) was dually purposed here. It not only gave the section of Art & Language in New York a distinct and intensely combative way to work together that would be suited to its own concerns but also provided a strategy for engaging and challenging the art world around it. As Ramsden wrote, "Pandemonium in the way we internally abrasively interact, and pandemonium in the relation between us and the culture."[14] If the discourse in *Art-Language* and the English indexing projects had become too strident for him, then pandemonium was a chaotic state—or total lack of state—in which to go on working and connect the resulting work with others who could amplify the din in which it was being produced.

The content of the annotations is as complicated and interwoven as the concept of pandemonium implies, particularly when combined with an unrelenting desire to go on bringing about more and more of it. Among the topics discussed are Art & Language's new conception of itself as researchers developing a learning situation through the use of heuristics; how it is to proceed with this work; how that work squares with the current status of art and the art world, including the linguistic gulf that Art & Language perceives between itself and other artists, especially painters; as well as the implications of Art & Language's borrowings from extra-artistic disciplines. An important set of annotations treats these avid interdisciplinary tendencies, which continuously transcend previous boundaries in search of new concepts and conceptual frameworks to put to use. At one point Ramsden hypothesizes that, as a result of these borrowings, works such as the annotations are "only *ad hoc* stratagems, heuristic devices" that "*do not* stand-in-line with the developing historical stylistic of 20th century Western Art" because their value is less as "products" or "pieces of paper" than as aids in a process of "proceeding" with such activities as "reading, conversing, talking etc [*sic*]" that are not necessarily artistic.[15] Of all the statements in the annotations, these are some of the most provocative because of what they suggest about identities Art & Language could assume by pursuing inquiry unbounded by concepts such as art, philosophy, and so on.

Taking Heller's first annotation as a point of departure, it is possible to trace by way of example how the participants in Art & Language develop one another's ideas in their search for knowledge and arrive at the ad hoc conclusions that they reach together. Heller begins by outlining a program for Art & Language's new undertaking that subsequent annotators take up and transform: "We seem to be faced with the task of starting/continuing the refutation of other theories though not so much through direct attack as through non-interest. Our own theories, however, are and will be subject to constant dissection and should be understood never to be secure—there seems to be no end in that theories may always be refuted."[16] In his second annotation, Menard responds to Heller's first annotation (as well as to the first annotations of Burn and Ramsden and to his own first annotation). He concurs with Heller that Art & Language's activity, at least for the time being, "will be self-referential" but suggests that it might be oriented by "our desire to create an optimal speaker-hearer (audience) context."[17] Within this kind of space, he proposes, the aim of Art & Language's work should be to facilitate "recognition of each individual's, as well as the group's, presuppositions."[18] Rather than continuously undermining points of view, as Heller advocates doing, Menard proposes continuously seeking to understand them better so as to facilitate discussion between people with different commitments.

Smith responds to both of these annotations (as well as to others) in his fourth annotation by proposing something less insular than Heller and less goal oriented than Menard. He suggests that the group "altogether forget that we are acting in an art context" or at the very least "reject any obligations to connect what we are doing to whatever notions we have about where art is at."[19] Only by letting "our artworld connections lapse" will it be possible to "avoid adopting either 'within art' or 'anti-art' postures."[20] He concludes, through reference to the concept of an "eventual context of use" that Burn advances in his own first annotation, with the hope that "our work will 'eventually' suggest its own 'context of use.'"[21] In Heller's twelfth annotation, which comments on Smith's fourth, he takes issue with Smith's ideas, asking "why leave the club, why not change it?"[22] He continues, "I do not think the entailment will foster either a 'within art or anti-art' posture but maybe an *art-critical* posture. How are we really different from any other persons attempting to be 'artists.' At any rate I fail to see how our/any work can suggest its own 'context of use.' It seems as though someone will have to make that suggestion."[23] Over the course of these annotations, Art & Language recognizes an increasing degree of complexity about its relationships to itself and to the art world that will have entailments for future work. On the one hand, it learns more about how limited and limiting both the art world and its own sociality can be for thought. On the other hand, it learns that it may not have any alternatives to these contexts and will in all likelihood have to work within their limits.

As the annotating process proceeds, Art & Language's awareness of these inextricabilities deepens. It is particularly evident in Ramsden's contributions. His tenth annotation also departs from Heller's first, and in it he contends that Heller's ideas about refuting past theories have "a lot of policemen of the art-world connotations about them."[24] Instead, he proposes, "we might simply ask for these theories—or better, ideologies—to be regarded as *problematical*."[25] He goes on to explain that "the formalized 'language of art' with its constituent 'artists,' 'display places,' 'ideologies' etc. need not be refuted, only seen as problematical," and, moreover, that "the vantage point from which these may be viewed as problematical could be that of our particular 'life-world,'" which he qualifies as "the 'trivialities' of New York circa the 1970s, Art & Language New York and England, recent contemporary art, Leo Castelli, The Bowery, a community of interested persons/a community of uninterested ones, them/us etc. etc."[26] "Problematical" is a new term in Art & Language's discourse. Ramsden borrows it from the work of Louis Althusser, who defines a "problematic" as "the constitutive unity of the effective thoughts that make up the domain of the existing *ideological field* with which a particular author must settle accounts in his own thought."[27] Having introduced this term into Art & Language's discourse, Ramsden links Art & Language's activity to it and, thereby, to a broader world of possibilities: "Speaking of *problematic Art & Language* is probably to refer more to [the] practico-social than the theoretical. That is, you speak of the ideological or the 'lived' relationship between 'our work' and 'the world.' This means you don't consider your 'work' outside of the problematic, or outside a relation with the world."[28]

The cessation of annotating shortly after the coinage of "problematic Art & Language" was, for Ramsden, a "way of preventing that split between 'talking in the pub,' 'reading,' and 'work.'"[29] It also corresponded to a search for practical ways to connect Art & Language's intellectual work to an audience larger than the immediate participants in the group. Annotations circulated within a small community could not accomplish this, and so another format would have to be found. The annotations had functioned for their writers as components of a learning environment in which they could collectively work out a purpose for their continuing to work together. Annotating genuinely helped them to identify pandemonium as both method and goal and to explore its workings, but the annotations were, when compared to the active environment in which they were created, rather lifeless documents of disorder that did little to re-create the intellectually riotous conditions in which they were produced. Shortly after the process of annotating stopped, then, a new project was quickly launched to reconfigure the text of the annotations into a livelier work that presents readers with situations not dissimilar to those Art & Language encountered during the process of annotating, thereby creating, even for an audience of one, a decidedly social situation in which discourse might appear problematic and pandemonium might go on. Titled *Blurting in A&L* (though also referred to as the Handbook), the resulting work is an artist's book that contains an introductory essay by Ramsden and Corris as well as 408 "blurts"—short statements presented without much immediate contextualization—extracted from the annotations and reorganized into a new whole.[30]

Copublished in 1973 by Art & Language Press and the Nova Scotia College of Art, *Blurting in A&L* is a soft-cover, staple-bound pamphlet of ninety-two pages that measures nine by six inches. On its front cover, printed diagonally from lower left to upper right, is a block of text that serves as a preface to the contents inside (figure 2.6). This text describes the book as "an index of blurts and their concatenations (the Handbook)," which, moreover, "constitutes a problematic; that is, you can't (at least not without deliberation) ignore possible pathways without losing embeddedness (ideolects); deliberation (here, the issue of going-on becomes a

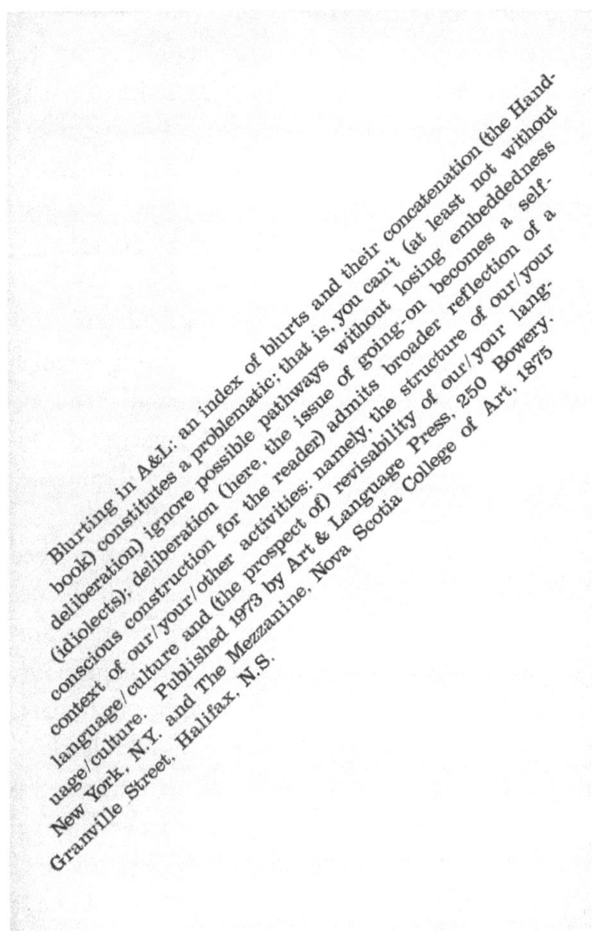

Figure 2.6 Art & Language, *Blurting in A&L*, 1973, front cover.

self-conscious construction for the reader) admits broader reflection of a context of our/your/other activities: namely, the structure of our/your language/culture and (the prospect of) revisability of our/your language/culture."[31] The use of a forward slash to simultaneously separate and join the words "our" and "your" as "our/your" implicates the reader of *Blurting in A&L* as a participant in Art & Language's work, and this helps to assuage concerns that its discourse remains closed to nonparticipants. Situating the work's impact within the broader "language/culture"—also conjoined and disjoined by a forward slash to implicate each in the other—that Art &

Language shares with its audience further ensures this. That the work was published as a mass-produced and inexpensive artist's book — a first for the New York section of the collective — also indicates its desire to reach a larger audience, which copublishing with the Nova Scotia College of Art, at the time an important press for artists' books, enabled.[32] Indeed, *Blurting in A&L* had wider distribution than any work Art & Language's New York section had previously done independently of its English collaborators.

The editorial process by which the annotations became *Blurting in A&L* was largely the work of Ramsden and Corris, although the process was discussed openly with the group during an April 13, 1973, meeting at which seven of the eight participants in the annotations were present. The transcript of this meeting, like most transcripts of Art & Language's discussions, does not indicate who is speaking so as to downplay the importance of individual contributions in favor of a collective and collaborative process, though it is safe to infer that the propositions about how to proceed with the editorial process are Ramsden's, given Corris's indicated absence from the meeting and the leading role that Ramsden took both in authoring *Blurting in A&L*'s introduction and in editing the work. He proposes, "We were thinking that perhaps what we would do would be not to make an index and include the annotations but instead we would compile a kind of glossary."[33] Ramsden further suggests that "we go through the annotations/transcript and we pick out key words and phrases" that would then serve as the basis for organizing an alphabetical list of the appearance of these terms in the text of the annotations.[34] The final result would be "a kind of combination glossary/dictionary/vocabulary list."[35]

Ultimately, when Ramsden and Corris edited *Blurting in A&L*, they incorporated aspects of this proposal but the work, as indicated on its front cover, remained an index of a sort, although a very different sort from what Art & Language was doing contemporaneously in England. To pull the contents together, they devised 108 "subject-headings or categories" drawn from the text of the annotations into which they sorted each of the 408 blurts they excerpted from it, and the keywords they chose read like a list of the concepts that preoccupied Art & Language during the previous six months.[36] They also created two "arrays" for each blurt: an "→" array that links each blurt to other blurts that follow more or less logically from it, and an "&" array that links each blurt to other blurts that are more loosely connected or part of a broader context for continuing with the reading process in a new direction. As Ramsden and Corris explain, "After our 400 odd blurts there are two possible relations to, potentially, every other single blurt. . . . The first relation is a '→.' There is also a '&.' . . . If you go from one blurt and you read into the '→' array then you are proceeding with a strong context. If you go into the '&' array then you are going into a weaker context."[37] Reading, then, would be a process of building up contexts and coming to see them from outside themselves just as Art & Language had done in working together on the annotations.

While these categories and arrays impose a structure on the blurts and on how a reader is meant to read them, Ramsden and Corris stress, "We could just as well call the 108 subject-headings 'user oriented landmarks.'"[38] Like landmarks guiding a traveler, the subject headings lead the reader through *Blurting in A&L* by offering a sense of direction without prescribing a path to take or stipulating much detail about what is to be found at a potential destination, and it is here that *Blurting in A&L* most noticeably differs from the annotations in structural terms. The annotations are organized chronologically as a series of overlapping sequences, which the reader is to follow in order to track the development of Art & Language's conversations. *Blurting in A&L* is not organized in such a predetermined fashion but instead anticipates the relative openness of hypertext. The alphabetical ordering of the blurts according to subject headings is arbitrary, and the reader is free to pick any of the 408 blurts as a valid starting point for entering the text. As Ramsden and Corris put the matter, "There are no strictly determined pathways, all you get is a set of possible next steps."[39] To read *Blurting in A&L* is, then, to create rather than trace pathways by reading blurts directly connected by the "→" symbol. When readers desire to exit a pathway they have created, they may read into the broader context of the "&" symbol, which terminates one pathway and opens another. It is, crucially, possible to create pathways that Art & Language could not have anticipated, and this also distinguishes *Blurting in A&L* sharply from the annotations as well as from *Index 01*, both of which provided a finite if large, even very large, set of relations between the items being indexed.

Following an example of this editorial protocol will reveal more about how *Blurting in A&L* works in practice. The fifty-fifth blurt is on the subject of the art world. It contains three sentences drawn from the annota-

& Anthropology 22, 23; Art 30, 31; Art-criticism 41; Collaboration 94; Context 100; Formalization 133; Historical reconstruction 161; Indeterminacy 176; Language 199; Radical 303; Reconstruction 307;

53 ART, WORK OF The claim for the primacy of the activity of making over any form of theorizing which could be brought to bear on it reveals the depth of Barnett Newman's claim for the autonomy of art-making.
→ Anomalies 20; Anthropology 25; Art, anthropologized 35; Art-community 37; Art-enquiry 46; Artist 48; Collaboration 93; Painting 254, 255; Philosophy 263; Positivism 271; Responsibility 312; Translation 359; Work 389;
& A priori 26; Art 29, 34; Art-criticism 44, 45; Art-world 55; Autonomy 58, 59, 60, 62; Context 105; Ideology 174; Painting 253;

54 ART, WORK OF Challenging habit and reflection is surely not limited to categorically ambiguous art. Rather, categorically ambiguous art forces labyrinthine ruminations about 'art', the 'category' art, the boundaries of art, art's 'nature' etc. —too often only this sort of art-bound reflection.
→ Ambiguity 15, 16; Categorical scheme 82; Certainty 84; Learning 213; Translation 363;
& Ambiguity 9, 12, 13; Art 32; Certainty 89; Education 121; Ideology 174; Opportunism 250; Opportunist A & L 251; Pragmatics 276; Work 395;

55 ART WORLD Critic, author, artist, enquirer, audience, should have the same status/ responsibilities. We still have the old 'meaningless' art blik about everything following from the natural creative magic of the artist. You can't accept the artist/ critic distinction anymore than you can glibly accept the theory/ practice distinction.
→ Collaboration 93, 94; Conversation 110; Meaning 235; Problematic 284, 286; Proceeding 292; Responsibility 311;
& Ambiguity 15; A priori 27; Art-criticism 39; Art-enquiry 46; Artist 48; Context 105; Conversational matrix 117; Ideology 170; Trivialities 369; Work 395;

56 AUTONOMY We should reject certain considerations on the basis of their being irrelevant to our context of discourse.
→ Alternatives 2; Ambiguity 9; Anomalies 20; Autonomy 57, 58; Formalization 134; Learning 212, 213; Radical 303; Translation 363; Work, pragmatics of 408;
& Ambiguity 4; A priori 26; Art, work of 54; Categorical scheme 82; Education 121; Falsification 131; Ideology 174;

57 AUTONOMY Calling an ideology autonomous implies that relevancy judgements can be made unambiguously. But what about 'provisionally autonomous ideology'?
→ Autonomy 56, 59, 61; Certainty 84; Ideology 164, 165, 167; Information retrieval system 180; Pragmatics 276; Relevance 309;
& Ambiguity 9, 11; Art 29; Art-enquiry 46; Context 95; Experience 123; Heuristic 139; Learning 213; Opportunism 246, 250;

58 AUTONOMY Husserl characterizes autonomy as objectivism. Science

30

has developed at a fantastic rate but has detached itself from the soil which originally gave it meaning. It ignores the trivial truths of the Lebenswelt.
→ Autonomy 60; Collaboration 93; Conversational matrix 117; Lebenswelt 217; Philosophy 264; Positivism 271; Pragmatics 276; Proceeding 293; Surface-structure 336; Trivialities 368, 369; Work 398;
& Art-criticism 42; Certainty 86, 89; Knowledge 192; Pragmatics 278; Responsibility 312;

59 AUTONOMY The difficulty with a provisional autonomy is that one could claim autonomy for one's acts (when you don't want to admit external critiques, etc.) and drop autonomy when the critiques are not challenging. Autonomy is not something that you can 'take' or 'leave'.
→ Autonomy 56, 57, 61; Ideology 167;
& Beliefs 67; Blik 75; Categorical scheme 81; Heuristic 137; Pragmatics 276; Responsibility 312; Theory 344; Work 387;

60 AUTONOMY The scientist does not ask himself about the historical presuppositions of his work while working. He takes the trivialities which he lives and works with (his Lebenswelt) for granted. Husserl has said that you can't ignore these trivialities if you want to understand the meaning of science.
→ Anthropology 25; Art-community 37; Autonomy 58; Ideology 170; Learning 205; Lebenswelt 217, 218; Philosophy 263; Positivism 271; Proceeding 293; Reading 306; Responsibility 311; Work 394;
& Art-criticism 45; Art, work of 53; Certainty 87; Education 121; Historical reconstruction 161; Knowledge 192; Translation 364; Work 378;

61 AUTONOMY It is clear that we utilize methodological autonomy. That is, we do not talk to 'just anybody'. It is interesting to examine this fact with respect to the notions of specialization, individuality and 'originality' that appear in art.
→ Autonomy 56, 58; Ideology 170, 174; Philosophy 263; Positivism 271; Reading 306; Specialization 325;
& Anomalies 20; A priori 26; Certainty 84; Collaboration 93; Radical 303; Translation 358; Trivialities 368, 369;

62 AUTONOMY Autonomy has been a condition of art's ideology. An art without autonomy would be an ideologically different art.
→ Autonomy 60; Blik 75; Historicism 162; Ideology 171;
& Annotating 19; Art, anthropologized 35; Art-community 37; Ideology 167; Painting 254, 255; Pragmatics 276, 277; Problematic 286; Radical 303; Work 403;

63 BELIEFS It is proper to say that some of our beliefs are fluctuating; they are neither as 'fixed' nor as 'passive' as may seem at first.
→ Conversational matrix 115; Pragmatics 276;
& Ambiguity 3; Belief 69; Blik 75; Certainty 90; Context 95; Ideology 174; Learning 205;

64 BELIEFS In some cases there are misunderstandings based more on the reaction of the 'hearer' to a statement, in conjunction with his/ her cherished beliefs, than those based on a professed ig-

31

Figure 2.7 Art & Language, *Blurting in A&L*, 1973, pp. 30 and 31.

→ Certainty 84, 85, 86; Surface-structure 334, 339; Work 394;
& Ambiguity 13; Annotating 17; Art, anthropologized 35; Autonomy 56; Beliefs 70, 71; Context 99; Conversational matrix 111, 115, 117; Heuristic 140, 152; Learning 205; Problematic 283;

88 CERTAINTY Wittgenstein does often say that we can know in ways that are well-grounded. For instance, 'The world would be inconceivable to me if I could not take 'x' as well-grounded'.
→ Artist 47; Certainty 84, 89, 90; Work 378;
& Art 29; Beliefs 70, 71; Experience 127; Knowledge 193; Painting 256; Work, pragmatics of 408;

89 CERTAINTY Uncovering 'deeper foundations', refuting past theories, and similar statements which pull epistemic-rank have 'policemen-of-the-art-world' connotations. It presupposes a kind of neutral cognitivity underlying all human activity. The model here is the natural sciences.
→ Certainty 84, 86, 87; Learning 205; Logical 220; Painting 256; Work 378;
& Ambiguity 9, 12; Autonomy 58; Beliefs 69, 70, 71; Conversation 109; Knowledge 191; Lebenswelt 218; Work 402;

90 CERTAINTY 'At the foundation of well-founded beliefs lies belief that is not founded.' What we do is subject to being groundless. Is there a possibility of logical soundness in our work?
→ Art criticism 42; Categorical scheme 82; Certainty 84, 86, 87, 88; Knowledge 191; Learning 205; Philosophy 266; Proceeding 294; Psychological 302; Surface-structure 339; Work 394;
& Art 29; Art criticism 40, 41; Art, work of 53; Autonomy 57; Context 107; Experience 125, 127; Ideology 174; Knowledge 189; Problematic 288; Surface-structure 334; Thesaurus 353; Translation 363;

91 COGNITIVITY The cognitivity of the world's most learned books may be used in middle-class academic studies. This is opposed to conversational blurting which creates a surface-structure.
→ Certainty 89; Context 107; Heuristic 152; Ideology 174; Learning 210; Surface-structure 337, 338; Work 379, 390;
& Ambiguity 13; Annotating 19; Beliefs 73; Heuristic 141, 153; Ideology 171; Knowledge 192; Logical 220; Semantic field 323; Trivialities 368, 369; Work 382;

92 COLLABORATION The group methodology is the best methodology.
→ Autonomy 61; Collaboration 94; Conversation 108, 109, 110; Conversational matrix 111, 115, 117; Intersubjectivity 188; Language environment 202; Learning 205, 215; Lebenswelt 218; Proceeding 293; Work 377, 385;
& Argument 28; Beliefs 64, 65; Collaboration 93; Context 96, 97, 99; Heuristic 135; Ideology 165; Practical 274; Speaker-hearer context 324; Work 380, 381;

93 COLLABORATION All specialized disciplines seem to have problems of communal organization: information exchange, group interaction, etc. Certain philosophers of science appear to be trying to cope with the uniqueness of some historical figures in relation to their own (i.e. the philosopher's) idealized picture of scientific

36

'continuity' or 'community'.
→ Context 105, 106; Historical reconstruction 161; Historicism 162; Opportunism 250; Paradigm 259; Reconstruction 307; Work 402;
& A priori 27; Autonomy 56; Context 98; Heuristic 138; Knowledge 193; Philosophy of Science 270; Responsibility 312, 313; Work 401;

94 COLLABORATION In many respects scientific information exchange and collaborative encounters provide us with an interesting alternative to the model of the art-world as it exists now. Rather than push the individual out of the picture, it provides a framework for maximum potential. De-personalization ought to be viewed as a reactionary fear about, rather than a product of, communal behavior.
→ Art criticism 39; Collaboration 92; Context 96, 102; Conversation 110; Conversation matrix 111, 112, 117; Individuality 178; Language 194; Language environment 201, 202; Learning 210, 215; Paradigm 259; Problematic 282; Work 375, 381;
& Ambiguity 8; Autonomy 61; Belief 65; Blurting 77; Context 99; Conversation 108, 109; Ideology 170; Intersubjectivity 188; Philosophy 264; Pragmatics 277, 278; Psychological 302; Semantic field 321; Stylistics 331; Work 394;

95 CONTEXT In an eventual context of use our statements are non-formally (i.e. semantically and pragmatically) ambiguous.
→ Ambiguity 3, 11; Context 99, 104; Information retrieval systems 180;
& Ambiguity 4, 5, 7; Autonomy 56; Belief 70, 71; Categorical scheme 82; Context 98, 100, 102; Heuristic 136, 137, 152; Learning 213; Opportunism 246; Semantics 317;

96 CONTEXT Context also accounts for the pragmatic dimensions of an individual's life.
→ Belief 65; Heuristic 141; Lebenswelt 218; Pragmatics 277, 279; Trivialities 368, 369;
& Ambiguity 8, 11; Argument 28; Conversational matrix 115; Ideology 165; Language environment 202; Philosophy 266; Pragmatics 278; Problematic Art & Language 289; Understanding 372;

97 CONTEXT Contexts, like languages, are governed by rules: rules which have been decided upon consensually.
→ Language 194, 195; Language environment 201; Proceeding 293; Responsibility 312; Semantics 320; Work 375;
& Art-community 38; Art criticism 45; Art & Language 49; Belief 66, 68; Collaboration 93; Ideology 172; Intersubjectivity 188;

98 CONTEXT What we should be looking for is not a characterization of a context that is a propos historical analysis, but a way of talking about context as a set of expectations/ related events.
→ Anthropology 25; Context 95, 100, 104; Language environment 201;
& Collaboration 93; Conversational matrix 117; Problematic 286; Reconstructions 307; Speaker-hearer context 324;

99 CONTEXT The value of an individual's expression is not determined solely by that individual's notion of context, but what that expression eventually obtains in the context of many expressions (its effectiveness).

37

Figure 2.8 Art & Language, *Blurting in A&L*, 1973, pp. 36 and 37.

tions (where they were not necessarily authored by the same person, nor did they necessarily appear consecutively as they do in the blurt) followed by two arrays indicating directions for further reading:

> 55 ART WORLD Critic, author, artist, enquirer, audience, should have the same status/responsibilities. We still have the old "meaningless" art blik about everything following from the natural creative magic of the artist. You can't accept the artist/critic distinction anymore than you can glibly accept the theory/practice distinction.
>
> → Collaboration 93, 94; Conversation 110; Meaning 235; Problematic 284, 286; Proceeding 292; Responsibility 311;
>
> & Ambiguity 15; A priori 27; Art-criticism 39; Art-enquiry 46; Artist 48; Context 105; Conversational matrix 117; Ideology 170; Trivialities 369; Work 395;[40]

The content of this blurt is, like all of the other blurts, short and declarative. It is disjointed, speaking in omniscient third person for a sentence, then collective first person, and then second person. It uses opaque jargon ("blik"), jumps from description to prescription, joins together an extraordinary range of topics and issues, and does not entirely cohere to make a clear point. It is also, according to Ramsden and Corris's arrays, related to eighteen other blurts. The reader who wishes to continue reading *Blurting in A&L* should (presuming he or she follows Art & Language's instructions) select a blurt from one of these two arrays, turn to the appropriate page, read that blurt, and repeat the process again for as long as he or she desires. So, beginning from blurt number 55, one could choose to enter the "→" array and select blurt number 94:

> 94 COLLABORATION In many respects scientific information exchange and collaborative encounters provide us with an interesting alternative to the model of the art-world as it exists now. Rather than push the individual out of the picture, it provides a framework for maximum potential. De-personalization ought to be viewed as a reactionary fear about, rather than a product of, communal behavior.
>
> → Art criticism 39; Collaboration 92; Context 96, 102;

Conversation 110; Conversation matrix 111, 112, 117; Individuality 178; Language 194; Language environment 201, 202; Learning 210, 215; Paradigm 259; Problematic 282; Work 375, 381;

& Ambiguity 8; Autonomy 1; Belief 65; Blurting 77; Context 99; Conversation 108, 109; Ideology 170; Intersubjectivity 188; Philosophy 264; Pragmatics 277, 278; Psychological 302; Semantic field 321; Stylistics 331; Work 394;[41]

Now, the reader's task is to make sense of this blurt in itself and in light of the previous one. Few if any of the terms doing heavy lifting in this blurt are found in the preceding one, and so it is up to each reader to decide how, for instance, to think "scientific information exchange" in relation to "the natural creative magic of the artist." How, similarly, is "de-personalization" as "reactionary fear" to be squared with the idea that everyone in the art world "should have the same status/responsibilities"? One may continue from there while always bearing in mind that these blurts are not definitive statements of Art & Language's position on the art world or collaboration (or any other topic) but serve instead as prompts to continue thinking in a trial-and-error fashion.

Depending on the pathways one constructs while reading through *Blurting in A&L*, any given blurt, chain of blurts, or claim within a blurt or blurt chain may appear either valid or not because the context in which it is read, that is, the sequence of blurts that precede it, changes; moreover, its inflection will change according to the context. What may seem to be a crazy notion can appear entirely sensible when arrived at in the right sequence of blurts and, vice versa, a sound idea can appear preposterous depending on how one's thinking has been proceeding. Indeed, by definition, blurts are statements that are unable to articulate the context in which they are uttered but rather rely on the interpretative capacity of receivers to supply it. As Ramsden and Corris note, "Much of this material will be incomprehensible at a glance. In order to get anything out of the material you would have to activate some of the potential pathways. Embeddedness becomes crucial."[42] Tellingly, each blurt ends with a semicolon, implying, as that punctuation mark does, the joining of complete thoughts that are separate but linked. The process of reading and constructing pathways in order to connect blurts and embed them in contexts that give them meaning may, therefore, continue indefinitely. The schematic layout of each blurt, with its links to other blurts via an elaborate structure of numbers and symbols, recalls a thesaurus, another "handbook" that a reader may explore endlessly, linking one word to the next, comparing them, and gaining a better understanding of "our/your language/culture." The key difference is that a thesaurus is clear about synonyms and antonyms, whereas *Blurting in A&L* leaves decisions about such things to the reader.

When someone reads the blurts according to Ramsden and Corris's instructions, "the issue of going-on becomes a self-conscious construction for the reader."[43] This idea is further emphasized in their introductory essay: "It's about constituting going-on, not describing going on."[44] It is here that the decisions facing Art & Language while drafting the annotations become those facing the reader of *Blurting in A&L*. Of the former work, Ramsden and Corris recall, "Looking at those annotations we wondered 'do I want to respond to this one?,' 'How will I respond to this?,' 'How will I go on?,' 'Do I want to go on?,' 'Will I go on in this way?,' 'Will I react against this?'"[45] Now, *Blurting in A&L* "makes reading explicit. It means that after reading a given blurt you have to ask yourself 'How do I go on?,' 'Do I in fact want to go on?' . . . The problem it shows is 'How do we, all of us, go on?'"[46] To read *Blurting in A&L* is, then, to become a quasi-participant in Art & Language, to straddle the line between "our/your" so that the boundaries between Art & Language, the art world, and the world itself reveal their insubstantiality and "language/culture" is opened to revision.

In the introductory essay, Ramsden and Corris speak of the annotations being "concerned with developing a teaching/learning, even social environment for eight individuals, all with a degree of shared interests and information."[47] With *Blurting in A&L*, they open this environment to broader participation by inviting their audience to further develop their work, and Ramsden and Corris openly consider the implications of Art & Language seeking converts to its way of working: "The generative potential of A&L has to do with practice. Maybe it might open an area of alternate potentials for those outside of A&L. The goal isn't to convert hoards to 'theoretical art' and similar nonsense, the goal isn't stylistic. All this means is that we don't offer a model (paradigm) for people to shift to; A&L is not an object of contemplation. The handbook isn't a model either. . . . What's very important now is that only the existence of an argumentation that is

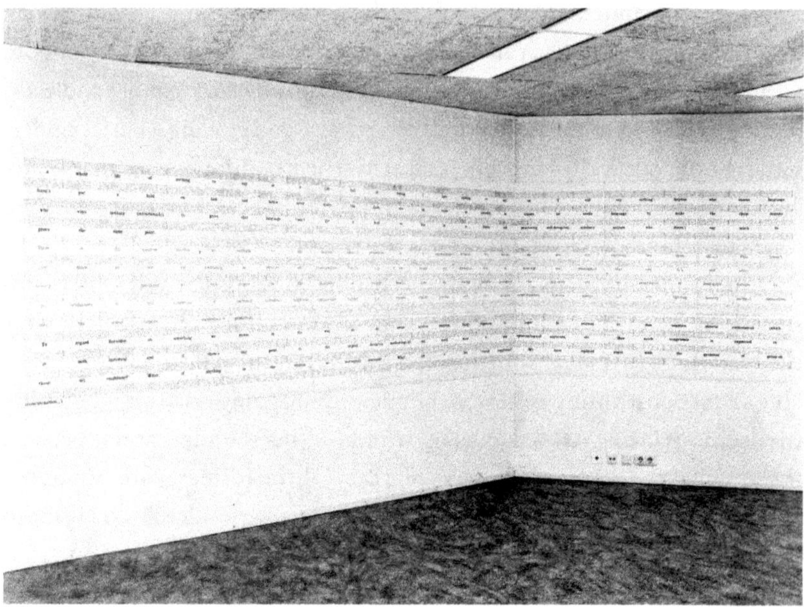

Figure 2.9 Art & Language, *Index 002 Bxal*, 1973.

neither compelling nor arbitrary offers the exercise of reasonable choice. That means that A&L is neither a model nor an attempt to convert—but, importantly, a bit of both."[48]

This desire to explore community through Art & Language's work was not shared in England, as the English response to *Blurting in A&L*, an index of 1973 titled *Index 002 Bxal*, indicates ("Bxal" is shorthand for "blurting in Art & Language"). This work came together after Baldwin and Pilkington visited New York in 1973 and got a firsthand sense of what Art & Language was doing there. They developed it as an alternative and competing way to index the annotations that the New Yorkers had reconfigured into their artist's book. To present it, a large printed text was hung on the wall of John Weber Gallery with the aim being to fill in blank spaces in it with concatenations of blurts supplied on an accompanying printed form (figures 2.9–2.11). Art & Language's New York section was to do the bulk of the concatenating. As had become customary of English indexes, Baldwin and Pilkington established a complex set of indexing procedures and rules for users to follow. Unlike *Blurting in A&L*, which utilized an exploratory

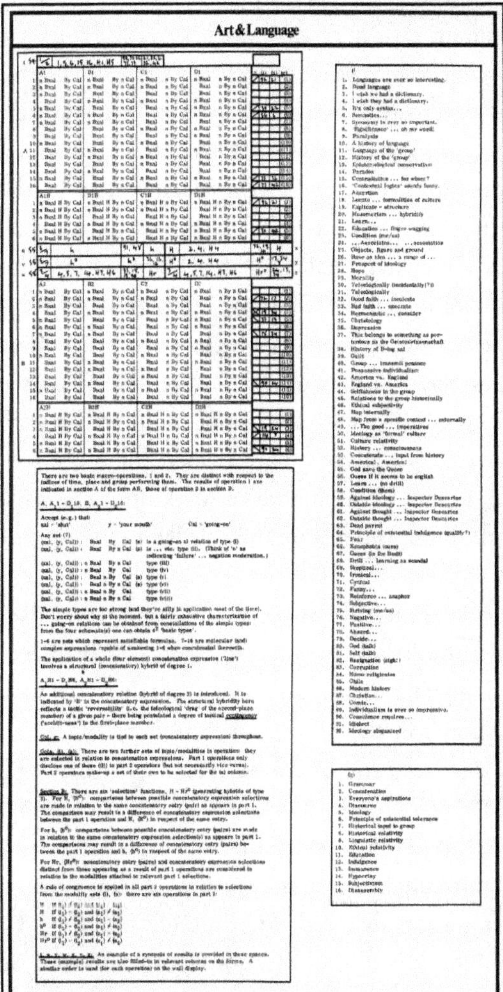

Figure 2.10 Art & Language, *Index 002 Bxal*, 1973, detail.

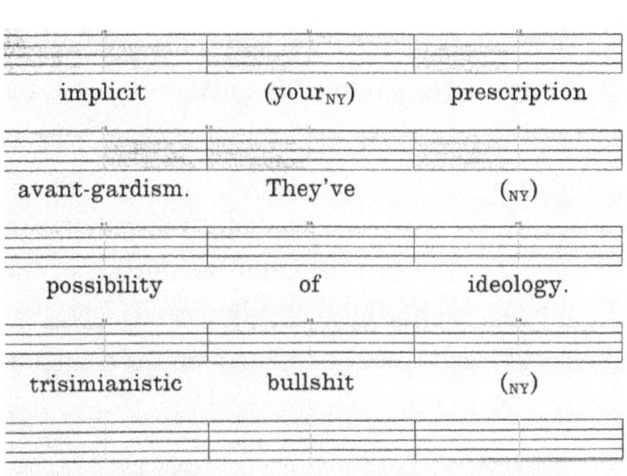

Figure 2.11 Art & Language, *Index 002 Bxal*, 1973, detail.

indexing procedure to place emphasis on the content of the blurts and the sociality by proxy that would arise from engaging with Art & Language's thinking, the concern of *Index 002 Bxal* is squarely on the formal structure for setting expressions into relation with one another. Less a prompt to thinking than a worksheet, its structure was so intricate that a supplementary text called "Handbook(s) to Going-On" appeared as an issue of *Art-Language* to further explicate the work.[49] Given the prominent status of John Weber Gallery, it is somewhat peculiar that Baldwin and Pilkington chose to exhibit there work meant more for the internal use of Art & Language than for any audience that came to see it. This was precisely the sort of thing that was leading the collective's New York section away from the indexing project and into conflict with its English counterparts over the social dimensions of Art & Language's work, which for it exerted a pressure that could not be ignored. The demands of working at the center of the art world in New York simply did not permit insular or cryptic work like *Index 002 Bxal*.

Burn and Ramsden formalized the differences between the two sections of Art & Language, at least from their perspective in New York, in an essay titled "Problems of Art & Language Space" that Burn largely wrote while Ramsden was away participating in the process of exhibiting *Index 01* at *Documenta*. It appeared in *Art-Language* under both of their names while the collective's two distinct approaches to indexing were still developing. In it, they highlight the need to pay greater attention to external contexts for Art & Language work, particularly insofar as future indexing projects would be concerned. After noting that indexing initially functioned in *Index 01* as a way to assess "the overall conversations in and around this journal," meaning *Art-Language*, they call for further explorations of not only how those conversations "fit together with normative art-activities (painting, sculpture and so-called 'post-object' art) and the writings concerning those activities" but also "how this framework fits into the expansive network of other frameworks and disciplines and activities."[50] Near the end of their essay, Burn and Ramsden suggest that a more sociological approach to Art & Language and its contexts is needed if indexing is not to run out of steam and become irrelevant to communities outside of the collective's own: "The notion of communities has only recently been researched by sociologists. A view of the history of art based on the changing

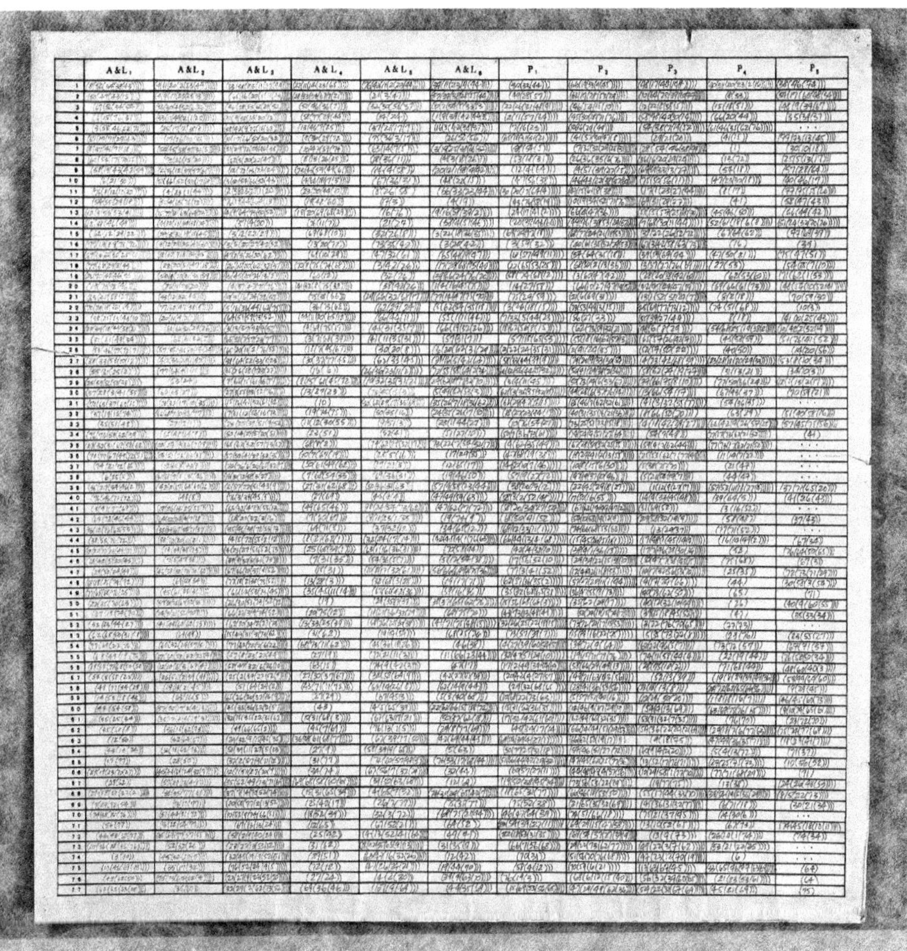

Figure 2.12 Art & Language, *77 Sentences*, 1974, detail of the concatenations. MACBA Collection, MACBA Consortium. Long-term loan of Philippe Méaille.

ambitions due to community ideologies should be revealing. What A&L is doing is making this community space explicit—deliberately social and institutionally based—intersubjective rather than subjective."[51]

In 1974, the New York section of Art & Language completed one final indexing project that insists upon the social direction it would continue to take thenceforward. *77 Sentences* is the work of Burn, Corris, Heller, Menard, Ramsden, and Smith (figure 2.12).[52] It uses short statements developed for the occasion of the work, but the process of concatenating them involved not only the group itself but also five people who had not previously contributed to its work. Karl Beveridge and Carole Condé, Canadian artists who came to New York from Toronto and met Burn and Ramsden shortly thereafter, would continue working with Art & Language from this point on. Paula Eck, Kathleen Mooney, and John Ruff also contributed to *77 Sentences*, though they would not work with Art & Language again. These five newcomers, along with participants in the collective's New York section, filled in a worksheet concerning the seventy-seven texts. Those texts, printed on a long vertical panel, were exhibited at Galerie Schema in Florence along with the completed worksheet, which asked respondents to envision connections between them and to develop ways of embedding them within one another. In this instance, the final product comes across as little more than a pretext for the process of having gathered together with new people so as to expand the ranks of the working group by producing it.

Around this time, acronyms begin to appear with greater frequency in Art & Language's writings to differentiate between the two sections of the group: "ALUK," "ALNY," and several variants thereof. The transcript of an internal Art & Language discussion held in New York on April 6, 1973, sketches one way that the New York section perceived its difference from the English section, and this difference has to do precisely with how its position near the center of the art world placed certain social demands upon its working that did not register across the Atlantic: "Andrew, what do you think is an important characteristic feature about being in NY?/ First of all, that NY tends to be much more intellectualized. . . . Beyond that, the high level of competition . . . large community of artists, you have a lot of people to talk to . . . communications./ [. . .] There's a heavy art-social scene . . . / And it becomes very clear to see the institutionalized way it works here. . . . Ya know what I mean? This would be a more sociological context than say (England) which is a more logical context. . . . I don't mean that they are more logical, but this would be more sociological. . . . / Surely, we give the more anthropological, sociological descriptions of what's ever going on. . . . /"[53]

By the end of 1974, the sections of Art & Language in England and New York were working entirely independently of one another. The event that confirmed this split was the reception of the September 1974 issue of

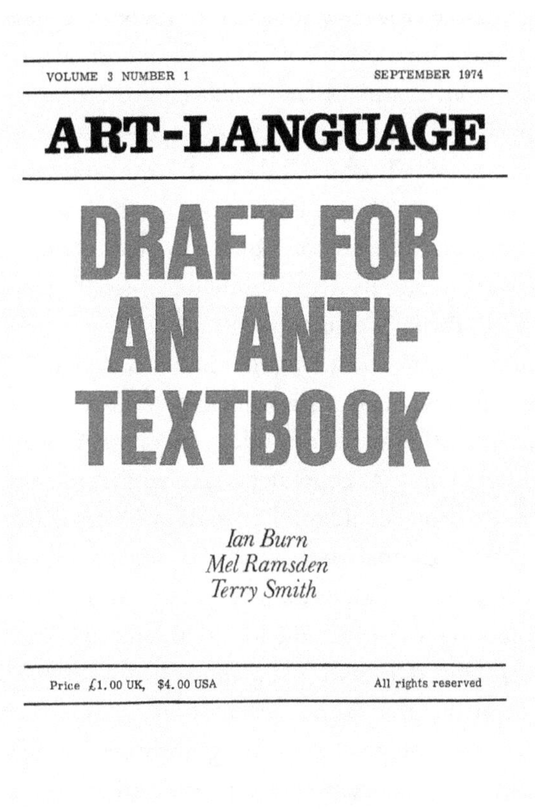

VOLUME 3 NUMBER 1 SEPTEMBER 1974

ART-LANGUAGE

DRAFT FOR AN ANTI-TEXTBOOK

Ian Burn
Mel Ramsden
Terry Smith

Price £1.00 UK, $4.00 USA All rights reserved

Figure 2.13 Art & Language, "Draft for an Anti-Textbook," *Art-Language* 3, no. 1 (1974).

Art-Language, which was given over to a series of transcripts documenting conversations Burn, Ramsden, and Smith had between May and June of that year about "the problematicness of our situation."[54] The title given to this project is "Draft for an Anti-Textbook," and its thirty-nine short chapters include many retrospective evaluations of Art & Language's work, of which the discussants offer a generally low assessment (figure 2.13). Essentially repeating the backward-looking project of *Index 01* by way of transcribed reflections on past work, "Draft for an Anti-Textbook" no longer seeks to find consistency within it. Earlier work with annotation and pedagogy had prepared the discussants for the sort of provisional and critical but nonprescriptive project that this new work's title suggests. The results of the conversations, which marked the New York section's definitive break with the indexing project and a turn toward work made almost entirely through transcriptions of its conversations that, as such, emphasize the sociality implicit in producing it, were, as Harrison notes, "largely disregarded in England," and "Draft for an Anti-Textbook" also marks the point after which a split between the two Art & Language sections is for the first time openly regarded as beyond repair.[55] A review of it by the English section in the next issue of *Art-Language* is entirely negative and dismissive. It bears the telling title "Rambling: To Partial Correspondents."[56]

"Draft for an Anti-Textbook" announces a big shift in Art & Language's approach to language that will eliminate from its work in New York any last traces of aspirations to locating solid foundations for continuing to work and bring to an end any last attempts to construct clear channels of communication through which the group could speak to itself or to others. The authors of "Draft for an Anti-Textbook" perceive the collective's difficulties in "'making lucid' the so-called 'relationship' to language, in any structural sense" as having something to do with the idea that language "can't be tackled directly, it's a matter of reflection . . . because we are already 'in' our language."[57] They argue further that "language has a hold on us," which means that "there's no way of standing off and getting, anthropologically, an overview."[58] These claims about language are connected to a reassessment of the collective's audience, which proceeds through a critique of the concept of "ideal speakers."[59] An ideal speaker or "ideal speaker-listener" is a central concept in Noam Chomsky's linguistics, which, in the first version of *Comparative Models*, Burn and Ramsden had invoked while putting forward a conception of their work as a "model of competence" in opposition to the art world's "model of performance." This distinction was often reasserted in the annotations, which began, at least for some of its participants, as an attempt to create something like an ideal speaker-listener environment within Art & Language. It recurs again in *Blurting in A&L*'s aspirations to equip its readers, through their construction of pathways through the text, with greater cognizance of their language. For Chomsky, the "ideal speaker-listener" is a language user who is—and here Burn, Ramsden, and Smith quote his *Aspects of the Theory of Syntax* directly—"unaffected by such grammatically irrelevant conditions as memory limitations, distractions, shifts of attention and interest, and errors (random or characteristic) in applying his knowledge of this [Chomsky actually writes 'the' instead of 'this'] language in actual performance."[60] Such a speaker enacts competence in a language with every linguistic performance, which is to say that his or her use of language is a performance of total competence, something that is never the case for actual speakers, each of whom is affected by the very things that Chomsky brackets out of consideration in constructing his notion of an ideal speaker-listener. By acknowledging the unattainability of this ideality, Burn, Ramsden, and Smith admit that their prior claims to be competent language users or to pursue competent language use is predicated on things that do not obtain outside of a conceptual framework deployed by linguists to theorize about language in the abstract. In actually obtaining circumstances, there are no ideal speaker-listeners. Following upon this realization, the authors of "Draft for an Anti-Textbook" also recognize that any audience for whom they would work will likewise never be composed of ideal speaker-listeners, and therefore failure is an implicit part of using language to relate to an audience.

In line with this assessment, the discussants posit the following hypothetical response to their conversation: "Assume all this chatter is published. People will probably read it and different things will interest different people for different reasons (maybe). Publishing this assumes a potential of generalizing, bits may interest people who might be called 'members of the art-world' but the same and/or other bits may interest other people. . . . that's all I want (and that's a lot)."[61] Here, there is an acknowledgment that no ideal audience exists for Art & Language's work and none is forthcoming. Instead, different perspectives out of its control are brought to bear on the collective's work, and the art world's multiplicity of perspectives are unavoidably among these, which means that, insofar as the art world is concerned, Art & Language is "not above it" but "in it as well."[62] Despite this admission of its participation in the art world after a period of withdrawal into its own collective activity, Art & Language's assessment of the art world is no softer than its earlier stern condemnations:

> "The artworld" is a highly stressed rhetorical situation in which roles are contingently related to constantly shifting sets of audience values, procedures etc. The artist is the prime-mover, the artwork the life blood, the critic the catalyst, the dealer the distributor, the

> audience the lapping-it-up fodder of glorious "art." . . . I mean this model of the closed image of the artworld as a natural order where everybody has a role which fits together as in an interconnected organism is half our problem. . . . it's what we're up against. It's easy to create another, more sinister picture: where the dealer is related to the stockbroker and the artist is related to the peddler.[63]

What is new in "Draft for an Anti-Textbook" is the collective's recognition that obstacles to communication and failures of language are not to be overcome so much as made productive when working together within art worlds. "Draft for an Anti-Textbook" therefore indicates a change in direction toward greater engagement with difficulties that arise in social settings mediated by language and a new willingness to seek out such engagements. This realization had been some time in coming, and the retrospective tendency in "Draft for an Anti-Textbook" offers an account of its coming to be: "The idea of 'collaboration,' if it ever worked with us, has certainly collapsed during the past couple of years into (vague) sociality. The problem with collaboration was the '*we* speak with one voice' implications; sociality might be more like '*I* speak with many voices.' . . . sociality would then be the inverse of collaboration."[64] Moreover, "any thought about the viability of a 'controlled' environment was explicitly exposed" and "all there was was some sense of social (group) obligation."[65] Between the impossibility of controlling the group situation and the obligation to recognize that sociality is not optional, there arises the "problem of not being able to distinguish 'message' from 'noise,'" which in turn uncovered "a position of realizing points of view where anomalies are no longer anomalies . . . the potentials of confusion . . . living with the difficulties . . . and how seemingly contradictory notions were no longer excludable."[66] Or, to summarize the recent history being reviewed here, "The Annotations were a mess . . . in many different ways . . . especially some of the social problems which came up and have come up since."[67]

In "Draft for an Anti-Textbook," the New York section of Art & Language completes and affirms its reorientation outward, and messiness is recuperated as exactly the state in which it and its audiences can socialize without rigid or monolithic concepts imposing themselves. One discussant proposes, in a way that recalls the reading procedure elaborated for *Blurt-*

ing in A&L, "I don't think there's anywhere you 'start.' . . . you start in the middle, anywhere, not from 'foundations,' not from a tabula rasa, but in a mess."[68] Elsewhere, someone suggests that the critic Lucy R. Lippard's mixed sentiments about Art & Language's work are in fact an excellent beginning for mutual learning: "Lucy Lippard said she 'enjoyed' A&L but still didn't understand it, which might show for her understanding is having an external view or overview, something we can't provide. . . . the best understanding she could have is to not-understand. . . . not-understanding is 'understanding.' . . . the best purchase on us is a confusion about the work . . . at least that might be the beginning of 'understanding.'"[69] The point at which a beneficial exchange between Art & Language and the art world may occur is here posited as the very point at which communication becomes impossible, a point from which it is not possible to proceed from understanding but only from confusion. "Draft for an Anti-Textbook" concludes with more remarks on this topic, including the important statement, "It doesn't make any sense to conceive of the social/cultural situation except in terms of encounter."[70] It is through encounter, then, that the New York section of Art & Language now conceives of its relations with one another and with others, and it begins to welcome and pursue encounters.

After two years spent contesting the art world from a constructed position of imagined exteriority facilitated by readings in the philosophy of science, Art & Language acknowledges in "Draft for an Anti-Textbook" that whatever gains it made by pursuing this position (and, in turning to the philosophy of science, it indeed gained knowledge about social relations, group collaboration, structural transformation, and many other things) are most useful when brought into tangible relations with audiences, however uncomfortable such relations may be or become. The philosophy of science quickly disappears from Art & Language's discussions as new concerns drawn primarily from political philosophy and cultural theory assume increasing priority for the kinds of insight they could provide into the sociality of working as artists. Smith voiced this newfound need to reengage the art world from a fresh perspective publicly in his 1974 *Artforum* article "Art and Art and Language," not only by publishing in a magazine that two years prior Art & Language had severely criticized, but also by acknowledging that a central paradox in Art & Language's work to that point was the fact that, despite striving to identify and overcome the limitations of the art world, its noisy channel was always the main conduit for Art & Language's work: "The hoped-for public is something like 'the general (intelligent) reading public'—a reality to at least certain publishers. In practice, however, the immediate audience for A&L work lies in the art world."[71]

After "Draft for an Anti-Textbook," the New York section of Art & Language becomes less satisfied with working for itself or with making work available to a largely anonymous public. To change "our/your language/culture," it henceforth becomes necessary for "our" to socialize and talk with "your" more directly and more frequently. In contrast to its English counterparts, whose numbers begin to dwindle following Atkinson's exit, the New York section strikes up collaborations with artists and others in Australia, New Zealand, and Yugoslavia, while also drastically rethinking its approach to working in New York. An existing preference for pandemonium now emerges not only in the discourse Art & Language creates but also in the way it socializes, as its attempts to reimagine art's worldly function become both transnational and intranational.

Three
Interplay

As part of its investigations into the conceptual facets of art worlds, the New York section of Art & Language produced a body of writings and a series of exhibitions concerning provincialism in art and culture that coincided with a broadening of its international sociality to include productive working relations with artists and critics in Australia and, slightly later, New Zealand. In Art & Language's work, interest in the concept of provincialism and its effects on art worlds in both the United States and abroad is strongest in contributions made by Ian Burn and Terry Smith, who both developed the double consciousness that comes with being Australian expatriates living in New York. This made them especially penetrating analysts of the uneven dynamics of cultural exchange between nations, which would be the major theme of several Art & Language exhibitions in Australia during 1975 and New Zealand during 1976. Burn's 1973 essay "Provincialism" provided direction for the group's efforts to reimagine cultural exchange across national borders by lamenting that "recent art has developed the rules of its 'game' to contain a trick ensuring all artists play by the American rules, while only Americans can win—and then not all Americans."[1] In other writings, Art & Language refined its understanding of provincialism into a general theory of cultural dependence, which it figured both as the ideology that keeps up art worlds and as their main product. The collective then sought to contest this ideology with a novel approach to international exhibition practice that reconfigured Art & Language's work along self-consciously international lines for the first time.

It is no accident that the Australians in Art & Language were most sensitive to these issues, as Australian intellectuals have accrued a lengthy history of reflecting on perceptions of their nation's cultural inferiority.

In perhaps the best-known formulation, the Australian writer and critic A. A. Phillips coined the term "cultural cringe" in 1950 to refer to the sense within Australia that culture produced by Australians did not compare favorably to European, especially British, culture: "We cannot shelter from invidious comparisons behind the barrier of a separate language; we have no long-established or interestingly different cultural tradition to give security and distinction to its interpreters; and the centrifugal pull of the great cultural metropolises works against us. Above our writers—and other artists—looms the intimidating mass of Anglo-Saxon achievement. Such a situation almost inevitably produces the characteristic Australian Cultural Cringe."[2] While not precisely a theory of provincialism, Phillips's account established a tone for the coming discourse on that topic, particularly by identifying the importance of the distant metropolis for writers and artists in Australia. It was, rather paradoxically, in the center of "Anglo-Saxon achievement" that Kenneth Clark would, in a 1962 lecture, formulate an art historical theory of provincialism according to which the dominant style of a period radiates outward from a center, becoming an international style that gets less and less metropolitan and more and more provincial the further into the periphery it gets.[3] Owing to the distance between England and historically prominent art centers such as Rome and Paris, Clark judged English art, the very art against which Australians judged themselves provincial, as itself thoroughly provincial in character.

Provincialism finds its first strong Australian articulation in the work of the art historian Bernard Smith, who, in 1971, characterized "the European art of Australia," as distinct from its Aboriginal art, to be "a provincial art carried on for almost two centuries now in a south-east Asian situation far from such metropolitan sources as London, Paris and, more recently, New York."[4] Like Phillips, Smith calls attention to the distance between Australia and major world cities in Europe and the United States, the main effect of which is "a time-lag in the reception, absorption and florescence of styles generated in those distant metropolitan centres."[5] Given that metropolitan art from these centers claimed significance for itself on the basis of the rapid stylistic turnovers characteristic of modernism, an Australian "time-lag" ensured that Australians who wanted to participate in developing metropolitan styles would always find themselves on the sidelines as belated imitators of art produced elsewhere. For Smith, Australia's escape from its provincial situation was intrinsically linked to developing metropolises in Australia, of which he wrote, "A metropolis creates a cosmopolitan urban situation by drawing upon many other centres and regions for its own growing population and creates a cultural dynamic from the urban environment so created."[6] At the beginning of the 1970s, Smith sensed that the provincial situation in Australia, "though continuing to prevail, was being transformed" by the creation of "nascent metropolitan situations of its own in its main capital cities."[7] The emergence of galleries dedicated to showing and fostering new art in Sydney and Melbourne—among them Central Street Gallery, Inhibodress, and Pinacotheca—created a network of artists, dealers, critics, and collectors intensely devoted to the latest developments in art, and these people were in frequent contact with metropolitan centers in Europe and North America via airmail and more affordable overseas airfare. The art produced within this network may have remained indebted to art from elsewhere, but it was better connected with that art than ever before, which presented the possibility that Australian cities could become metropolitan art centers for the first time and Australian art could overcome its provincialism and reciprocate the influence it drew from elsewhere.

Terry Smith was a student of Bernard Smith's prior to his expatriation to New York, and he began to articulate his own ideas about provincialism not long after his teacher did. In response to "Notes on the Centre: New York," an essay celebrating American modernism that the Australian art critic Patrick McCaughey published in the Australian journal *Quadrant* while living and studying in New York on a Harkness Fellowship, Smith wrote "Provincialism in Art," which appeared in the same journal less than six months later.[8] Smith identifies in McCaughey's essay "a problem especially pertinent to Australian art at this time, that of the metropolitan/provincial relationship in art," and he makes this problem the main subject of his own essay.[9] He also introduces the idea of an "impossible double bind" facing the provincial artist, who must respond to international art in order to innovate but who is unable to do so because his or her distance from the place where that art originates blocks access to the moments of innovation upon which it stakes its claim to being modern.[10] Smith, however, challenges the time-lag theory of provincialism by observing that provincial artists generally only ever have access to the mature expression of a style, not the inchoate state from which it emerged. Without access to this prior state when the style was still in formation, the provincial artist cannot innovate because he or she is denied access to the early work in which formative innovations took place. Modernism arrives fully formed in Australia. Time lag is less an issue than the fact that the immature stages of a style never, not even belatedly in most cases, reach its shores. Provincialism is not a result of how long it takes for American art to reach Australia but a matter of which American art arrives and why. Nascent in Smith's commentary here is a shift away from naturalizing geographical explanations of provincialism that will eventually culminate in Art & Language's account of it as an ideology of cultural dependency that manifests in precisely the kind of geographical thinking that previous accounts of provincialism emphasize.

Initially, Smith, like his mentor, harbored hopes of an end to provincialism, which he identified with the emergence of an avant-garde in Australia. With Tony McGillick, he curated an exhibition titled *The Situation Now: Object or Post-Object Art?* informed by the term "post-object art," which the critic Donald Brook, another of Smith's teachers in the Department of Fine Art at the University of Sydney, coined to describe the proliferation of new approaches, including performance, installation, earthworks, and conceptual art, that were then emerging in the aftermath of modernism in Australia as in the United States and elsewhere.[11] Mounted at the Contemporary Art Society in Sydney in 1971, the exhibition presented recent developments in Australian art, which Smith claimed had "yet to break down the limitations that have always been present in Australian art" but which at least represented "an avant-garde relative to previous Australian art."[12] Among those in the exhibition were Burn and Mel Ramsden, whose correspondence with Smith during preparations for *The Situation Now* precipitated his contacting them upon arriving in New York the following year.

These ideas and aspirations provide background for Art & Language's writings about provincialism, the first of which is Burn's essay "Provincialism," which he published in the inaugural issue of the short-lived Melbourne-based journal *Art Dialogue* roughly simultaneously with its appearance in the catalog to the Belgian exhibition *Deurle 11/7/73*. Its primary concern is not distance but context. Specifically, Burn is highly critical of the way that artistic exchange between nations imposes values developed within one context onto another, and he also introduces the idea that such exchanges are bound up with the more general values of the nations involved.[13] After proposing, "The meaning or sense of art activities are governed by the contexts they derive from and occur within," Burn then puts forward a long list of contextual factors that contribute to how art acquires meaning: "Something may be determined by geographical, or linguistic, or sociological, or political, or economic, or ethical, or anthropological, or experiential, or theoretical grounds."[14] An adequate description of a context would need, therefore, to be "extensive enough to reveal the correspondence of a praxis to its various ideological conditions," and Burn contends that the main force holding contexts together is education, because those who share a context "have *learned* in similar ways and are therefore capable of communicating with each other."[15] This understanding of context as a result of learning built upon a diverse array of values implies connections between American art and a broader American ideology: "It can be asserted, for example, that a society which produced and supported the best American art also produced and supported the ideological initiatives for the Vietnam War."[16]

Having put art broadly into relation with other social and cultural factors, Burn criticizes artists for their "tacit assumption that art is not affected by economics, politics or geography."[17] He also warns against assuming "that one's activity is neutral on ideological grounds" and singles out Carl Andre's often-repeated remark, "Art is what we do. Culture is what is done to us," as characteristic of this misguided belief.[18] For Burn, the internationalization of art and culture involves the importation of standards of judgment from one context to another, where they may have deleterious effects. As an example, he cites the case of Hard Edge abstraction in both the United Kingdom and the United States: "To judge that style in England by the values of the American style is to judge the British style as being of a lower value—whereas one should judge it in relation to its own context."[19] When these misapplications occur, Burn claims that a hierarchy establishes itself as one context subjugates others, which it renders provincial: "A provincial context may be internally defining, but what defines the context as 'provincial' is significantly externally determined."[20] He then advances a clear definition of provincialism: "What provincialism really means is that *significant judgments are being made according to the rules governing behaviour in an ideologically different context*."[21] Artists' agency is neutralized when they act as if they were elsewhere and ignore the conditions in which they produce, hence the two major effects of provincialism that Burn identifies: "a cultural impotence for artists of provincial contexts and, intentionally or not, . . . a cultural imperialist policy on the part of those in the dominant context."[22] Provincialism produces a situation in which "what is good for the dominant American art is good for world art," and this "guarantees American art a special autonomy and immunity to external criticism and even dialogue, while guaranteeing impotency for other contexts. These," according to Burn, "are the characteristics of a hierarchical 'art-world.'"[23]

Implicit in this description of provincialism, its causes, and its effects are two important ideas: First, neither the dominant nor the provincial context is exclusively responsible for enforcing the hierarchy of dominant and provincial contexts, and thus neither can single-handedly undo it; second, provincialism need not be intended to occur. Given this, Burn's proposal for contesting the provincial situation is particularly apt. In his words,

> What is the missing element? It is some sense of *interplay* between divergent contexts and ideologies, of dialectical opposites to one's own beliefs and concepts. It is also the strength of the interplay which counts and in turn strengthens and develops divergent contexts. Rejuvenation and the genesis of new ideas depend largely on cultural cross-fertilisations. This does not mean the present kind of "exchange" with foreign artists whose success is already tacitly sanctioned by an American context. It means accepting other contexts for what they are, for what we can learn from ourselves, and not accepting them on the basis of how well they mirror (reinforce) the dominant program.[24]

For Burn, interplay could create relations between contexts that would not create hierarchies of dominance and submission. It might, instead, become "the basis of a different self-describing 'art-world.'"[25] In other words, transforming how cultural exchange occurs across national borders could be a way forward for efforts to combat provincialism as well as a way forward for Art & Language's larger project of conceptually interrogating art worlds in pursuit of alternatives to them.

A clearer picture about how provincialism functions as an ideological force emerges in Terry Smith's essay "The Provincialism Problem."[26] Smith wrote this essay at the invitation of Lawrence Alloway, then an editor at *Artforum*, who asked him to contribute a piece on art in Australia. As requested, "The Provincialism Problem" considers Australian art. However, Smith argues that provincialism, which he defines as "an attitude of subservience to an externally imposed hierarchy of cultural values," is not unique to Australia but pervades all art worlds as an enabling but also disabling condition.[27] Indeed, Smith opens the essay by proposing that provincialism is the common situation for artists everywhere, including in the metropolitan center of New York: "[Provincialism] is not simply the product of a colonialist history; nor is it merely a function of geographic location. Most New York artists, critics, collectors, dealers, and gallery-goers are provincialist in their work, attitudes, and positions within the system. Members of art worlds outside New York—on every continent, including North America—are likewise provincial, although in different ways. The projection of the New York art world as the metropolitan center for art by every other art world is symptomatic of the provincialism of each of them."[28] In claiming that provincialism is "a viewpoint which, while effectively governing majority behavior, is as culturally relative as any other," Smith raises the possibility of contesting it at the level of ideology.[29] However, past efforts to contest it seem only to have reinforced its power, and Smith refers to the alternating pull of "a defiant urge to localism" and "a reluctant recognition that the generative innovations in art . . . are determined externally" as the "provincialist bind" that traps those desirous of solutions to the provincialism problem.[30] This bind is so constricting that Smith emphatically contends, *"As the situation stands, the provincial artist cannot choose not to be provincial."*[31]

Not even relocating to the "strong" metropolitan center will ease the provincialist bind. As Smith notes, "provincialism pervades New York, precisely in that the overwhelming majority of artists here exist in a satellite relationship to a few artists, galleries, critics, collectors, museums, and magazines."[32] He then asserts that the structure of provincialism is a general condition of cultural dependency not determined by geography but organized around what he calls "bright stars" in the art world: "There is a structural hierarchy in the operations of the international art world which centers on the bright stars in the constellation, the few artists, galleries, etc. who are 'on top' this decade. . . . Whereas most artists are rule-following, these are both rule-following *and rule-generating* creators. . . . Above all, they are in a situation which is culturally privileged for making their moves count."[33] Smith names several of these stars: Frank Stella, Donald Judd, Sol LeWitt, Allan Kaprow, Robert Morris, Robert Smithson, Mark di Suvero, Joseph Beuys, Kenneth Noland, Jules Olitski, and Anthony Caro. Andy Warhol is conspicuously absent from this list, but apart from pop art, this tally encompasses every major movement, tendency, group, and style to emerge in New York during the 1960s and early 1970s with the further exception of feminism, which mounted criticisms analogous to Smith's that originated in concerns about patriarchy rather than provincialism. "Breaking the bind" and becoming one of these art-world celebrities is no solution to the provincialism problem because "the system is structured so that several artists every few years *have* to break the bind."[34] Therefore, Smith concludes, "artists who permit their works to be used in these ways by curators and critics need to reassess just what their ideological commitments amount to," and the essay ends with a pointed reminder that "there are no ideologically neutral cultural acts."[35] In a response to Australian critic Elwyn Lynn's letter to the editor of *Artforum* criticizing Smith's text, Smith states his position even more emphatically: "I tried to underline in my article that we do not have a problem, because that suggests the possibility of a neat solution. Rather, we are all (in no way excluding myself) in a *problematic situation* and, in struggling within it, we try to build not just an alternative, but an oppositional, structure."[36]

While Burn and Smith were preparing their respective essays for publication, they were also discussing what an oppositional structure might be like within the context of Art & Language, particularly with Ramsden, and excerpts from their discussions that focus on the relationship between American and Australian art appear as two of the thirty-nine sections of "Draft for an Anti-Textbook," the September 1974 issue of *Art-Language*. As a trio, they develop a picture of Art & Language's activities as a form of what Burn called interplay, in which it would be possible to learn together in ways that would not reproduce provincialism. In other words, Art & Language draws on its work as conceptual artists engaged in a collective mode of sociality as a model of a practice that could create an alternative to the art world in which provincialism prevails.

The first of these two sections of "Draft for an Anti-Textbook," titled "The Unreality of This Culture," introduces concerns drawn from Marxist philosophy. Art & Language had previously used Marxist terms, especially "reification" and "problematic," but its Marxism is amplified in "Draft for an Anti-Textbook," where Marxist theory provides analytical tools that enable Art & Language "to go beyond reified objects" and "see art, not just in an object but in the notion of detachment, of detached 'appreciation' as a way of life."[37] The authors describe "detached" American art as both capitalist and classed, a "bourgeois Culture" that aims "to promote *detachment*, the unreality of Culture."[38] This "Official Culture" is exported by "MoMA, *Artforum* etc.," who promote it but, Art & Language claims, do not "acknowledge the ideology of what they are doing."[39] The bureaucratized situation in which this culture thrives is "Kafka-esque" because "there is no one to accept responsibility, no one in control of 'policy,' no one to 'blame.'"[40] As Burn previously noted, no one party intends for such a situation to arise. What the group sets out to do in "Draft for an Anti-Textbook" is demystify how this condition arises and how it might cease to arise.

For Art & Language, the danger of disseminating Official Culture is not the potential transmission of American values as explicit content but the imposition of cultural dependency in the very procedure by which any content is transmitted internationally from the United States to Australia. This is made possible because such transmissions present art as prepackaged and ready for consumption: "a part of our leisure, part of our 'time off.'"[41] When one of the discussants—the names of individual speakers are not indicated—poses the question, "What is the result of sending shows to Australia, S-E Asia, Latin America, etc?" the answer proffered is, "It promotes an unreal sense of culture . . . that culture is in safe hands, so don't you worry about it . . . and you can vicariously participate in it, by seeing exhibitions, reading about them, and so on. What I am arguing against here is this whole spectator concept of 'culture.' If a population can tolerate an unreal cultural life, it may tolerate anything."[42] In the end, Art & Language claims, this situation, according to which people are excluded from the production of culture in their roles as spectators, becomes monolithic: "Once you have the bureaucratic machinery set up, it's going to keep running in essentially the same way."[43] There is, seemingly, no escape: "Your choices are: play the game and be subsumed, or don't play the game and be banished, literally out of sight."[44]

Nowhere is this arrangement more clearly embodied for Art & Language than in exhibitions organized by the International Council of the Museum of Modern Art in New York.[45] The example on which it fixates in its discussion is *Some Recent American Art*, the eighth International Council exhibition to tour Australia and the first since the influential *Two Decades of American Painting* did so in 1967.[46] *Some Recent American Art* picked up where its predecessor left off, bringing to Australia the proliferation of new styles in American art that followed modernism, pop, and minimalism in the second half of the 1960s as well as new mediums such as video. For this sequel exhibition, a number of the exhibiting artists flew to Australia to discuss their work with Australian audiences. Because "'the locals' were exposed to a particular artist's cultur*ing*," Art & Language contends, "nothing of that artist's enculturation was available. So, in order to respond to that artist's culturing, for it to be a meaningful encounter, the local is forced into tacit reconstruction of the enculturing ideology."[47] The distinction between "cultur*ing*" and "enculturation" is crucial for Art & Language's account of provincialism. The former refers to the effects that art and culture have on their audiences, while the latter is the set of values one acquires when learning about culture. Enculturation is what Art & Language's approach to conceptual art as deliberation about concepts sought to shape consciously by creating access to cultur*ing* within a collective discourse. For Art & Language, the cultur*ing* of Official Culture imposes itself far more tacitly than what occurs within its own group: "You're not directly influenced, it sneaks up from behind."[48] This is so because when art arrives in Australia from the United States, little if anything of the enculturation that led American artists to produce it is made available. The intellectual conditions of its production are concealed, and so there can be no interplay between contexts because the relationship between parties is asymmetrical; no American artist is subjected to the cultur*ing* of an Australian.

At a broader societal level, the tacit acceptance of American culture that results provides "*the ideal conditions for imposing 'internationalism*,'" the risk of which is a mismatch between what Art & Language calls "social reality" and "cultural reality."[49] This detachment of culture from society becomes especially dangerous when social interests are imposed through culture, and, in the case of the Museum of Modern Art, the collective contends that these interests are equivalent to those of the Rockefeller family, a prominent trustee of the museum that had extensive ties to the U.S. government, especially the Central Intelligence Agency. Following from this insight, Art & Language traces parallels between the international interests of the U.S. government and the shifting international foci of the International Council's exhibitions: "Latin America in the 1940's, Europe during the 1950's, Latin America again then Asia, including Australia, during the 1960's and 1970's."[50] This policy, when combined with the Museum of Modern Art's tendency to exhibit in the United States international artists "who 'fit' best with MoMA's notion of 'international art,'" leads to "the uniformity, the one-sidedness, the predictability, and the dullness of art everywhere!"[51]

This situation, however dire it seems to Art & Language, is not entirely hopeless. In the second of the two sections on the United States and Australia in "Draft for an Anti-Textbook," it hypothesizes about what an "'authentic' culture" as opposed to the Museum of Modern Art's "'high' pain-in-the-arse culture" might be, and it proposes the need for an "alternate *institution*" of which, at the time, it can identify "*no model at all.*"[52] Unwilling to accept "alternatives like folk-art . . . as serious options," Art & Language proposes that "something like teaching" might provide a platform for developing an alternative cultural model, and it considers its own group activity, modes of socialization, and collective pedagogy as a possible model.[53] This potential alternative is not as institutionalized as the Museum of Modern Art. Instead, it is, Art & Language claims, more "social . . . *and there is no clear demarcation when our socializing becomes work.*"[54] This indeterminacy scrambles "the relationships between artist and exhibition and gallery-goer," which "have been reified and officially institutionalized along the lines also of teacher/learner . . . affirming spectator culture."[55] Art & Language contrasts this to its own work: "we have tried to screw-up that particular relation between people . . . at least as it bears on us."[56] The proposed alternative institution effaces the hierarchical distinction that institutions usually maintain between teacher and learner in favor of a social situation in which these roles are less defined but teaching and learning remain goals. In short, Art & Language proposes something very much like the work it was then doing in New York, but for this model to be put into practice, proximal contact between contexts must first be arranged, since "there is no institutional access to A&L, there is only social access, an *encounter*."[57]

"Draft for an Anti-Textbook" was not well received by Art & Language's English section, and more disagreement about internationality followed. Another, similar transcript of New York conversations appears under the title "Brainstorming—New York" in the May 1975 issue of *Art-Language*. (In addition to Burn and Ramsden, Andrew Menard is listed as a contributor to this discussion.) The most significant aspect of this text for the disintegrating relationship between Art & Language's two main sections is its appendix, which is framed as a response to a transatlantic telephone conversation with Harold Hurrell, one of the founders of Art & Language in England. "Hurrell," Burn and Ramsden report, "asked us on the phone if we would consider the ramifications of 'Brainstorming 19/9/74' being read 'behind the Iron Curtain'—in Poland."[58] Hurrell's mention of Poland is far from arbitrary; in 1975, Art & Language showed work at the Foksal Gallery in Warsaw. Hurrell apparently intended his remark dismissively to suggest that Art & Language's concerns in New York were too local to be taken seriously anywhere else, particularly in a place as different from New York as Poland, or at least this is how Burn and Ramsden interpreted him. They respond by imagining Poles reading their text, which gives rise to "a remarkable epistemological problem: how can it be interpreted 'transituationally'?"[59] Their answer, couched in Art & Language's jargon, is that however Poles interpret the text reveals something potentially important about it from which the collective might learn: "There is a heuristic learning situation potentially present in the mapping of the indexicality of the text and the transituational 'objectivity' of Polish interpretations."[60] At the same time, Burn and Ramsden dismiss the kind of international reception their own work was receiving from their colleagues in England by suggesting that it was no better than what an unknown Polish audience might provide: "A lot seems to happen when something crosses the Atlantic, even with people we know."[61]

Art & Language's ambivalence about internationalizing art surfaced prominently in September 1974, when the collective's New York section

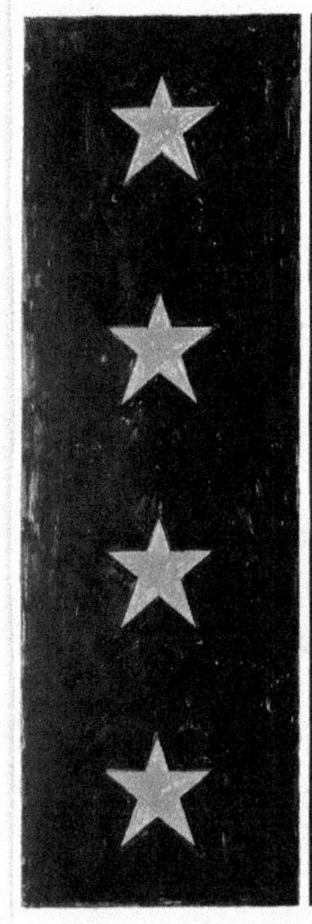

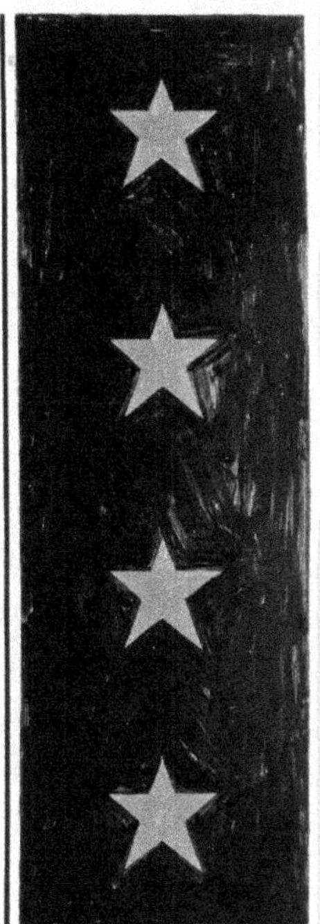

Figure 3.1 Art & Language, *To the Commission of Homage to Salvador Allende*, 1974.

was given an opportunity to exhibit a work at the Centro de Arte y Comunicación (CAYC) in Buenos Aires to protest the 1973 military coup in Chile, which replaced Salvador Allende's democratically elected socialist government with a brutal, American-backed military dictatorship led by Augusto Pinochet. Invited to submit work to an exhibition called *Homage to Salvador Allende*, Burn and Ramsden produced a poster titled *To the Commission of Homage to Salvador Allende* (figure 3.1). Beneath this title and bordered on left and right by stars reminiscent of the star on the Chilean flag is a lengthy text in the form of a letter to the project organizers that reflects ambivalently on the internationalization of art with specific reference to the CAYC's aspirations. The poster text opens with a hesitant response to the invitation to exhibit in Argentina: "There are two possible consequences of exposing 'the people of Latin America' to what is called the 'avant-garde art of the big international centers.' The first would be to make it easier for them to criticize the art, to open eyes to its social and ideological problematic. This would be good. The second consequence would be to affirm the already ubiquitous unreality of Official Culture: under the cloak of 'aesthetics' to encourage people to feel 'real' culture is something done elsewhere is alien from what they themselves do. This would be bad."[62]

Burn and Ramsden's concerns about the project stem from a fear that the latter, "bad" outcome of internationalism is far more likely to result if work is sent from New York to Buenos Aires without substantial reflection on the possible effects it might have at its destination: "The effect of this exhibition, if we read the situation in Latin America correctly . . . , will be to enable the corpse of New York dominated Official Culture, the domain of silly adventurism, the gathering place of reactionaries and other peddlars [*sic*] of aesthetic pretense, to imperialistically dictate 'culture' to the people of Latin America—a situation which strikes us as being positively mad."[63] Their broader assessment of the kind of internationalism of which they believe the CAYC project to be an example is equally damning:

> Internationalism simply means that the moguls of world media power get to say what is international. Under the guise of "sharing between people's [*sic*] of various cultures" it is in fact the means whereby a power elite arrogantly assume their own localized values are somehow "universal." Thus internationalism, by condemning "local variations" as provincial and inferior, reinforces its own hegemony and disrupts any possibility of a non-reified culture emerging locally. What better way to promote authority, predictability and dullness! What better way to hide the frailty of subjectivity, to remove the rewards of action, than behind some warped professional idea of "culture."[64]

Burn and Ramsden's proposal for an alternative to this hegemonic relationship is a reassessment of exhibition practice, but no practical approach is put forward at this stage: "History is, in part, the transformation of social relations into cultural ones. What needs to be done is retrieve social relations from the dominance of reified mystifying cultural ones."[65] How precisely to do so is unclear, but the problem is, seemingly, shared and therefore the basis for further collaborative work: "These are problems faced in any exhibition, though they are increased in 'international' ones, especially 'international' ones in 'underdeveloped' countries. They are the problems we are 'in' ourselves."[66]

Art & Language was able to devise a more satisfying approach to the problem of international exhibitions by developing a proposal Smith made in "The Provincialism Problem" into an actual undertaking. Near the end of his essay, Smith identifies the source of provincialism in international exhibitions that bring the art of the metropolis to the provinces, and he suggests the need for an exhibition practice that contends with the provincialism problem by addressing it at this level in a direct manner: "At present, it seems that the most responsible kind of exhibition would be one that took as its aim, not the supposedly 'neutral' presentation of a selection of artworks, but the display of the very problematic which its own incursion into a provincial situation raises. This would be difficult, certainly, requiring an unusual degree of reflexivity and some rethinking of the nature of exhibitions, but it is surely not impossible."[67] Following his return to Australia in 1975, Smith was invited to exhibit at three major state galleries in Sydney, Melbourne, and Adelaide, and he began organizing Art & Language exhibitions with input from his colleagues in New York that are exactly the sort of intervention he identifies as most necessary in "The Provincialism Problem." The "impossible" double bind of provincialism begins to loosen in these instances precisely because Art & Language, itself composed of such a transnational milieu, is able to be reflexive in its internationality and make as explicit as possible the dynamics of cultural exchange as they happen.

Smith seized opportunities presented to him to show Art & Language work at the Art Gallery of New South Wales in Sydney, the National Gallery of Victoria in Melbourne, and the Art Gallery of South Australia in Adelaide as an occasion to provide Art & Language's theoretical account of provincialism with a more practical dimension. In posters announcing the exhibitions, the plans for which Smith developed in correspondence with Burn and Ramsden, who remained in New York and contributed from afar, Art & Language lays out the set of concerns that it will address (figure 3.2):

ART & LANGUAGE

Discussions 11am to 1pm Wednesday to Sunday

The hegemony of Official Culture perpetuates a market-place intelligibility. This is fast becoming a tawdry surrogate for existence.

We have come to realize we are already shaped by our 'given' roles - the institutionalization of artist, critic, curator, audience-our lives/experience are following as a formality: now the role determines the person, not the other way about: ask not what you can do <u>for</u> Modern Art but what Modern Art can do <u>to</u> you.

This latest form of art-imperialism can only be assailed by first assailing our given producer-consumer 'natures'- are we in good hands with the Museum of Modern Art and the U.S. Information Service, the professionals the specialists the artocrats/bureaucrats who hand us culture, not something we do but something <u>they</u> do, who'creat-ively' wrap themselves around the creations of <u>others</u>, not something <u>we</u> do but something <u>they</u> do?

At regular intervals during the exhibition, <u>Art & Language</u> will cable blurts/fragments of discourse from New York to the Gallery. These will be received by Terry Smith who, at the times indicated, will conduct 'dialogues' with invited guests and the gallery public. This means Terry will deal with each blurt praxiologically-concerning himself with the question of embeddedness, the problems of re-embedd-ing, the specific contexts of reference. Look on this exhibition as perhaps a kind of model of what an 'international' exhibition might be like (?). Don't look on it as part of the iniquitous history of 'art-show' morphological 'innovations'. It's separate from the adventurism of current art-surface-styles as well as from 'an exchange of information' in the gee whiz communications theory sense.

Blurting in A&L...I generate a surface of language and this surface is embedded: its embeddedness is in respect to specific social, cultural and contextual points of reference. What happens when my surface (language...grammar(?)) is abstracted from its set of references and represented in another set of references (yours)? does it matter? can we say various points of reference match? what does not-matching mean? what does fit and mis-fit imply? what does all this tell you about <u>your</u> points of reference, <u>your</u> practice, poss-ibilities-what does <u>all</u> this tell me about <u>mine</u>?

This is not just another trans-oceanic lecture, but a dialogue, our fragments or conversation. These fragments (the cables) are anticipated to pick up a lot of (your) socio-cultural 'noise', as well as reflect a lot of ours...there isn't, between you and me, a 'clear channel'. Making the 'noise' explicit or accessible is making ordinarily habitual processes self-conscious, transformations can be projected from surface to depth, and hence - and here is the point - we have some potential for revisability of our languaging/cultural situations...

Some (Australian) entrepreneurs and art-pundits don't recognize 'culture' except insofar as it perpetuates their own and others aesthetic half-life. Some people in Melbourne or Sydney appear to be more enamoured with the centre of consumer pretense, the avant-gardist and careerist market-place (NY), than some of us are. This is all a lot more confusing than talking about gross geographical/national chunks like 'Australia' and the 'USA'-cosmopolitanism and localism are only symptoms of a cause which is traceable to the way our ability to actually learn (practice...culture...) is frustrated by our socialized submissions to the alienation of the exchanges (and the word is appropriate) between people.

National Gallery of Victoria May 28 to June 8 ,1975

Figure 3.2 Promotional flyer for Art & Language exhibition in Melbourne, 1975.

> The hegemony of Official Culture perpetuates a market-place intelligibility. This is fast becoming a tawdry surrogate for existence.
>
> We have come to realize that we are already shaped by our "given" roles (the institutionalization of artist, critic, curator, audience) our lives/experience are following as a formality: now the role determines the person, not the other way about: ask not what you can do *for* Modern Art but what Modern Art can do *to* you.
>
> This latest form of art-imperialism can only be assailed by first assailing our given producer/consumer "natures." Are we in good hands with the Museum of Modern Art and the U.S. Information Service, the professionals the specialists the artocrats/bureaucrats who hand us culture, not something we do but something *they* do, who "creatively" wrap themselves around the creations of others, not something *we* do but something *they* do?[68]

These concerns were unexpectedly timely, as Art & Language discovered that the itinerary for its exhibitions would inadvertently overlap times and venues in Sydney and Melbourne with *Modern Masters: From Manet to Matisse*, a major exhibition of European modernism organized by the International Council of the Museum of Modern Art, the first such exhibition since *Some Recent American Art* in 1974. "The coincidence of the Art & Language show and the exhibition 'Modern Masters: From Manet to Matisse' at the major State galleries in Australia during May, June and July created a battleground of contrasting conceptions of culture," Smith wrote shortly after Art & Language's exhibition program concluded in a report for Art & Language's new journal *The Fox*: "The clash has significance both in and beyond New York—where both shows, in different senses, 'originated.' Imperialist/colonialist hackles were raised, and there was enacted a drama of censorship rebuffed or ratbaggery curtailed (depending upon your viewpoint)."[69]

Indeed, the series of exhibitions got off to a controversial start when, following pressure from Liberal Party politician Peter Coleman, the Art Gallery of New South Wales's trustees and director Peter Laverty voted to cancel the Sydney exhibition at a meeting on February 28, 1975. The previous year, Coleman, who served on the Australian Council for the Arts from 1968 to 1973, published a book titled *Obscenity, Blasphemy, Sedition:*

Censorship in Australia, in which he argued that Australia had overcome its history of censorship.[70] Clearly, it had not. In the June 1975 issue of the journal *Quadrant*, which Coleman edited, Elwyn Lynn, the same critic who previously objected to Smith's "The Provincialism Problem" with a letter to the editor of *Artforum*, published a lengthy essay about *Modern Masters* that aimed to dismiss Smith's concerns about cultural imperialism as "a gross simplification."[71] The second Art & Language exhibition, scheduled for Melbourne, nearly met with the same fate as the one scheduled for Sydney after *Modern Masters* curator William S. Lieberman, who was in Melbourne at the time, saw the poster Smith created to publicize the Art & Language exhibition there and "promptly threatened to sue the Gallery," citing specifically Smith's mention of the Museum of Modern Art in the poster's text.[72] After an initial cancellation, Gordon Thomson, director of the National Gallery of Victoria, permitted Smith to go forward with the exhibition but only if it was staged "in the Art School in the back of the gallery."[73] Back in New York, Annette Kuhn covered the controversy for the *Village Voice*. In her "Culture Shock" column, she reports that Art & Language remained "in high spirits. They believe that by attempting to suppress their show the MoMA proved the collective's point."[74]

As staged in both Melbourne and, later, Adelaide, where *Modern Masters* did not tour and, accordingly, no censorship controversy occurred, the exhibition took shape as an installation designed to fill a room (figures 3.3, 3.4). Ostensibly a retrospective of Art & Language's work, it featured no works of art but instead catalogs from past Art & Language exhibitions, issues of its journals *Art-Language* and *The Fox*, and other Art & Language texts, including typescript drafts of "The Provincialism Problem," all of which appeared on tables for visitors to peruse at their leisure—and, tellingly, without an index structuring that perusal, as had been the case for so much previous work by Art & Language. Instead of a set of rules for reading the collective's work, a conversation would occur. Copies of the promotional poster for the exhibition hung on the walls and announced its other component, for which the installation served as a rostrum: a series of discussions between Smith, guest speakers from the Australian arts community, and interested visitors to the gallery that were planned to take, as their points of departure, blurts supplied by Burn and Ramsden from ongoing Art & Language work in New York. In Melbourne, these texts arrived via

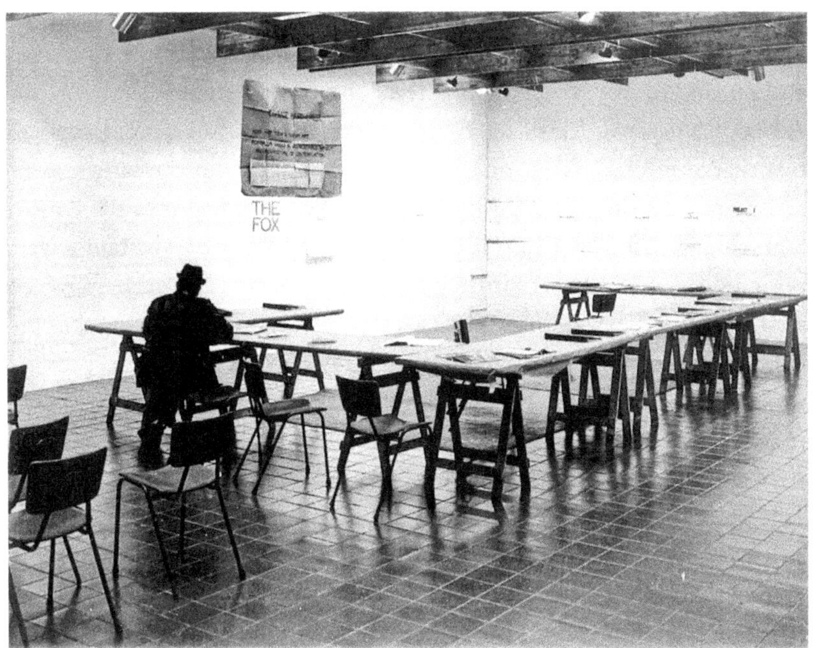

Figure 3.3 Art & Language exhibition in Melbourne, 1975, installation view.

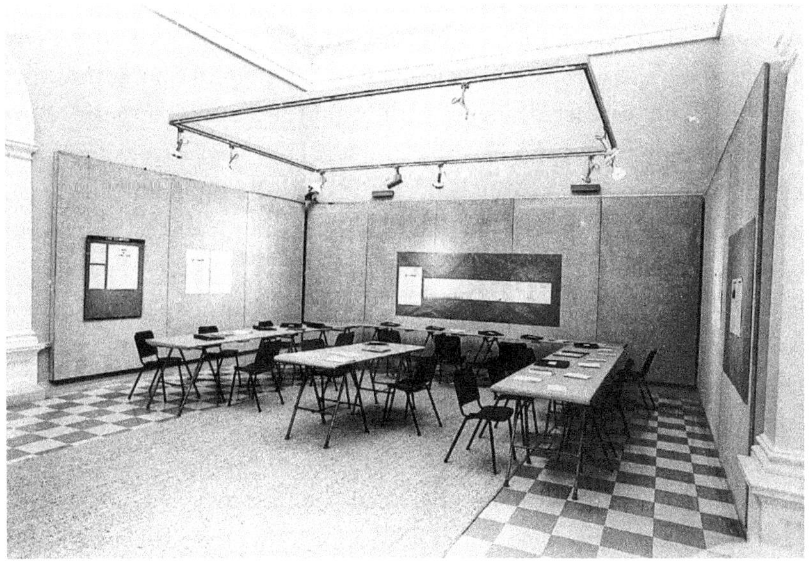

Figure 3.4 Art & Language exhibition in Adelaide, 1975, installation view.

a Teletype machine, which transmits text along telephone lines at a high rate of speed, thereby creating a rapid connection between the two cities and putting to rest any remaining fears of a provincializing time lag. The Adelaide blurts were extracted from a working draft of an Art & Language text that Smith received in advance. It could stand in for the early state of artistic process that generally did not arrive in Australia from the United States along with American "masterpieces." In either case, the blurts were posted on a large sheet of brown paper for visitors to examine before each session. On it, under the heading "COMRADE HARD-LINER" are the core ideas of Art & Language's intervention phrased in the most direct possible form as slogans: "MOST ART TODAY IS MUSEUM ART" and "FORMALISM WOULD BE INCONCEIVABLE WITHOUT AN ARCHITECTURE OF CONTEMPLATION."

If the state galleries wanted an exhibition that would bring Australia up to date regarding the latest developments in conceptual art, they got more than they bargained for, as Smith turned the exhibitions themselves into those very developments, implicating Australian audiences in the production of the work and inviting them into Art & Language as participants through the discussions in the galleries. The promotional poster outlines the format these discussions took: "At regular intervals during the exhibition, *Art & Language* will send blurts/fragments of discourse from New York to the Gallery. These will be received by Terry Smith who, at the times indicated, will conduct 'dialogues' with invited guests and the gallery public. This means Terry will deal with each blurt praxiologically—concerning himself with the question of embeddedness, the problems of re-embedding, the specific contexts of reference. Look on this exhibition as perhaps a kind of model of what an 'international' exhibition might be like (?)." Specifically, Art & Language aimed to "pick up a lot of (your) socio-cultural 'noise,' as well as reflect a lot of ours" in order to emphasize that "there isn't, between you and me, a 'clear channel.'" Making "ordinarily habitual processes self conscious" frees up the possibility of investigating the deeper "social, cultural and contextual points of reference" within which "a surface of language... is embedded." The hoped-for result is that "we have some potential for revisability of our languaging/cultural situations." In other words, by working on the difficulties to which cultural exchange gives rise, language can be extracted from the contexts in which it is "embedded," whether American or Australian, and put to new uses, including the facilitation of exchanges. By juxtaposing this alternative format to *Modern Masters*'s mode of international exchange, Art & Language's exhibitions provided occasions to oppose centrist projections that produce provincialism. The politics of art at stake makes explicit the concepts informing artists' worldviews so as to open to all involved new possibilities for thought and action. At the same time, this activity is itself conducted in a manner that already embodies these values insofar as it emphasizes dialogue and scrambles distinctions between here and there, center and periphery, metropolis and province. In short, the exhibitions enact a conceptual revolt so as to develop an international mode of enculturation through interplay between art worlds.

However, this more equitable mode of exchange proved far from harmonious. "In a way," Smith says at the beginning of the first Melbourne discussion, in reference to Burn and Ramsden's first Teletype message, "them sending a message from NY, with the obligation in this set-up that we pay special attention to it, is just as offensive as the Modern Masters package."[75] However, he adds, "in our case the main reason for us getting together now is that we have a chance of, through me, taking the message apart, treating it as problematic."[76] If Smith found Burn and Ramsden's transmission of texts potentially too close in character to *Modern Masters* and something that he, with his audience, would subject to analysis, that very audience took issue with Smith himself as potentially embodying the very dynamic he claimed to subvert. An unnamed participant in the first Melbourne session complains, "Nothing radical can happen here because of the way you've structured it with you and your students sitting around the table and the microphones up the front of the room. That's the same structure as Modern Masters."[77] Later, at the first Adelaide session, Liz Sheridan protests, "Your jargon is prohibitive—it's like an Englishman speaking German to a Frenchman."[78] By the end of each week of discussions, however, these concerns were largely assuaged or, more to the point, seen as the problematic situation in which work needed to be done. Assisting with that work were a number of invited guests, including a group of art students from Melbourne universities, philosopher of science Henry Krips, Marxist historian Humphrey McQueen, art critic Patrick McCaughey, poet Garrie Hutchinson, director of the Art Gallery of South Australia Earle Hackett, art historian Donald Brook, Noel Sheridan of the Experimental Art Foundation, members of the Progressive Art Movement, and the critic and curator Lucy R. Lippard, who was visiting Australia from New York at the time.

The concerns addressed in these discussions get to the heart of the contradiction animating Art & Language's exhibitions in Australia: on the one hand, Smith's position as the collective's sole representative enables him to open a conduit between New York and Melbourne or New York and Adelaide where cultur*ing* is reciprocated, and a process of enculturation suited to the demands of international exchange is established through encounter and interplay; on the other hand, Smith's role, in its exclusivity and privilege, threatens to reproduce the logic of subservience that the exhibitions aim to undercut, and the fact that he begins each session with what he calls a "translation" of Burn and Ramsden's blurts out of Art & Language's argot implies that its discourse is so alien to his audience that dependence on him is inevitable.[79] Despite the obstacles impeding Smith's attempts to generate conversation, the discussions do make considerable strides toward addressing what Smith calls "the key problem: how does one engage in art activity, form unspecified, which can be relevant in a way which goes beyond the confines of art history, the elitist artworld which entraps us?"[80]

By far the most contentious discussion was the third in Adelaide, in which Smith squared off against representatives from the Progressive Art Movement and defined his position on the politics of artistic activity relative to their populist vision of an art for the people. On June 30, in anticipation of the discussion, Christine McCarthy, secretary of the Progressive Art Movement, sent a letter to Ian North, curator of paintings at the Art Gallery of South Australia, announcing that the group "decided that it cannot participate in the organization" because of its concerns "that art should be put to the service of ordinary people rather than remaining a diversion for privileged intellectuals."[81] McCarthy also noted that the group would send observers to the discussion, who, if they deemed it suitable, would participate in it. At the session, Smith began by restating his position on provincialism and cultural imperialism as effected by recent touring exhibitions organized by the International Council of the Museum of Modern Art. An unnamed participant stated the Progressive Art Movement's position: "But the option is clear. You simply don't work for that art world. Forget it. We should work for the people, in a way they can understand."[82] What follows was a lengthy, at times protracted, discussion about the politics of making art. Smith deemed "the people" too abstract an entity and contended that abandoning the art world neither exempts art from participation in a capitalist system nor counteracts the deleterious effects of the art world on society, hence Art & Language's position and efforts at building a dialogue on provincialism within the art world. The discussion concluded with Smith's response to artist Julie Ewington's question about his position and whether it had a positive program: "What I'm proposing is that we act as terrorists toward our language, i.e. toward all our isms. We should start with the worlds we are in, and reproduce our learning as we go, so that we at least prefigure our ends in our means. We should organize, in order to counteract our histories of soft subjectivism. We should condemn 'political art.' We forge praxis only in struggling against our rulers, oppressors, manipulators--I've been pointing out who they are and how they operate for the past three days. Is that direct enough?"[83]

The fifth and final session in Adelaide, for which Lippard joined Smith as the only American to participate in these discussions about provincialism, returned to many of these issues in a way that summarized much of what emerged during the course of the two exhibitions (figure 3.5). Lippard came to Australia to give the Power Lecture in Sydney, and afterward she traveled through the country lecturing and exploring her interest in women's art. Not surprisingly, she raised a number of feminist concerns and claims that "A&L has nothing to do with women's problems."[84] Despite this, in her analyses of the art world, Lippard had much in common with the group. For instance, she said,

> Feminism has led me to abandon that idea of endless change in art. Avant-gardism, the notion that everything has to be *beyond* something else, terms like "Post-object Art." Medium and progression are misleading: the emphasis should be on how the work gets across, to what audience; on how far it goes towards subverting the system. We are trapped in a capitalist society. We can go a little way to the left or right, but in either direction you come up against this gigantic wall which you can't pass through if you live in a society which doesn't respect art or artists. The artworld is entirely conservative, and so are artists. This radical wildness and freedom image is nonsense.[85]

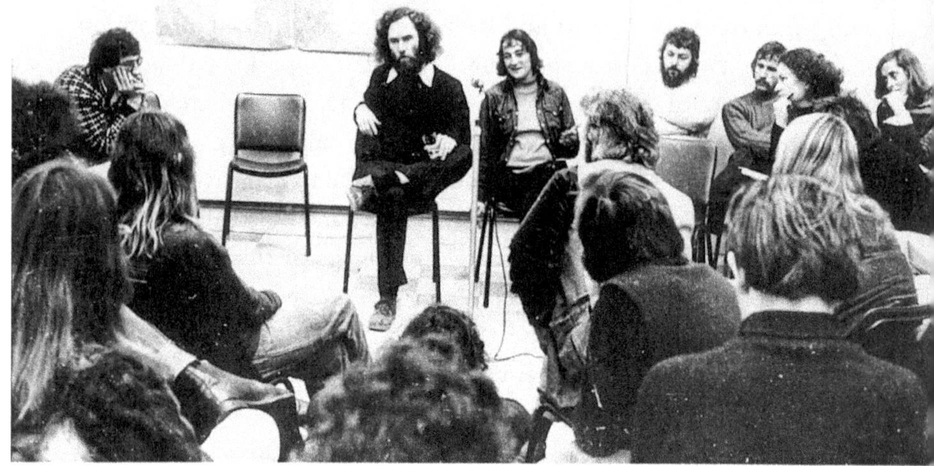

Figure 3.5 Terry Smith and Lucy Lippard speaking with others during the Art & Language exhibition in Adelaide, 1975.

Lippard then addressed this picture of the art world to the ambivalences of internationalism, noting that she had previously visited New Zealand to speak in connection with the exhibition *Some Recent American Art*, her visit having been arranged by the Museum of Modern Art. Speaking to the political complexities of that situation, she asserted, "I was well aware I was being used and was able to use them a bit too."[86] Here, Lippard captured the profound uneasiness of operating between an activist desire and the threat that one's own activism can be neutered by an institutional authority that appropriates it to preempt claims that what it is doing might be politically damaging. "But they could say: 'We're so liberal, we can send as our representative someone who has been threatened with arrest in the Museum several times.' I knew what I was getting into and discussed it in an article in the *N.Z. Quarterly*."[87] Lippard also affirmed a program Smith outlined for combating provincialism in Australia, and saw its applicability to the United States. Smith's program included three points: "The three things I see as crucial for Australian culture . . . the gap between high culture and mass culturing—we've got to get through that. We've got to get through the bluff dichotomy of internationalism/localism. And, thirdly, the issues involved in governmental/state patronage have got to pass 'The Arts' and 'Culture' as their main references. These are where the issues cluster."[88] Lippard responded by indicating that these problems are not limited to the Australian situation, stating, "The problems are exactly the same in America."[89] As for why this is so, she suggested, "The art scenes reproduce each other because they imitate each other as markets. There's so much that is economically determined."[90]

Of course, the discussions that accompanied Art & Language's Australian exhibitions could not resolve all the issues they raised, but Smith judged the overall project a success for at least beginning a process of wrestling with them. In a letter to Burn and Ramsden that recapitulates the proceedings in Melbourne, he writes, "it worked far better than I had dreamed—above all, I found myself witnessing the amazing sight of thirty/forty people, who came to each session, very clearly, publicly, evidently *learning*—making connections they hadn't before, pushing themselves beyond what was previously safe to know, then going further."[91] Smith's letter, along with a report on the exhibitions that he published as an essay in *The Fox*, furthered the transcontinental exchange by reciprocating Burn and Ramsden's transmission of blurts to Australia. Ramsden's reply, in a letter of June 16, 1975, suggests that Smith's reports were beneficial in New York: "I've learnt quite a bit so far from the Australian show: It's no doubt one of the most important things we've done. Following it up should be even more interesting."[92]

Two things followed more or less immediately from Art & Language's exhibitions in Australia. The first was a publication containing transcripts of the discussions in Melbourne and Adelaide along with other material related to the exhibition, including press clippings, interviews, and documents. Smith and Burn made initial plans to publish this as an issue of *Art-Language*, but they fell through.[93] Instead, the material Smith assembled and edited ultimately appeared as a volume titled *Art & Language: Australia 1975*. The vast majority of this book's pages are given over to transcripts of the discussions that took place in Melbourne and Adelaide. Unlike a conventional exhibition catalog, works by Art & Language are not reproduced

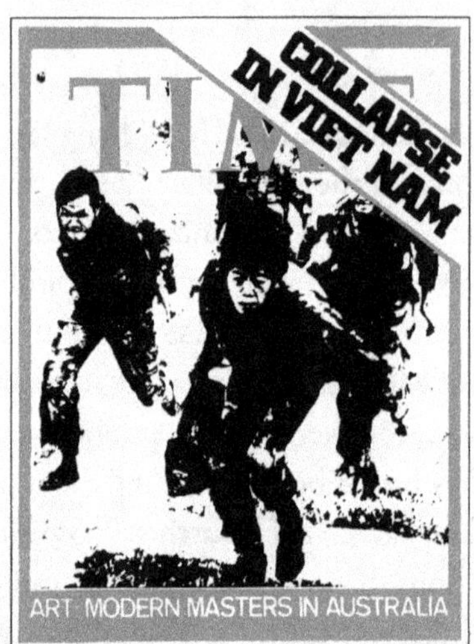

Figure 3.6 Art & Language, *Art & Language: Australia 1975*, 1976, front cover. Design and layout by Chips Mackinolty.

except in documentary images of the talks, where various items can be seen only obliquely, resting on tables. A brief checklist of the items on display is included, but dialogue takes center stage.[94] Art & Language's concerns about cultural imperialism are highlighted on the book's front cover, which features a design by Chips Mackinolty (figure 3.6). Mackinolty, an artist affiliated with the Earthworks Poster Collective, which worked at the Sydney University Art Workshop also known as the Tin Sheds, began producing political posters, including many anti–Vietnam War posters, in the early 1970s. His cover for *Art & Language: Australia 1975* appropriates the April 14, 1975, issue of *Time*, which devoted substantial coverage to the Vietnam

War under the banner headline "Collapse in Vietnam" above an image from the war zone. At the bottom is a second headline that reads, "Art: Modern Masters in Australia." Presented like a found collage, the cover image juxtaposes American foreign policies on the military and cultural fronts to reveal the diverse manifestations of imperialism affecting the world at the time.

The last page of *Art & Language: Australia 1975* includes a notice that announces a second outcome of Art & Language's exhibitions in Australia:

> Also available:
>
> (Provisional) ART & LANGUAGE: AUCKLAND 1976
>
> Transcripts of the discussions held at the Auckland City Art Gallery, August 1976, with related texts and illustrations of the installations "Media Massacre," "Medibunk," and "The Story of Cur, Piggy and the Prefect."[95]

This volume never came to fruition. It would have documented an Art & Language exhibition and discussion series that Smith conceived and executed to introduce the collective's work to audiences in New Zealand and to examine provincialism outside the bounds of the art world as a general cultural condition that conceptual art allied to a kind of media activism could analyze and contest. The exhibition ignored New York and the United States altogether to show how cultural dependency operates in other contexts, taking a regional approach based not on international art exhibitions but on Australian media, including coverage of New Zealand, and its connection to political relations between those countries.

John Maynard, exhibitions officer of the Auckland City Art Gallery, first contacted Smith about doing an Art & Language exhibition in the gallery's Project Programme series while Smith was resident in the United States. Unable to do so at the time, he eventually agreed to the dates August 4–10, 1976, and a format similar to Art & Language's exhibitions in Australia, including a gallery presentation supplemented by public discussions. Initially, two were planned for August 8 and 9, but according to transcripts of the discussions, five occurred, one on August 4, and two each on August 7 and 8. The gallery presentation consisted of two major elements: a mixture of Art & Language projects, including the publications and binders displayed in Melbourne and Adelaide, accompanied by a series of new projects

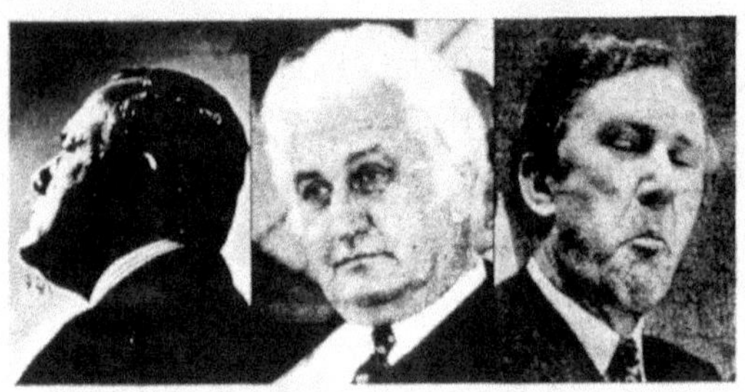

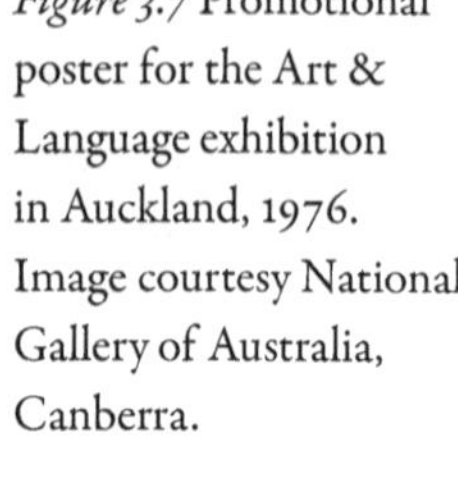

Figure 3.7 Promotional poster for the Art & Language exhibition in Auckland, 1976. Image courtesy National Gallery of Australia, Canberra.

Smith created on the theme of Australian media culture that responded to current events.

In 1975, New Zealand elected the socially and economically conservative National Party politician Robert Muldoon as prime minister. His election coincided with a shift to the right in Australian politics that occurred after Governor General John Kerr named Malcolm Fraser, head of the Liberal-National Country Party coalition, to form a caretaker government and replace Gough Whitlam, leader of the Labour Party, as prime minister. To publicize his exhibition in Auckland, Smith, in collaboration with Mackinolty, produced a poster featuring photographs of Muldoon, Kerr, and Fraser with the words "Piggy," "Cur," and "Prefect," respectively, above them (figure 3.7). It received initial approval from the Auckland City Art Gallery Subcommittee after Maynard presented it to them, and copies were put up around Auckland. However, on August 2, shortly before the exhibition was to open, Ernest Smith, director of the gallery, informed Maynard and Terry

Smith that the poster could not be shown publicly. A meeting was called, and Smith agreed to black out the words above the photographs on the remaining posters that had not already been posted in the city. On versions displayed in the gallery, he added, in addition to black bars, a rubber stamp that reads, "THIS POSTER HAS BEEN CENSORED." The controversy surrounding the poster became a minor media event in New Zealand, with a short illustrated article appearing on the front page of the *Auckland Star*, a daily evening newspaper.[96]

Despite this act of censorship, the exhibition otherwise went ahead as planned, and Smith used the banned words freely inside the gallery. On the gallery walls were three installations composed primarily of sandwich boards featuring enlarged headlines from Sydney newspapers (figures 3.8, 3.9). The first, titled *The Story of Cur, Piggy, and the Prefect*, narrates, in the large block letters of sandwich board headlines, the recent shift to the right in Australian and New Zealand politics by revealing how political consciousness was produced and manipulated in and through the media. Second was *Medibunk*, which concerned the proposed general strike that followed Fraser's changes to Medibank, Australia's universal health care program. *Media Massacre*, the third installation, concerns Australian stereotyping of New Zealanders through a collection of sandwich boards that sensationalize the case of Phillip Western, a New Zealander murderer and prison escapee. Smith conceived these displays "as a *ta tze pao*, a wall newspaper on the model of the Democracy Wall in China, to which anyone could add their views. Some did."[97] As installations, they use collage techniques of juxtaposition to compare the ideological commitments of mainstream and underground media so as to expose discursive limitations and put forward alternative forms of knowledge. Sometimes, similar sandwich boards are grouped together to show repetition and emphasis; other times, differing perspectives from a tabloid and a radical newspaper are placed side by side to offer two views of the same event. The language used on these sandwich boards is also subject to critique through its displacement into the gallery space, where condensed headlines, which may make sense within the immediate flux of Sydney street life, become strange, and the media's mystifications of everyday experience come to the fore.

The sandwich boards take over the role that Burn and Ramsden's blurts played in Art & Language's Australian exhibitions and serve as focal points

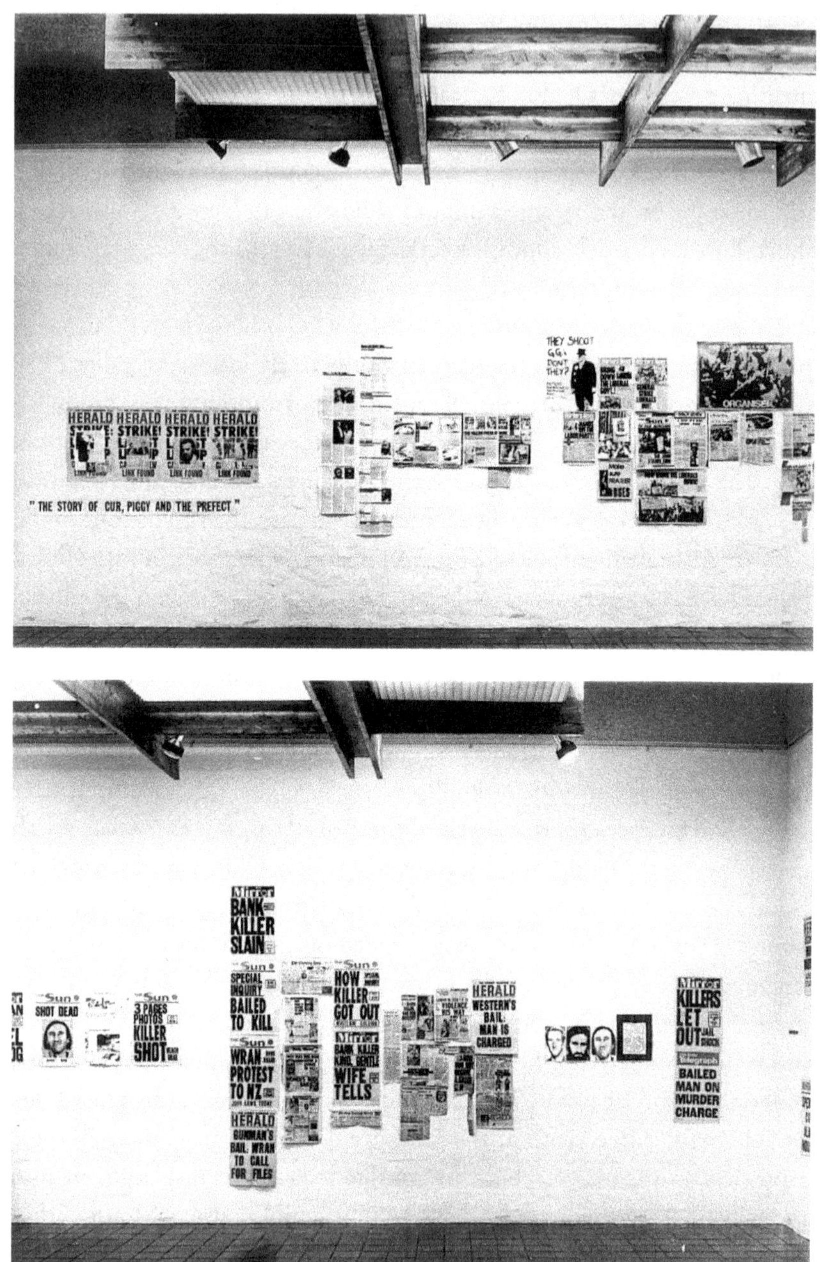

Figures 3.8 and 3.9 Terry Smith, Art & Language exhibition in Auckland, 1976, installation view.

for discussions that Smith framed "generally under the heading of art and politics."[98] These began with a decoding of ideological assumptions present in the media, fully shifting Art & Language's earlier critique of provincialism in the art world to the issue of cultural dependency in general. The five sessions ranged over a number of topics including the social function of institutions and the role of the artist within them, ownership of the media and its concomitant limits as a forum for public discourse, the conditions of cultural production in New Zealand (including comparative discussion of the radically different conditions in China at the time), and more. As in Australia, invited guests accompanied Smith, including artists Bruce Barber and Elizabeth Morley; poet and critic Wystan Curnow; journalist Geoff Chapple; representatives of the Progressive Bookshop, a left-wing bookstore in Auckland; and art historians Tony Green, Ian Buchanan, and Mike Dunn. The audience was vocal as well.

With this Auckland exhibition and discussion series, which Smith conceived without significant input from New York, the institutions of the art world come to figure as ambivalent sites. After working in and through them in Australia, Smith treats such institutions as less monolithic than malleable. He argues that, despite the institutional capacity for reproducing power, its appropriation of opposition can never be total, and thus it is feasible, even preferable, to work from within institutions:

> It is possible for people to work oppositionally within universities and oppositionally within galleries because they want to construct them differently, because they believe they are right and they've got arguments for it and got experience to show it. . . . I mean precisely that the activity of creativity, of generating imagery[,] of setting up contrasts, of making intuitive leaps and grasps, producing symbols, that whole human process can't be annexed—not all of it, but most of it can and most of it has been. What's left are people who, because of contradictions in the bourgeois takeover, are produced as opponents, and in that opposition is where the hope for the future lies.[99]

These people who are "left" proffer no solutions to the provincialism problem or to cultural dependency in general. Instead, they work to bring about its dissolution with discussions and arguments that transform the institutions and exchanges that bring it about in the first place. This lesson would have been valuable in New York, where, by the time of Smith's Auckland exhibition, Art & Language was disintegrating after debates about how to organize itself relative to the art world led nearly all of the collective to depart. Smith too departed Art & Language not long after he returned to Australia from New Zealand. At an earlier date, the diverse ideas held by members of the collective could have been reconciled as vital components of a larger oppositional strategy, perhaps as interplay of the sort that Smith had been facilitating, but the sociality through which the collective's practice sustained itself was, by this time, so strained that a breach was inevitable.

Four
Foxes and Hedgehogs

"Us old warlords of conceptual art have gotten together," Joseph Kosuth told Annette Kuhn of the *Village Voice* in April 1975, to enact "the formalization of the schism between theoretical conceptualists and the stylists."[1] Late the previous year, Kosuth had called several participants in Art & Language's New York section together to form an editorial board. Alienated from the collective's English section, Kosuth envisioned a new publication called *The Fox* that would operate as an alternative to Art & Language's already established journal, *Art-Language*, which had been edited in England since 1969.[2] As with previous work by Art & Language, *The Fox* was conceived as a forum for conversation about how best to organize artistic practice relative to the current state of the art world. Sarah Charlesworth, a photographer who had been brought into the fold of Art & Language by Kosuth around this time and proved instrumental in founding the new magazine, spoke of it as an endeavor that was not begun "as a project of Art & Language" but rather as a way to confront "the extremely oppressive nature of a very elitist and rather irrelevant (in terms of effective practice) theoretical debating society which was Art & Language."[3] That the magazine ultimately did appear as a product of the Art & Language "Foundation, Inc." happened, as Charles Harrison notes, at the insistence of Mel Ramsden, who felt it necessary "that antecedence should be acknowledged."[4] From the outset, then, those participating in *The Fox* acknowledge that disagreement could be constitutive of a robust collaboration, and the introductory note published at the front of the first issue welcomes responses "pro and con" to its call for the creation of "some kind of community practice." Indeed, the debates that played out across the pages of *The Fox*, particularly those concerning art's relationship to politics, would prove so contentious as to threaten the existence of Art & Language and call into question the continuing relevance of conceptual art.

Inviting plurality and even contradiction was entirely appropriate given the particular fox from which *The Fox* took its name. A fragment attributed to the ancient Greek poet Archilochus compares this fox to a hedgehog: "πόλλ' οἶδ' ἀλώπηξ, ἀλλ' ἐχῖνος ἓν μέγα." Douglas E. Gerber translates this passage as "The fox knows many tricks, the hedgehog one, but it's a big one."[5] Isaiah Berlin references this fragment of Archilochus's in his 1951 essay "Lev Tolstoy's Historical Scepticism," later revised and expanded to become the book *The Hedgehog and the Fox: An Essay on Tolstoy's View of History*, which is where Art & Language encountered it. Berlin writes of hedgehogs and foxes:

> For there exists a great chasm between those, on the one side, who relate everything to a single central vision, one system less or more coherent or articulate, in terms of which they understand, think and feel—a single, universal, organizing principle in terms of which alone all that they are and say has significance—and, on the other side, those who pursue many ends, often unrelated and even contradictory, connected, if at all, only in some *de facto* way, for some psychological or physiological cause, related by no moral or aesthetic principle; these last lead lives, perform acts, and entertain ideas that are centrifugal rather than centripetal, their thought is scattered or diffused, moving on many levels, seizing upon the essence of a vast variety of experiences and objects for what they are in themselves, without, consciously or unconsciously, seeking to fit them into, or exclude them from, any one unchanging, all-embracing, sometimes self-contradictory and incomplete, at times fanatical, unitary inner vision. The first kind of intellectual and artistic personality belongs to the hedgehogs, the second to the foxes.[6]

By naming their new journal after Archilochus's fox as glossed by Berlin, the editors of *The Fox* consciously contrasted themselves to the English section of Art & Language. In New York, the collective continued to welcome participation from an increasing number of people, who brought fresh interests and concerns into the group and into *The Fox*'s editorial board. In contrast, the growth of Art & Language in England had slowed. Eventually, the group there began shrinking, and its work increasingly became identifiable with one person: Michael Baldwin. Within the pages of *Art-Language* and *The Fox*, to which participants in both sections of Art & Language continued to contribute, a debate about the future of the collective plays itself out, with lines drawn and redrawn as the hedgehog-like consensus attitude in England conflicts with the fox-like pandemonium in New York. As this conflict developed into a debate about politicizing art, the roles of fox and hedgehog shifted with the changing alliances formed in an increasingly precarious collective. Hedgehogs would pop up in New York, and those in England would get tricky.

The Fox was not, however, intended entirely as a vehicle for a protracted transatlantic debate. Its primary audience was the art world, particularly the New York art world, and again Archilochus's fox appealed to Art & Language's desire to avoid what it saw as its peers' single-minded, hedgehog-like embrace of the commodity form at a time when conceptual art was beginning to be heavily collected. Against this, *The Fox* was polemical even in its appearance, which eschewed the glossy pages and full-bleed color images characteristic of most art magazines in favor of inexpensive newsprint with cardboard covers and entirely black-and-white contents. Only the covers of each issue were printed in color, and then only a single color: green for the first, red for the second, and blue for the third (figures 4.1–4.3). *The Fox*'s aesthetic is so pared down that the stylistic decision to use Copperplate Gothic on the cover and for titles can feel like a concession to decorativeness. The few images that do appear are reproduced in high contrast and poor quality. Brittle, an issue of *The Fox* gives the impression that it might disintegrate in its reader's hands at any moment. This bare-bones look and feel places a certain emphasis squarely on *The Fox*'s textual contents, which mark a return to the essay format that Art & Language had largely eschewed for several years while it pursued other methods of presentation. Now, desiring to address the art world as clearly and directly as possible, the comparative straightforwardness of the essay—as well as its historical role as a vehicle for polemic—appeals again, and the absence of Art & Language's characteristic argot is evident throughout the confrontational addresses that compose the bulk of *The Fox*. At the same time, essays returned the group to individual authorship, albeit through a writing pro-

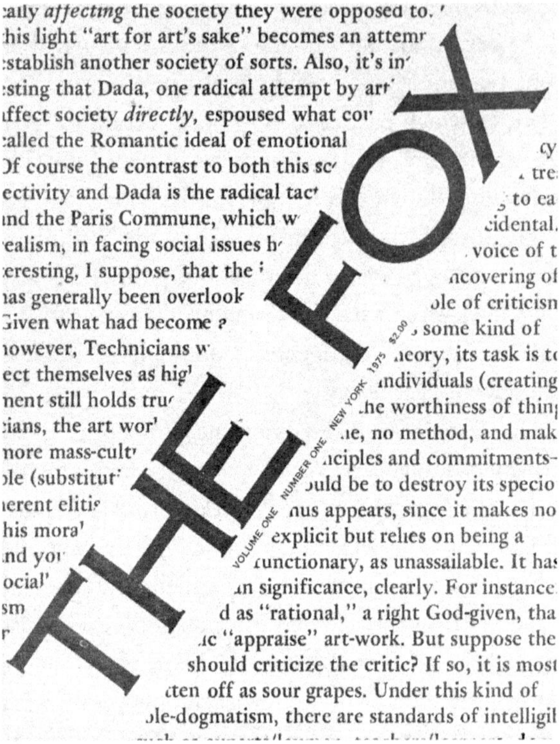

Figure 4.1 Art & Language, *The Fox* 1, no. 1 (1975).

cess that generally involved the circulation of working drafts for comments, which had a tendency to amplify differences between writers rather than subsuming them into a unified collective voice. As Art & Language came together to address the art world, it fell apart as a group.

If the collective's audiences previously complained about the obscurity of its prose or of its presentation, they now took issue with that prose's precision, which made abundantly evident the collective's hostility to the art world, and *The Fox* was not well received by certain of its initial readers. Mona da Vinci provided a presumably pseudonymous and particularly harsh review of the second issue for the *Soho Weekly News*. She (he?) accuses *The Fox* of "mobilizing offensive attacks against art, art history, *Artforum*, artists, art education, formalist and phenomenologist criticism, the phenomenon of Don Judd, art politics, art museums, public art, in fact,

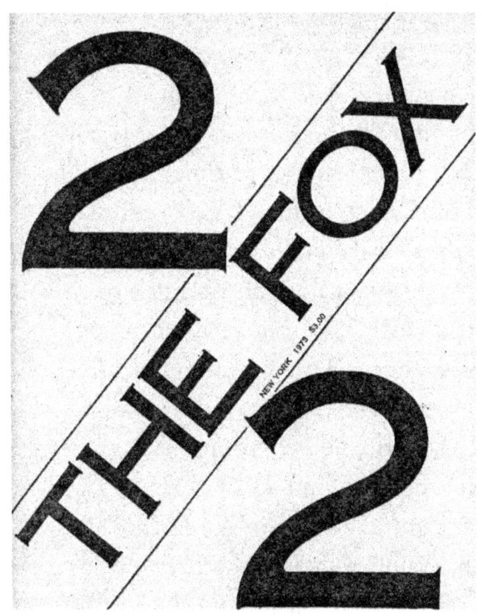

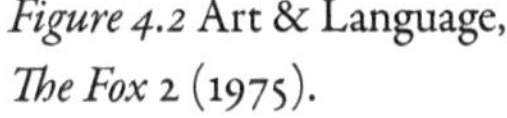
Figure 4.2 Art & Language, *The Fox* 2 (1975).

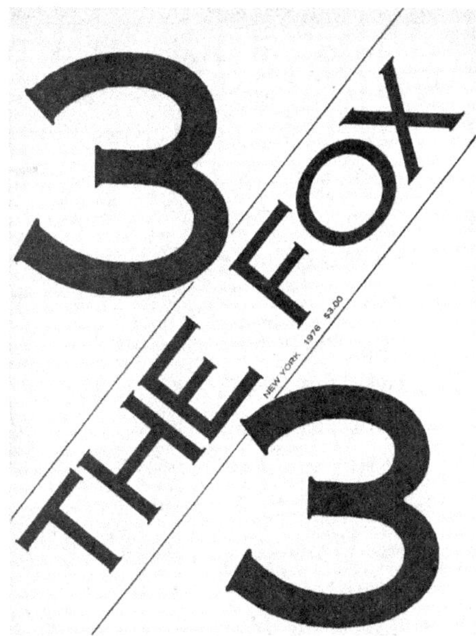

Figure 4.3 Art & Language, *The Fox* 3 (1976).

anything that relates to our American 'capitalist ethos,' which is everything, including *The Fox* itself."[7] The editors of *The Fox* would not have taken much issue with da Vinci's complaint—from their standpoint, it was a compliment—but her claims that Art & Language consisted of "'failed' conceptual artists" who formed "a secondary community of beaten survivors" would have cut closer to the bone.[8] Though the intentionally contentious journal garnered mostly negative reviews of this type (many of which were published in its own pages as letters to the editor), it left a distinctly different impression on some, particularly a younger generation of artists confronting the nascent legacy of conceptual art. Jenny Holzer, for instance, recalls that *The Fox* "introduced me to politics in art."[9] A number of art students, including several studying with Kosuth at the School of Visual Arts, began dropping in on Art & Language's meetings. If nothing else, by this point, the group's internal struggles appear not as the insular idiosyncrasies of wayward conceptual artists but as something from which the art world might learn.

The foxes listed on the editorial board for the first issue are Sarah Charlesworth, Michael Corris, Preston Heller, Joseph Kosuth, Andrew Menard, and Mel Ramsden. Of these names, only Charlesworth's is new to Art & Language. Conspicuously absent from the editorial board is Ian Burn, who had been on bad terms with Kosuth for some time but who nevertheless appears on the masthead of the first issue as reviews editor.[10] Over the course of its short life—the third issue, published in early 1976, would be the last—the editors, who were also major contributors, published a considerable amount of writing, mostly about the relationship between art and politics, though *The Fox* was not in any conventional sense a political journal. Rather, it responded to the politicization of the art world during the 1960s and 1970s that led to the formation of groups such as the Art Workers' Coalition (AWC), which sought to improve working conditions for artists.[11] Several of the most insightful articles in *The Fox* are less attempts to politicize art or artists than examinations of whether art's politicization is achieving its purported goals. Neither antipolitical nor apolitical, *The Fox* is rather a politically cautious journal that sought to elucidate what would constitute a satisfactory politicization of art. Through the texts contained within, as well as discussions of *The Fox* in debates published in *Art-Language*, Art & Language posed hard questions about the amenability of the conceptual art in which it had been involved to the radical political aims that it now felt with a heightened level of urgency. It also posed hard questions to itself about which set of radical political aims was correct. All told, the journal marks an important shift in the collective's practice away from sustained inquiry into the conceptual frameworks of art worlds and of its own collaboration toward a new interest in the consequences of those frameworks: classism, racism, and sexism in art worlds and the subsequent challenge for the group of identifying how it could best confront those things.

Examination of the relationship between art and politics allowed the fox-like tendencies of the journal's editorial board to open onto an especially wide range of subjects. Corris, Menard, Heller, Burn, and Adrian Piper discuss the pricing of artworks and other economic considerations to do with art; Dave Rushton and Paul Wood reflect on art education; Kosuth considers and reconsiders the legacy of conceptual art; Terry Atkinson theorizes on language use; Terry Smith reflects on the practice of art history; and so on. Reviews of recent publications or exhibitions by T. J. Clark, Linda Nochlin, John Berger, Hans Haacke, and Ian Wilson situate *The Fox* within a milieu of Marxist and feminist art history and conceptual art. Kuhn, in her brief blurb on *The Fox* for the *Village Voice*, notes that the first issue was slated to appear on April 15, 1975, in an edition of four thousand copies at a cost of two dollars (Charles Harrison lists the print run of the first issue at three thousand, and that of the second and third issues at five thousand each).[12] Whatever the exact size of the run, its relatively low cost and the large number of copies in circulation indicate the editors' desire for wide distribution, which was handled by Jaap Reitman, a New York bookseller, whose shop in SoHo was a gathering place for artists. Reitman also made *The Fox* available internationally through his contacts in the United States, Canada, Italy, France, Germany, and England, and letters to the editor from around the world reveal a wide readership.

The Fox's examination of art and politics extended well beyond New York, and it received significant contributions from many of the places where Art & Language had forged or was forging working relationships. Smith reports about his concurrent Art & Language work in Sydney, Melbourne, and Adelaide, and Zoran Popović and Jasna Tijardović, collaborators based in Yugoslavia, write about the situation facing artists in Belgrade. (The latter two would also open *The Fox* to other Yugoslavian artists, including Goran Djordevic, who also cohosted Art & Language during its visit to Belgrade in 1975.) And, of course, *The Fox* includes parts of the protracted debate over political concerns that further strained relations between the sections of the collective in New York and England. At the same time that *The Fox* was an exceptionally transnational result of Art & Language's working life in New York, it was also concerned with New York in new ways, focusing on a set of issues that could be called intranational, insofar as Art & Language began to demonstrate a burgeoning consciousness of the political complexities in New York—especially the triangulation of race, class, and gender—that its previous criticisms of art world discourse there had overlooked. If the years 1975 and 1976 were Art & Language's most transnational, with the collective allying with artists and intellectuals in Australia and Yugoslavia, they were also in some ways its most intranational, seeing Art & Language collaborating with feminist and black nationalist groups in the city, and *The Fox* was the main outlet for this new direction in the collective's thought and work.

When the first issue of *The Fox* appeared in April 1975, its lead item, Charlesworth's article "A Declaration of Dependence," provided an initial salvo that introduces themes that other contributors to the journal also address. Her title, which invokes the Declaration of Independence and anticipates the two hundredth anniversary of its signing during the forthcoming American bicentennial year of 1976, calls attention to the fact that artists remain fundamentally dependent on the art world that surrounds them, and the essay reasserts many ideas familiar from Art & Language's earlier work, though the increasing prominence of Marxist terminology provides new analytical tools for framing these old concerns. Charlesworth puts forward a base-superstructure model of the relationship between society and ideology, though not an altogether deterministic one. She differentiates between "political and economic order" and "ideological and intellectual traditions," and she further proposes, "the ideological structure of society integrates and legitimizes the institutional order by explaining and legitimizing its objectivated meanings."[13] For art to transform society, Charlesworth maintains that not only ideology—art and culture—but also this "institutional order" must be taken into consideration: "the structural system of the art-world, which provides a context for the social signification of art, is itself contextually situated in a social system, the structure of which it in turn reflects. At this point, attempts to question or transform the nature of art beyond formalistic considerations must inevitably begin to involve consideration not only of the presuppositions inherent in the internal structure of art models, but also critical awareness of the social system which preconditions and drastically confines the possibility of transformation."[14]

As in previous writings by Art & Language, "the bureaucratic structure of the New York art world" is held up for criticism, as are "socially convenient (marketable) formal models of art (i.e. painting and sculpture)" supported by "more abstract socially convenient (non-controversial) theoretical models (formalism, art for art's sake)."[15] Added to this is the persistence of "the individual artist" who produces work of "quality."[16] If these criticisms seem similar to those already voiced by Art & Language, Charlesworth's next move shows that these issues continue to be the most important because they "are *implicit and internalized* to such a degree that they inform *every aspect of our self and social consciousness* upon which all praxis is founded."[17] Furthermore, "The artist may then be unwittingly supportive of ideals or conditions in relation to which he sees himself as neutral or even opposed."[18] Overcoming these limits can only occur, Charlesworth contends, if individual artists "begin to accept a responsibility for the social implications of their actions."[19] From this, she hopes, "a collective spirit or consciousness conducive to social change can occur," and she points to her "involvement with *The Fox*" as, in her own case as an individual artist, an example of precisely this kind of activity.[20]

Charlesworth also suggests that conceptual art offers some release from the art-for-art's-sake attitudes of modernism that fail to adequately address the sociality of the individual artist, albeit in a limited manner. While she notes, "So-called conceptual art represents, among other things, an attempt to redefine art value or significance in terms of its ideational rather than physical ('experiential') attributes," she also concedes that "it *functions in society* in a manner not unlike previously more morphologically oriented work."[21] In the end, "art as idea as art product, alas, moves in the world of commodity-products and hardly the realm of 'idea.'"[22] However, in this failure, there is cause for hope: "We can *learn* as much, in a sense, through the 'failure' of concept art as we do through its partial success."[23] Regardless, Charlesworth claims, "we exist as its inevitable heirs."[24] Having described where art and the art world stand in her estimation, Charlesworth offers a potential direction forward: "What is called for is . . . the gradual creation of a community, a discourse, an art, which is not so much the reflection of our competitive and antagonistic pursuits as it is a common vehicle through which we might continually examine not only our own values and assumptions, but those of the culture of and to which we ideally speak."[25] How this "gradual creation" should occur and how it would "continually examine" the cultures to which it addresses itself is heavily contested in the other essays that compose the first issue of *The Fox*, even if there is a general consensus that Charlesworth has correctly diagnosed an incontrovertible condition of dependence and proposed a direction forward in community.

Loosely speaking, two positions on community emerge in the inaugural issue of *The Fox*. Each develops lines present in Charlesworth's essay, and both rest on the distinction, which she leaves largely unresolved, between the individual and the community itself. Characterizing the first of these positions, Kosuth, who had taken up the study of anthropology at the New School during the early 1970s with the politically and philosophically inclined anthropologists Bob Scholte and Stanley Diamond, envisions the artist as "a model of the anthropologist *engaged*."[26] He accounts for art as a form of theory brought to bear on practice: "In the sense that it is a theory, it is an overview; yet because it is not a detached overview but rather a socially mediating activity, it is engaged, and it is praxis."[27] Unlike anthropology, which, as an academic pursuit, is "*dis*-engaged," art "is manifested in praxis; it 'depicts' *while* it alters society."[28] In contrast to scientific anthropologists, who are "not part of the community" they study and thus remain "outside of the culture," the artist as anthropologist endeavors "to obtain fluency in his *own* culture."[29] This is "a dialectical process which, simply put, consists of attempting to affect the culture while he is simultaneously learning from (and seeking the acceptance of) that same culture which is affecting him."[30] If Charlesworth identifies community with the editorial board of *The Fox* that she, as an individual, chose to join, then for Kosuth, community is defined more broadly as society itself, to which he, as an individual, belongs. The task of art is to understand and shape that society's culture.

Ramsden, in his essay "On Practice," represents an opposite pole by questioning whether the radical ambitions of practices such as what Kosuth describes are capable of changing the communities in which they intervene. Recalling Charlesworth's remarks about the internalization of ideological structures, Ramsden questions whether an individual is capable of identifying the culture that affects him or her since the individual's existence is contingent upon that culture. "I know, for example," he writes, "that rabid ambition and careerism—almost the New York art world's raison d'être—are present in myself, even though I'm perfectly aware of their presence. This would lead me to believe, assuming there are others like me, and I know there are, that the market isn't just contingently there, that we don't just create freely and only afterwards get bulldozed by the market. That we now practice with the market in mind (and I'm not loftily excepting my own writing here)."[31] Ramsden indicates clearly that he does not think "that New York artists want to be Imperialist puppets"; however, he suggests that "even those who profess unique political awareness — having no doubt been 'radicalized' at one point or another of their lives — just don't make the connections they ought to between their work and (e.g.) the spread of a marketing expedient like 'international art.'"[32] Ramsden is specifically critical of the AWC, though his remarks about it extend to the category of political art generally: "I remember finally coming to the conclusion that the impotence of the AWC lay in this refusal to deal with 'work' — what we each *do*; that is, *practice*. It appeared sure that part-time *politicking* wasn't enough, that we now must have a revision of the commodity status of the work itself."[33] To "facilitate some hope of 'authenticity,'" Ramsden, like his colleagues, proposes the creation of "a tradition (community) which does not embody a commodity mode of existence," but he is not particularly optimistic about actually building one, even if he does have a clear idea about the prerequisites for establishing one.[34] He suggests that "such an 'oppositional alternative' (or numerous such alternatives) . . . can only arise within communities whose *sociality* (language . . . grammar . . .) is its own."[35] He proposes teaching and learning as different sorts of practice capable of evading the tendency to regard art as a form of commodity production: "Commitment to teach and learn is a commitment first to dialogue, to commonality, not point of view or authority. Teaching is constituted through a particular person's praxis. This is what we're after."[36] Even though teaching and learning have long been central to Art & Language's activity, the final twist of Ramsden's phrasing acknowledges that its present work is at best only transitional and yet to achieve its aims. He describes *Art-Language* and *The Fox* as "at least mouthpieces of a community," but they are also "functionaries of a market."[37]

Faced with "an automatic system" in New York that is set up "to further augment the gray-official alienation of culture," Ramsden is also skeptical of working outside New York in "the international *Kunstwelt* carousel."[38] He rejects international exchanges such as "Seth Siegelaub's so-called 'network of booksellers and mailing lists'" as the embodiment of "a nasty guiding art-imperialistic concept of spreading 'information' globally as if it existed impersonally somehow, independent of anybody in particular having practical needs (frailty)."[39] Ramsden has additional, economic concerns about working internationally: "The reason art can be 'international' (a rubric which, as Ian Burn points out, is correctly a market not a cultural term . . .) is not the result of any daft McLunacy like the growth of a 'global village' but because of a global acquisition system, always needing to expand, automatically operating apart from, and systematically bulldozing, any local practice."[40] At the same time, "a 'search' 'outside' the art bureaucracy" for "making our work 'public'" is also troubling, and Ramsden rejects the search for larger audiences as "the rating worries of TV executives."[41] He further suggests that "this concept of mass audience" is inappropriate for the kind of sociality he envisions, as it is "more a question of a manic rational power construct than a question of mutual exchange or encounter."[42] Only a community that meets to dialogue and learn is capable of producing and sustaining the social change that Ramsden desires, and the prospects for this surviving and thriving are, he wagers, dim at best.

Art & Language's English section shared Ramsden's dour assessment of the situation in New York. Michael Baldwin and Philip Pilkington's "For Thomas Hobbes," their contribution to the first issue of *The Fox*, begins:

> The editors wanted something written about New York. What a bizarre idea.
>
> One prevailing emotion (is that what it is?) is our snobbery in relation to the community allegedly under scrutiny. "Why are so many of them so thick?" is perhaps not the sort of question we should be asking.
>
> Another question: "Why are there so few 'real' conflicts?" There seems to be support for Parsonian Open-Society-recommendations in the critical to-ing and fro-ing of New York's art community.[43]

Response to *The Fox* itself was equally grim in England. Writing in *Art-Language* in May 1975, Art & Language—the specific authors and contributors are indicated as Charles and Sandra Harrison, Philip Pilkington, Dave Rushton, Paul Wood, and, foreshadowing realignments to come, Ramsden—dismissed *The Fox* as "Utopian Prayers and Infantile Marxism."[44] In a short polemic, this group attacks the journal for lacking "any recognition of an historical materialist conflict within ideology," without which "it would be difficult to suggest a de facto dysfunction-condition wherein 'learning' may take place."[45] These harsh words call into question the validity of Art & Language's work in New York, and they did little to reconcile the hostility between the two sections of the collective.

Nowhere is this conflict more clearly presented than in a clash between Baldwin and Burn that comes to a head in the same issue of *Art-Language*. A note at the back of the journal advises readers about "something like incompatibility between the various pieces of writing in this collection."[46] Specifically, "Objections were raised to an article which Ian Burn published in 'Artforum,' and he was sent a somewhat carefully composed document (published here). His response to this, also published here, appears to compound the original errors. We can only assume either that Ian Burn did not read what he was sent, or that he read but felt that he was in a position to ignore it (which he was not)."[47] A footnote to this passage adds insult to injury: "For example, as Dennis Wright said of a 'political artist' in Belfast: 'The silly fucker, hasn't it occurred to him that one side might be right?'"[48]

The article in question is Burn's essay "The Art Market: Affluence and Degradation," which appeared in the April 1975 issue of *Artforum*.[49] The sections into which the text is divided are given headers that, when put together, pose the question to which the text is addressed: "WHILE WE'VE BEEN ADMIRING OUR NAVELS/WE HAVE BEEN CAPITALIZED AND MARKETED/BUT THROUGH REALIZING OUR SOCIALIZATION/MIGHT WE BE ABLE TO TRANSFORM OUR REALITY?" Contending that, under obtaining conditions, "works of art *start off* as commodities," Burn advocates in favor of "scrutinizing certain historically unique aspects of our market relations," and he follows with the historical materialist account of the art world that the English section found lacking in *The Fox*, albeit one that would not meet with its satisfaction.[50] He also proposes, "The work of (fine) art has become the ideal exchange commodity in our society" because it finds its value almost "strictly in an exchange market (not involving production)" and is thus subject to impersonal market manipulations.[51] As a result of this, the artist is "'created' by the market as merely part of a labour force" as a "politically conservative" figure.[52] Concomitant with the proletarianization of the artist, there is an "increase in the numbers of drab 'non-production workers' (middle-people)" including critics, dealers, curators, and so on, whose task is to promote, market, and sell art in commodity form.[53] Burn is particularly sensitive to the role the

United States plays in enforcing a corporate culture "demanding a uniformity dominated by New York art" by insisting that artists "affirm and perpetuate at least one of the dominant styles" that originated in New York.[54] Burn concludes his essay on "a note of guarded optimism" by hoping for the same thing as his colleagues in New York: "a distinctive consciousness and solidarity developing out of a 'community of artists.'"[55]

There are two responses to this essay in the *Art-Language* article "'Mr. Lin Yutang Refers to "Fair Play" . . . ?'"[56] The initial response is presented in the especially hostile voice of "Professor Norman Trotsky" and the second in the milder voice of "Petrichenko." The primary author of this two-voiced text is Michael Baldwin, but, in accordance with the contributor list at the front of the issue, four other names are indicated as either coauthors or sympathizers with the authors' views: Sarah Charlesworth, Charles Harrison, Harold Hurrell, and Lynn Lemaster. Baldwin's disagreements do not concern Burn's prescription of community—Sandra Harrison's text "Pedagogical Sketchbook (AL)," which appears in the same issue of *Art-Language*, advocates in favor of a collectivity that in its broad outlines is similar to what those in New York support—but rather his diagnosis of the situation facing artists in New York, particularly Burn's discussion of capitalism.[57] Specifically, Baldwin argues that artists are bourgeois and not, as Burn contends, working class, and furthermore, that artists are mistaken if they believe or act on a belief that they belong to the same social class as laborers. Instead, Baldwin suggests that artists can achieve solidarity with the working classes only by first recognizing their own complicity as part of the bourgeoisie and acting in accordance with this insight.

"Professor Norman Trotsky" takes a particularly hard-line stance and posits the following general argument about his problem with class in Burn's article:

> The surmise that those contradictions that are faced by the artist may be resolved in a sort of penetrative artistic counter-culture without fundamental reference to the class struggle is a denial of the historical basis of social change. Artists are, variously, members of a social "section" which, from an historical (class) point of view, is "indeterminate." Every kid knows that this "section" and its relatives fundamentally reflect capitalism. "While We've Been . . ."

> recommends that social transformation which gives security and comfort to the artist as petty-bourgeois and regrets the images of quasi-proletarianization that certain (strange) politico-economo-ethical observations provide.[58]

"Trotsky" prefers "a demystifying meeting of the intelligentsia (sectional bourgeoisie), students and workers."[59] This is to take place through "The 'maturing' of the conditions of socialism (or socialization for that matter)," which is both "the accumulation of the real conditions of an adequate consciousness" and "the product of the actions of the class 'for-itself.'"[60] In essence, "Trotsky" argues for the reorientation of existing working-class consciousness so as to transform the proletariat from an effect of historical processes into a historical agent. In contrast, the more moderate "Petrichenko" opens by calling "Trotsky" "a bit harsh," but he too is skeptical of Burn's argument about the art market.[61] Against "Trotsky's" uniform vision of sociality as the historical process of classes coming to self-consciousness, "Petrichenko" argues for "not just one kind of socialization."[62] His concern is that socialization is "often in danger of being devoid of structural content" and "doomed to flicker about in a crystalline contradiction that remains merely decorative and inert . . . or what . . . worse?"[63] A footnote casts further doubts on "such confections as 'Let's construct art on the basis of "social criticism/praxis"'" and further criticizes "half-hearted ambiguities" that "come across as swashbuckling calls to arms."[64] In short, both "Trotsky" and "Petrichenko" share a sense that Burn has misunderstood the social position of the artist and the role art plays in class struggle.

Unsurprisingly, Burn did not acquiesce to these criticisms. In a response essay, "Strategy Is Political: Dear M . . . ," he calls attention to the way that class is organized differently in old world countries, such as England, with long-established conventions regarding labor and sociality, and newer nations, including the United States and Australia, where class consciousness is less developed, class is less rigidly defined, and social relationships are more commonly formed across class divisions.[65] In America, "if you treat class as a thing, there are classes . . . ; as an experience, there aren't. . . . The experiences necessary for the creation of working class consciousness haven't existed."[66] Similarly, Australia "lacks any rigid class structure" and "the working class there has a petty bourgeois consciousness."[67] Having established that his original article "was written in (for) socio-political conditions different from your own," he dismisses Baldwin for making criticisms that do not apply within the context of the United States: "'Capitalism is capitalism, that's all we need to know' is what you seem (Trotskying) to suggest. That is just to ignore the significance of the difficulties we encounter."[68] Burn's insistence that "class isn't just a thing, a mere factor of your social relation to production, but a living experience" matters because in New York, Burn suggests, "Practice is overwhelmed by a cultural 'reality'" that must be taken into prior consideration, hence the importance to politics of art and culture that, in different circumstances, might prove to reinforce class distinctions.[69] In particular, he cites "a media-intensified intellectual division of labour" that "has virtually destroyed the practice of cultural criticism."[70] Burn describes Art & Language "talking a lot about an 'art' as an active agency in changing people and their social relations, about the ideological role of <u>an</u> 'art'" as a way to counteract this dearth of criticism.[71]

Burn also scolds his interlocutors in England for forgetting the importance of broadening dialogue as widely as possible: "You know as well that the only hope of any sort of authentic (*sic*) practice lies in being able to keep our dialogue growing . . . more conversations . . . the moment we let it all go, fade away, we don't have any hope and can just as well be thrown onto the garbage heap of modern art."[72] Rather than opportunism, a charge Baldwin levels against Burn, Burn suggests that broadening Art & Language's sociality provides occasions for developing new ideas about how to proceed as well as a broader audience to participate in shaping those ideas. In a second rebuttal, published in the second issue of *The Fox* as a review of the May 1975 issue of *Art-Language*, Burn turns the tables on Baldwin's criticism by claiming that his "psychologized (rather than socialized) personality coming to dominate community" is the real danger to Art & Language's future as a group.[73] In contrast, Burn presents his proposal for a constantly expanding sociality as an ongoing process that is appropriate and necessary if some kind of basis for class struggle and resistance to capitalism is to emerge in the United States, which, in addition to a rabid and privately controlled media culture, lacks a viable leftist political alternative comparable to England's Labour Party. Burn's proposal also represents a response to Baldwin's criticism that socializing lacks content. He concludes by suggesting that the search for a base for criticizing capitalism has yet to reach the stage of positing content and, for the time being, finds its politics in challenging modernism's mistakes about content as it searches for an engaged sociality appropriate to the situation in the United States: "far from indulging in utopian panaceas, we are, as it were, trying to practice (create) the conditions. . . . We haven't arrived at our own content. Subverting form-as-content is political, that's all. But we won't end up as more objects of history . . . yet."[74]

Art & Language's English section develops its own political program elsewhere in the May 1975 issue of *Art-Language*. Sandra Harrison, citing Burn's question "BUT THROUGH REALIZING OUR SOCIALIZATION, MIGHT WE BE ABLE TO TRANSFORM OUR REALITY?," answers, bluntly, "No. . . . The transformation of reality," she suggests instead, "will only take place as a result of proletarian-based revolution of the total economic structure."[75] Of artists, Harrison says, "Artists are self-employed. They do not sell their labour. They do not receive salaries. They are supported in various ways. To use the language of proletarian class struggle is to sink into fantasy."[76] A collaboratively authored text in the same issue of *Art-Language* proposes an alternative approach to allying art to political struggle: "Our tasks will be: 1) to establish appropriate forms of contact with self-active groups in working class movements (not necessarily 'official' ones); 2) the attempt to integrate the resulting dialogue in a reciprocal historic practice—so that the self-transformation of that practice avoids the socio-historical mistake of 'permitting' a merely marginal or adjustive response to the critical aspect of that dialogue."[77] Burn, for his part, was skeptical about the English section's proposals about meetings with the working class. In a private notebook from the period, he wrote, "ALUK—it's hard to see how their words can become deeds."[78]

Following this disagreement, an alienated Burn began to distance himself from Art & Language. He accepted teaching positions in San Diego and Halifax that took him away from New York for much of 1976. Despite his increasing disillusionment with Art & Language, he continued to participate when in New York, and his championing of expanded sociality found considerable support with participants in the collective there, a number of whom, envisioning themselves as workers, advocated withdrawal from what they perceived to be a hopelessly bourgeois art world. They began to form associations and alliances with other groups and collectives, some composed of artists, others of a more directly activist orientation. In establishing this social base, they hoped to find new audiences for Art & Language's work and draw strength from wider association with other politically oriented collectives active in struggles against sexism and racism. Corris, who was deeply involved in this phase of Art & Language's politicization in New York, recounts the collective receiving "a postcard from the artist Lawrence Weiner bearing the cryptic message: 'a meeting is desired'" in the fall of 1975.[79] Weiner's overture drew Art & Language into a coalition of artists and critics, including Carl Andre, Leon Golub, Hans Haacke, Lucy R. Lippard, Miriam Schapiro, and many others affiliated with a variety of feminist and African American groups, that became Artists Meeting for Cultural Change (AMCC).[80]

This group's first public statement, a broadside addressed "To the American Art Community from Artists Meeting for Cultural Change" and dated December 14, 1975, objects to the exhibition *Three Centuries of American Art*, which was drawn from the personal collection of John D. Rockefeller III and organized by the De Young Museum in San Francisco but scheduled for exhibition at the Whitney Museum of American Art in September 1976. Those involved with AMCC "object to the collusion of the De Young and Whitney Museums and John D. Rockefeller III in using a private collection of art, with its discriminatory omissions, to promote upper class values and a socially reactionary view of American art."[81] More specifically, it objects to the inclusion of "no Black artists and only one woman artist," which it sees as an extension of the Whitney's lack of "Black professional staff in curatorial or even sub-curatorial rank" and the absence of African American and female artists in the museum's exhibitions.[82] As a countermeasure, the broadside announces a picketing of the Whitney to take place on January 3, 1976, as "the first step in setting up a national network to protest such misuse of art and artists for the Bicentennial—and afterwards" (figures 4.4, 4.5).[83] Though Art & Language's New York section would no longer exist by this point, the Whitney picketing led ultimately to the publication of *An Anti-Catalog*, which included a number of texts critical of *Three Centuries of American Art* and the ideological position that their authors took the exhibition to represent.[84] Of Art & Language's former participants, only Kosuth and Charlesworth saw this project through to completion.

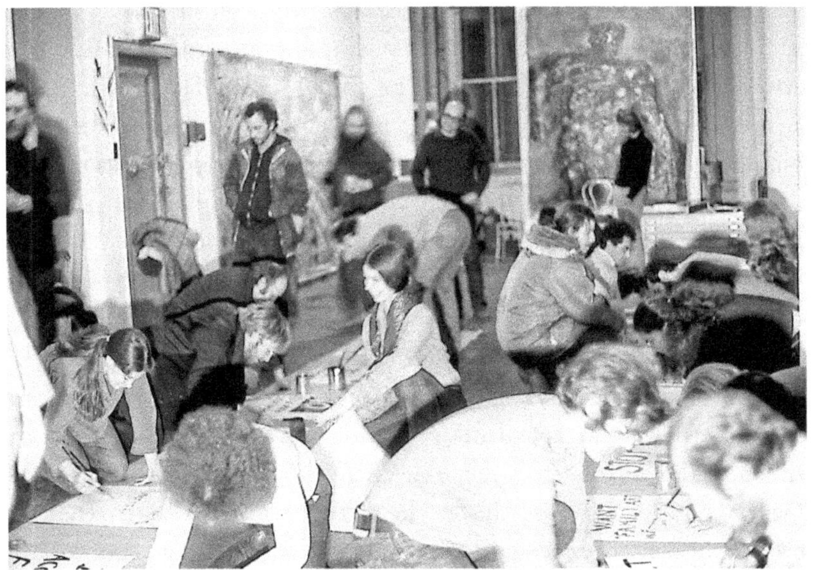

Figure 4.4 Artists Meeting for Cultural Change, in the studio of Leon Golub, preparing for its protest at the Whitney Museum, 1976.

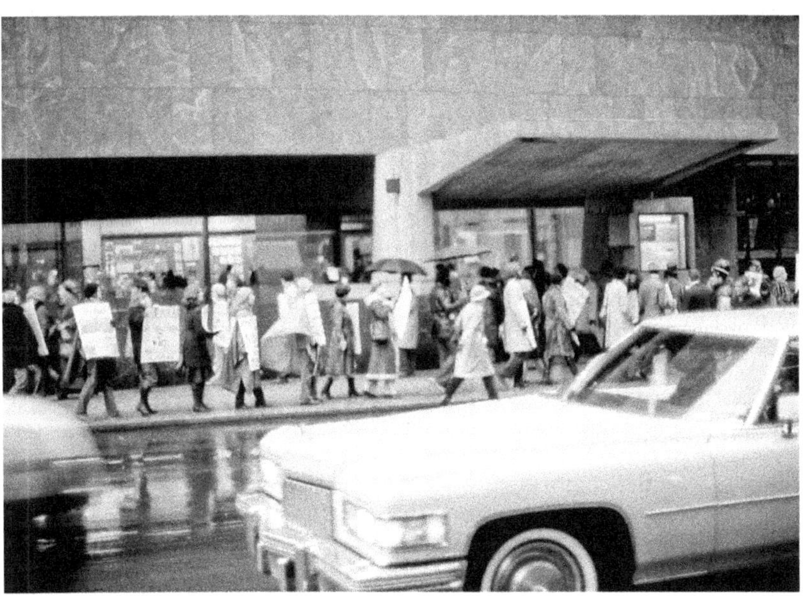

Figure 4.5 Artists Meeting for Cultural Change protesting at the Whitney Museum, 1976.

The third issue of *The Fox* contains a portfolio of statements by and about AMCC collected and presented by Charlesworth under the title "For Artists Meeting." She introduces it by noting, "Some feel they have the answers; others are looking, and I often feel that it is in the uncertainty of our often naive and awkward search that we begin to approach the unfamiliar territory (discovery) which lies beyond conditioned response."[85] Indeed, she further ventures that "rather than being 'non-productive' in terms of arriving at clear-cut 'solutions,' such discussions and collective struggle toward understanding are not only valuable and healthy in terms of personal growth and change but provide in and of themselves, a *very tentative basis* of social change, through a process of social interaction which occurs *outside of* (but not independent of) specific institutional forms."[86] Nearer the end of her introductory remarks, Charlesworth offers a succinct statement of position regarding the benefit of groups such as AMCC: "The process of our collective recognition of the 'problems' and our move toward their 'resolution' are one."[87]

Held first at the loft of artists Rudolf Baranik and May Stevens and later at Artists Space, regular congregations for AMCC's open meetings generated a number of the statements that fill out Charlesworth's portfolio in *The Fox*. In addition to the Whitney boycott proposal, she includes the AMCC Position Paper Committee's "A Tentative Position Paper," presented at a meeting on February 22, 1976, that sought to establish "a real and viable basis for continuing" to meet.[88] At the risk of becoming "a rather dull super-ad-hoc committee" after the Whitney protest, the authors propose that, in the absence of "a particular set of beliefs" held in common by the group, "a sense of uncertainty" is "where we begin."[89] Given the number of Art & Language participants whose initials appear at the top of the document, it is not surprising that "with these problems in mind, the committee would like to recommend that the group devote a regular and considerable amount of time to study, discussion, learning—as a group—seeing this dialogue as already being a step towards a new form of practice."[90] It is further proposed that this practice not "detract from the continuous and careful attention to immediate, external problems, such as Whitney-type situations" but act instead as a "long-term function of the group" that would persist in the absence of such concerns.[91] In essence, this proposal, if it were adopted, would have remade the AMCC as an extension of Art & Language. It even includes a proposed list of topics for further consideration that closely resemble the subjects of Art & Language's ongoing conversation: "Art & Feminism, Collaboration, Imperialism, Artist as Intellectual, the Culture Industry, the Role of Museums."[92] The other papers Charlesworth includes in the portfolio take up many of these issues, including contributions from Ginny Reath, Elizabeth Hess, and Carolee Schneemann on feminism; V. King on imperialism; and Leandro Katz on the role of men in the women's movement.

Art & Language also associated with a black nationalist organization that called itself the Anti-Imperialist Cultural Union (AICU) and, from 1978 to 1981, published the Maoist journal *Main Trend*. Corris relates that during "the winter of 1975" the AICU "began to recruit members from AMCC" in order "to enlarge their social base to include SoHo artists to form a new, 'mass organization.'"[93] This group set itself up, similarly to AMCC, as a coalition of groups and individuals with shared aims and interests, and the Congress of Afrikan People (CAP), one of the constituent groups, led by the poet Amiri Baraka, accounted for the AICU's name and direction in a draft proposal for the organization's "Principles of Unity": "'Anti-Imperialist' because our class stand opposes Imperialism wherever it exists, 'Cultural' in order to include all the arts and artists who through their creative labor take the raw materials found in the life of the people and shape them into the ideological form of literature and art serving the masses of the people, and 'union' to reflect the proposed mass character of the organization. We unite to take action to end our oppression and exploitation caused by the system of Imperialism."[94]

Response to the New York section's involvement in AMCC and the AICU was not positive in England. Baldwin did not share CAP's stance on the role of artists in the political process, and he dismissed the AICU as "Maoist pipsqueaks."[95] Ramsden was equally disaffected with what he took to be a wrongheaded politicization of art practice in New York. In an open letter to Art & Language dated August 10, 1975, he displays the depth of his skepticism: "The question remains: who do we direct our activism at and who is it for? Do we simply assail 'the art-establishment'? Our very own privilidges [*sic*]? In which case, who listens? Joseph's [Kosuth] and Sarah's [Charlesworth] radical academics? Terry Smith's radical academics? Michael's [Corris] Marxist chums? Maybe, maybe? The greatest subversion of the privilidged [*sic*] *Kunstwelt* would be to refuse to make art for that *Kunstwelt* whilst making an art as ambitious as that usually seen in that *Kunstwelt*. I have no idea of course how to do this."[96] Ramsden, who, in the same letter, claims a need "to break contact with ALUK," which would effectively isolate him from the entire collective, would, shortly thereafter, begin to recognize common ground with Baldwin.[97] In a retrospective account of AMCC and the AICU published in *Art-Language* in October 1977 after the breakup of Art & Language's New York section, the remainder of the collective, still including Ramsden and now based entirely in England, complains about "Beleaguered art-world artists . . . fixated upon 'radical politics.'"[98] Referring to AMCC, it writes, "These artists are in no position either to volunteer to have, or to accept an invitation to have, the interests of the working class."[99] Of the AICU, it wagers, "To threaten 'non-proletarians' with immanent [*sic*] 'proletarianisation' is not to keep anyone awake nights."[100]

Unreceptive to what he felt to be oversimplified politics coupled with art world careerism among Art & Language's New York section, Baldwin decided to reclaim the name Art & Language for those working under it in England. He gave Mayo Thompson, an American musician who began to associate with Art & Language in 1973 while living in England, the task of assuming distribution of *Art-Language* in New York upon his return there in 1975. Shortly after Thompson's arrival, Burn and Ramsden made clear their commitment to Art & Language, and Baldwin's plans were amended. Kosuth, whose individual artistic pursuits Baldwin, Burn, and Ramsden had all found for some time to be in conflict with his declared stake in the group, was, by this point, the odd man out from the original trio of New York–based participants in Art & Language. A plan was devised to oust him. Thompson, Burn, and Ramsden decided to convene meetings at which collective authorship of all future work by participants would be an absolute and strongly enforced precondition for membership in Art & Language, something to which they knew Kosuth would not agree. Enforcing collective authorship would also mean that the English section would henceforward have more say over what transpired in New York than ever before, which would enable Baldwin, moving forward, to curtail the political work that he found so disagreeable. Helping spearhead this initiative had the added advantage for Ramsden of strengthening his burgeoning alliance with Baldwin, who consented to the plot and threw his proxy behind him, and this, in turn, solidified Ramsden's leadership position within the New York section.

Hostility toward Kosuth had simmered in New York for some time but came to a boil after Burn co-authored an article for the second issue of *The Fox* with Karl Beveridge. Beveridge and Burn's essay covertly attacks Kosuth in the guise of attacking the minimalist sculptor Donald Judd for his individualism and inadequate understanding of sociality. It begins with an overture: "Don Judd, is it possible to talk?" and continues to address Judd in the second person with a series of questions, beginning with this one: "How do we deal with an almost sacrosanct figure, a reputation seemingly above ordinary criticism, a powerful reference point for so much during the sixties and apparently still 'fundamental' to a lot of high art produced today?"[101] They treat Judd not as a person but as a construction of the art world, asking him about his writings, his work, his theories about art, his favorite terms, what has been written about him, his political statements, his vocal attitudes about America and American art, and so on, citing his writings and statements along the way as if the text were an interview or dialogue. These questions mount up until they ask the key question: "Against all this, how could you see your work as *political*, as *subversive!*"[102] They quote Judd twice to the effect, "My work didn't have anything to do with society, the institutions and grand theories" and "I've always thought that my work had political implications."[103] Beveridge and Burn's questions now turn incredulous: "Do you still believe that? Do you still believe that the *individual* qua individual can be political or subversive? Haven't you realized that it is exactly what the interests dominating this society *want*, that it is its most insidious form of social control?"[104] They carry on in this manner before reaching the conclusion, "*You can't be subversive to institutions and at the same time presuppose a form of art which reproduces, thus increases, the power of those institutions*. If you really want your art to be subversive, it must be a form of art which doesn't reproduce the Big Cultural Lie."[105]

As a piece of strategy, "Don Judd" worked. The real Donald Judd read the essay and got upset with Kosuth for allowing it to be published in a journal of which he was an editor. According to Beveridge, Judd made his anger with Kosuth known "through the dealer Leo Castelli," who represented both of them at the time.[106] When the planned Art & Language meetings

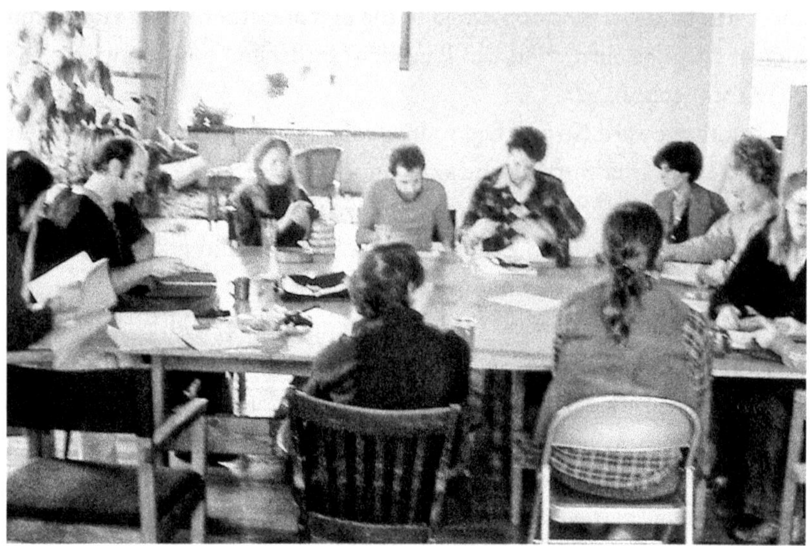

Figure 4.6 Art & Language meeting, 1976.

began in late February 1976 (figure 4.6), Burn, Ramsden, and Thompson further maneuvered against Kosuth and his supporters. Transcripts of the discussions that ensued are the lead item of the third and final issue of *The Fox*, where they are presented under the editorship of "Peter Benchley," a pseudonym rather than the popular novelist of the same name. "Benchley" was asked to present his "edited transcripts of the group's proceedings during three 'struggle sessions' (*sic*) at the close of February, 1976. There were seven such sessions in all. I selected the first and the last two."[107] The edited transcripts appear under the title "The Lumpen-Headache," and "Benchley" indicates that present for the discussions were "Michael Corris, Joseph Kosuth, Sarah Charlesworth, Karl Beveridge, Christine Kozlov, Ian Burn, Carole Conde [*sic*], Mel Ramsden, Andrew Menard, Preston Heller, Jill Breakstone, Mayo Thompson, Nigel Lendon, Alex Hay *et alia*."[108] In the transcripts, these names were replaced with the names of different species of fish, which many of the participants kept as pets, to protect their public reputations from the more rancorous assertions made during the meetings. However, in a number of copies of *The Fox*, a key connecting the names of discussants to their corresponding fish species is stamped on the inside front cover.[109] That the real Peter Benchley is best known as the author of

Jaws, then, is all too fitting given the dangerous waters into which Art & Language was venturing.

The first session begins with Ramsden introducing the core topic of "social change," which has become the crucial problem facing Art & Language as both an insufficiently theorized concern and its supposed reason for continuing to work together as a collective.[110] With the floor open for debate, many familiar issues resurface, including whether Art & Language's social class prevents it from stimulating social change, whether the society in which it lives prevents its work from having the effects it desires, whether it has a satisfactory understanding of its circumstances, and whether real alternatives—Ramsden proposes socialism—exist, are practical and practicable, and are open to Art & Language's participation. Wide gulfs separate the points of view that emerge. Charlesworth represents one extreme when she states her opposition to Far Left options and announces her sympathy with a multifront politics that addresses sexism and racism as much as classism: "I'm not interested in working for a dictatorship of the proletariat. I am interested in working for a society that would be truly egalitarian which has a whole different basis of social relations, that confronts the problems of capitalism. . . . And I think there are other problems, such as sexism and racism that are very much part of the problem, that just talking about the role of the working-class doesn't help clarify."[111] Thompson, with faith in the historical inevitability of a proletarian revolution, states the opposite: "The dictatorship of the proletariat . . . *is not up to us*. The working class will change things, will transform society."[112] The discussions sway between these two opposed points of view, covering such topics as "internal group hierarchy, feminism, male-chauvinism, etc."[113] Ideas accumulate, but they are largely abstract; few concrete decisions are made, feasible strategies are lacking, and no definitive plans are made. Uncertainty and contradiction prevail, as those advocating socialism remain narrowly committed to class issues and reluctant to admit concerns about sexism and racism into their discussion of sociality, while those advocating a more complex politics that also treats these topics in addition to class privileges have difficulties envisioning a program as coherent as the socialism for which their more class-focused colleagues advocate. The collective's internationality is little discussed, and whatever model it could have offered to reconcile these positions by mediating between economics and identity goes unconsidered, as does Art & Language's earlier interest in incommensurability and other topics derived from the philosophy of science that concern how groups can organize themselves in the absence of a clear direction forward. The result is an impasse, and an open struggle for power ensues.

From the opening of the sixth and penultimate session, the group's proposals become more concrete, as the original purpose of the meetings finally comes to the surface. Thompson begins, "We've been talking about unity and a lot of terminology has been bandied about. I've tried all week long to make clear that we are involved in a socialist process, something with which we have an active, ongoing relationship."[114] Burn develops Thompson's concern about unity into a need for "clear ideological direction. . . . Something we haven't done in the past is take our form of organization very seriously. That's been a disaster. We've had, really, a *laissez-faire* organization. . . . Either we stand still and have a non-progressive group, or we take organization seriously."[115] He continues, "What I would like to see is work start to all come out as Art & Language, without names, that includes articles and shows. I want, also, a mandate that you *can't* do things as an individual. That makes the sociality into exploitation."[116]

At this point, Kosuth, sensing a turn against his better interests, stakes out his ground by suggesting that Burn's concerns about labor relations in Art & Language are misguided. He accuses those in the group desiring socialism of bad faith for relying on the prestige associated with participating in Art & Language as a means of financial support and individual entrée into the art world:

> The economic, social, and psychological motives are propelling some of us toward a socialist program along lines that can transform in an immediate way our specific living and working context into a more equitable and beneficial arrangement. While these short-term means are important on the same human grounds that we have elected a long-term strategy for socialism, they do nevertheless constitute a kind of operational reformism insofar as they attempt to make life in the capitalist system acceptable. . . . I don't understand why we should keep Art & Language? Keeping it for some of us is a form of keeping their individual identity, and if particular individuals are asked to give up the power they think they have in the artworld as

individuals, then I think those whose individuality in the artworld rests upon the mantle "Art & Language" should also be forced to change similarly.[117]

The solution he proposes—"I suggest we form a political party"—takes the socialist desires of Burn, Ramsden, and Thompson to their logical conclusion, preempting their impending move against him by suggesting that the collective from which they are moving to exclude him will not enable them to achieve their political goals and that all are better off abandoning it in favor of politics.[118] At the same time, though, Kosuth is calling attention to his importance to the group as its best-known participant; without him, the rest of Art & Language's members will lose whatever power they have that derives from belonging to the collective in which he participates.

From here, the discussion shifts away from competing preoccupations with the place of class within political struggle to the conflict between individuality and collectivity, with Kosuth reiterating his aversion to total collectivization. Charlesworth also supports individual work on the grounds that it enables participants in Art & Language to contact others outside the group as potential new participants or at the very least as a larger audience for the collective's work. Against this, Burn, Ramsden, and Thompson, increasingly joined by Corris, Menard, Heller, and others, insist on a more coherent platform and organizational structure for the group with socialism being a desired goal and guiding strategy. By the beginning of the seventh and final session (the third transcribed), those in favor of collective authorship and socialist politics are ready to force their issue and put their cards on the table in the form of a list of provisions:

1. All work which is "made public" will be represented under the collective name. This applies to exhibitions, publishing articles, teaching and any other working which has a "public" form.

2. All work which is "made public" has to be discussed and accepted by the general body. This will set up a framework for criticism/self-criticism of work (something which has been lacking in the past). In this matter the will of the general body has to prevail.

3. Working "publicly" in an individualistic manner will be considered as self-disqualification from this process.

> 4. What are the implications of this for the economics of each of us?
>
> 5. What do we do about the question of expansion and the prospects of working with other people (this was subsequently changed to: our strength is based in our ideological struggle)? New participation in the group is likely to emerge through development of working relations with existing participants.
>
> 6. Do we retain the name Art & Language?[119]

Tabled for future consideration are the possibility of "'Decentralized' (from New York City) working," "'the definition' of collective work," and the possibility of "'thematic' exhibitions."[120] Ramsden then proposes,

> Those who are in general agreement with the above provisos should form a splinter group to be called (Provisional) Art & Language. . . . Those not in agreement with the provisos can retain the name Art & Language. The issue must be made clear: we are not trying to push anybody "out," we are simply trying to go on. In other words, those who want to stay in the position we're in now, can retain the name Art & Language, those who want to go on must go on with a different name and with a new form of organization.[121]

The discussion now centers squarely on the future of Art & Language's membership, and Kosuth, aware that he is being marginalized, proclaims, "I feel there's a certain kind of social dynamic going on here and I have a hard time getting a fair hearing."[122] There is some mulling over the earlier clash between Kosuth and Burn. Kosuth laments how so many participants in Art & Language seem to be siding against him and with Burn, and Ramsden suggests that Kosuth has "never seen the social base of working," while Burn "has been talking to a lot of other people."[123] As a vote looms, Ramsden states his case against Kosuth in direct and straightforward terms:

> You have always had, and we have always allowed you to have, a certain say as to what goes on in A&L but we've never had a say in what goes on in your work because as "an individual" you have this pioneering attitude. Now let's be realistic, we have to have some

> organizational control over the way this group gets mined, the way people go into it and out of it and stop the opportunism. Now you are either going to be completely separate from A&L or completely in it and that's all that we're asking around the table. Not half and half.[124]

After some discussion about the individual provisions to clarify their implications, Ramsden asks, "Who's going to be here in 2 weeks and submit to the provisos of provo?" and Thompson declares definitively, "Let's do it. Let's take our stands."[125]

The rest of the group, who all agree to the provisions, take Charlesworth's "I abstain" and Kosuth's "I half agree, I half abstain" as refusals to agree.[126] With the establishment of (Provisional) Art & Language—the name evokes the Troubles in Northern Ireland and the Provisional Irish Republican Army—Kosuth and Charlesworth were effectively blocked from future participation in the collective. *The Fox*, which had been Kosuth's initiative, ceased publication after its third issue. The ultimate ramifications of Art & Language's decision played out over the months to come. It had gained a new purpose through uncompromising commitment to sociality as a means of proceeding with its work, but it lost the comfort with plurality that had driven its sociality to this point. There were now two positions with real vitality remaining in Art & Language: One, with total support in England and increasing support from Ramsden and Thompson in New York, that envisioned Art & Language as an essentially petty-bourgeois group devoted to solidarity with the working class and collective learning about art, politics, and the relations between them, and another, subscribed to by the rest of Art & Language's New York participants, that sought expanded sociality as a means of leaving art behind and engaging more directly in political activity. Without Kosuth and Charlesworth, the group lacked third or fourth alternatives, and without a fox-like mind-set, these two incommensurable, hedgehog-like approaches would gradually find themselves opposed and in open conflict, particularly as the group now relied more and more on Baldwin's art world profile, having lost Kosuth's. This favored Ramsden and Thompson's position, and, with Burn continuing to be mostly absent from New York, further marginalized those who shared his views.

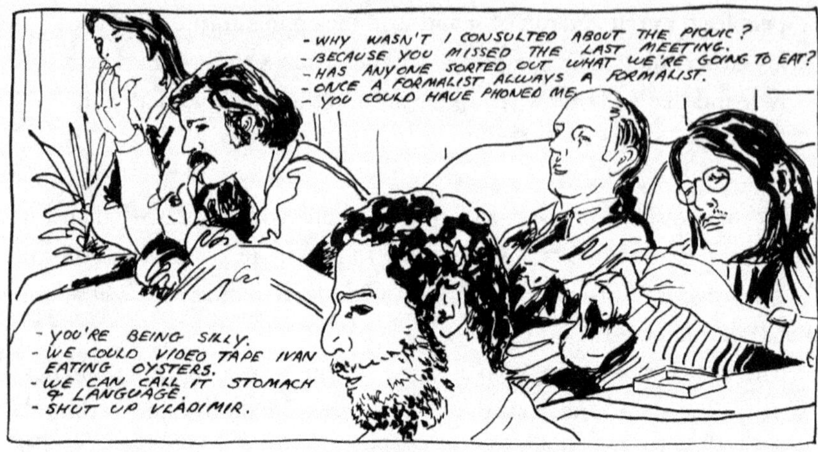

Figure 4.7 Carole Condé and Karl Beveridge, cartoon from *The Fox* 3 (1976).

A series of humorous cartoons by Beveridge and Condé that appear in the final issue of *The Fox* capture the power struggles and disillusionments of the group as it descended into infighting, and they provide a gloomy picture of the New York section of Art & Language as its final months approached (figures 4.7, 4.8). Beveridge and Condé depict the trials and tribulations of two "'foreign' artists" named "Chuck" and "Kitty" (clearly noms de plume for themselves) presented like an episode in an ongoing adventure series, titled comically "The Edge of Edge."[127] "Like thousands of others," and like many of the other participants in Art & Language, "they came to New York seeking those elusive muses, fame and fortune."[128] Dissatisfied with the "authenticity of their 'quality' avant-garde-kunst," they fall in with the "Art & Languish" collective, who share their disillusionment with the art world, but Art & Languish is not without its own problems.[129] At Chuck and Kitty's first meeting with the group, "The atmosphere was guardedly tense, ideas and information were cautiously 'traded.' Some (no

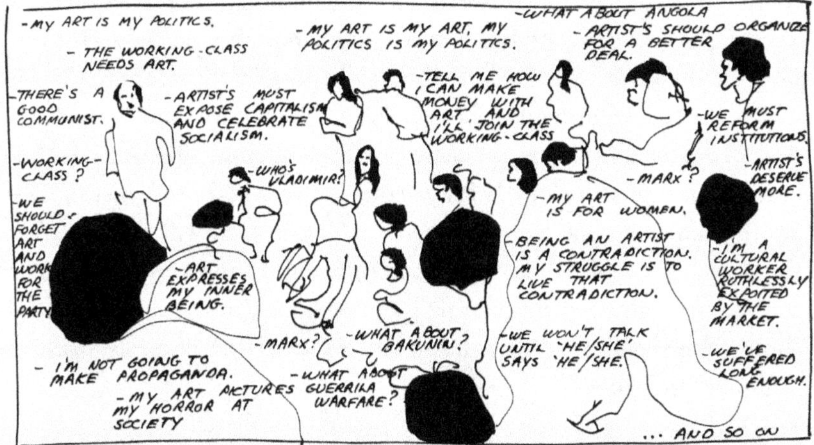

Others in the art community sniffed a 'crisis'. Regular meetings were called. Opinions and positions covered the spectrum from dimwit to dilettante. The Artists Mania for Confused Claptrap (A.M.C.C.) was probably the most radical 'movement' around, but ego-trips reigned and ideological progress was negligible. Some local pundits were amazed that artists even got together! Strange as it may seem, people still came, and some actions were taken. The members of Art & Languish weren't much help, behaving much as everyone else. Why were they as hopeless?

Figure 4.8 Carole Condé and Karl Beveridge, cartoon from *The Fox* 3 (1976).

names) had a better position in the kunstmart, thus a better 'trading value,' which no one challenged for fear of 'power-failure.'"[130]

As Chuck and Kitty's relationship with Art & Languish deepens, the group's squabbles become increasingly pathetic. In one drawing, figures that closely resemble Burn, Corris, and Lendon complain about not being "consulted about the picnic."[131] In another, a discussion about an Art & Languish "platform" involving five members, two of whom appear to be Kosuth and Ramsden, in a room full of plants that bears a resemblance to Burn and Ramsden's studio at 250 Bowery devolves into complaints about the "W.C."[132] An AMCC ("Artists Mania for Confused Claptrap") meeting appears to offer no respite, as half-sketched figures scattered throughout the panel gripe cacophonously about art without anyone seemingly listening to anyone else.[133] The last panel, the end of the episode, seems to show Art & Languish agreeing to membership provisions. However, a closer examination reveals that the topic actually under discussion is who will water the plants, as if the function of *The Fox*—to pursue a theoretical rather than stylistic conceptual art—collapsed from a claim to art world relevance into a mere spat between roommates over a mundane domestic chore. The caption accompanying this final panel rather appropriately mocks the way in which Art & Languish talks about politics: "We'll leave Chuck and Kitty, Art & Languish, and their problems. Can they fight individualism and find unity in the capitalist world? How are they going to make ends meet? What are the concrete conditions they face? What, in fact, will they do? Can they develop a positive relation, given their cultivation and privileges, to the class struggle? Yes, the class struggle! And make no mistake, 'When it comes to the revolution' it was heard said '*we know* we'll be up-against-the-wall-motherfuckers.'"[134]

Five
Keep All Your Friends

(Provisional) Art & Language, the tenuous alliance of those participants in Art & Language who, in March 1976, adopted provisions to enforce strict criteria for membership, lasted less than a year, and its termination coincides with both the dissolution of the Art & Language section in New York and the end of Art & Language's international collaborations. Ousting Joseph Kosuth and Sarah Charlesworth, who did not adopt the provisions, did little to resolve the group's tendency to factionalize according to different conceptions of how to politicize art. If anything, reducing the number of factions exacerbated divisions within the group that had been suppressed by the temporary moment of unity occasioned by agreement about the provisions. Two irreconcilable positions emerged, both of which share a Far Left orientation and a belief that the category of political art is insufficient as either politics or art, but the conclusions each faction drew from these commitments differed considerably. One, insisting that the art world is irredeemably bourgeois, proposed abandoning it, allying with dedicated political collectives, and attempting to win converts to its position away from the art world, while the other faction felt that such abandonment was not so easily achieved, and it sought to challenge recent pretentions to politics as themselves manifestations of the art world's bourgeois ideology. Together, these two halves are recognizably an extension of Art & Language's pursuits, but they were, by this point, no longer conducting themselves in a communal way.

Both factions were on display in a June 1976 exhibition at John Weber Gallery in two distinct bodies of work that Art & Language produced over the previous year. At the peak of the collective's tense artistic and political brinksmanship and mere months before it would collapse altogether, its New York section finally made the first comprehensive presentation of its own work in an exhibition of its own. Unsurprisingly, it was a scattered one. However, because it appeared under the collective's name, the lines of division in the group would not necessarily have been apparent to gallery goers. Sometimes referred to as the "Music-Language" exhibition, this show included the first results of Art & Language's musical projects: audio and video recordings that played daily in the gallery at scheduled intervals. Continuously visible on the walls alongside sheet music for some of the songs Art & Language had written was a second body of work composed of three documentary projects—the producers of which had no overlap with those involved in the Music-Language projects—concerned with art institutions in Canada, Yugoslavia, and the United States. The documentary projects develop Art & Language's interest in encounter and the problems of intercultural exchange in new directions, and all take up the theme of art's institutional complicity with the state and its geopolitical consequences. Carole Condé and Karl Beveridge's small work titled *What Would Canada Do without a Flavin?* captures, in concentrated form, the key themes of the entire enterprise: state governments, media, and their relations to art in institutional settings (figure 5.1). It appropriates a *New York Times* article by culturally conservative critic Hilton Kramer containing a photograph of artworks, most of them in styles that recall American high modernism, minimalism, and postminimalism, in the collection of the Canadian Art Bank, a government program in Condé and Beveridge's native country that purchases art and supplies it to government buildings and offices.[1] Beneath this is a text by Condé and Beveridge that advocates the need to politicize art rather than imitate the manner of New York artists like Dan Flavin. It reads, "What Would Canada Do Without a 'Flavin'? / 1) Make Its Own (Bourgeois Nationalism). / 2) Struggle to Expropriate the Expropriators of National Culture (Proletarian Internationalism)."

The other two documentary projects are more extensive undertakings that develop the same themes present in Condé and Beveridge's work (figures 5.2–5.3). One concerns the function of art in Yugoslavia and was set into motion when the Yugoslavian artist and filmmaker Zoran Popović and critic Jasna Tijardović arrived in New York from Belgrade during 1974 and quickly made contact with Kosuth, who provided them with access to studio space at 24 Bond Street in the NoHo neighborhood during their

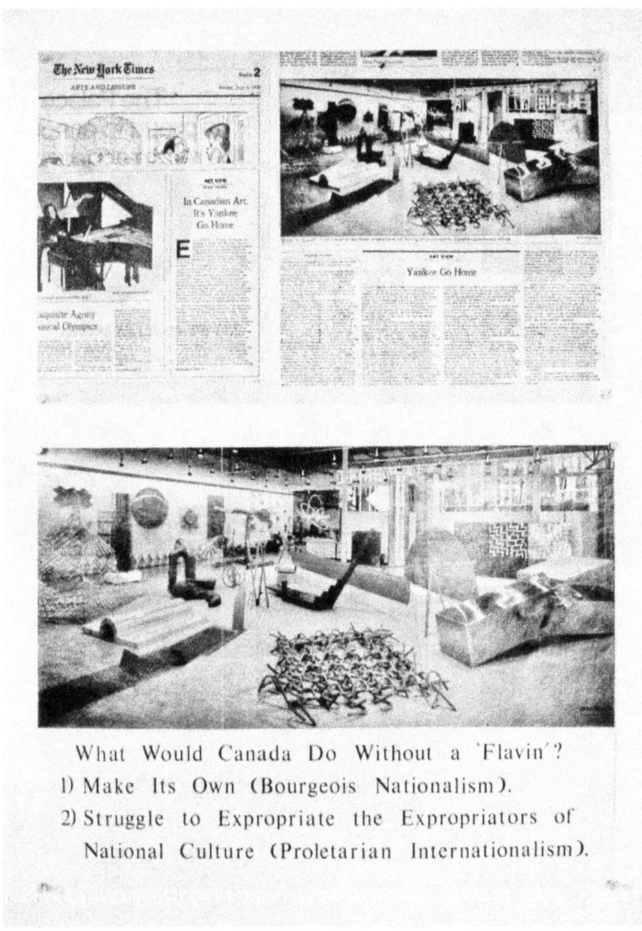

Figure 5.1 Art & Language, *What Would Canada Do without a Flavin?*, 1976.

initial year-long stay in New York. They soon began a collaboration with Art & Language that culminated in Popović's documentary film *Борба у Њујорку* (*Borba u Njujorku* or *Borba u New Yorku* in Latin script and *Struggle in New York* in English translation), filmed during a second visit in 1976, which concerns the politicization of art in New York and captures the factional lines along which the Art & Language section there dissolved.[2] Despite fundamental differences in their situations as practicing artists, the collaboration between Popović, Tijardović, and Art & Language enabled

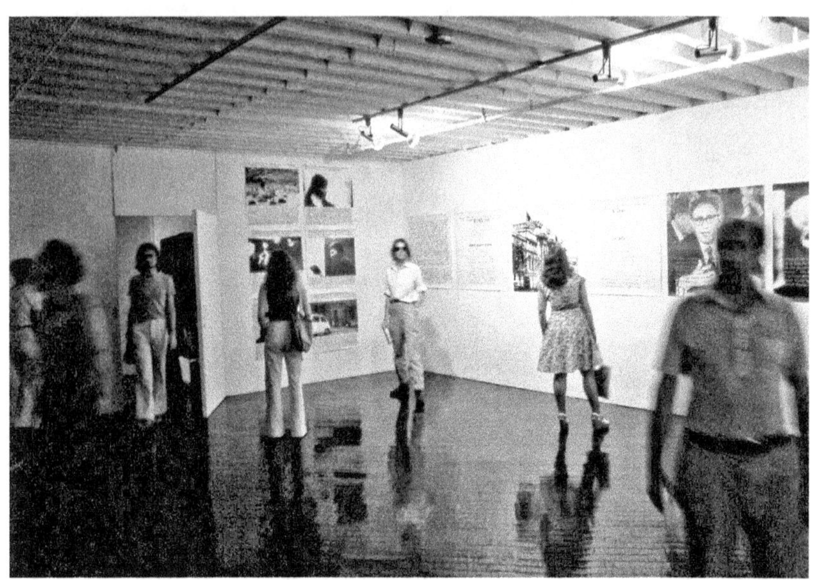

Figure 5.2 Art & Language exhibition at John Weber Gallery, 1976, installation view (left: Art & Language, *The Organization of Culture under Self-Management Socialism*, 1976; right: Art & Language, *The Organization of Culture under Monopoly Capitalism*, 1976).

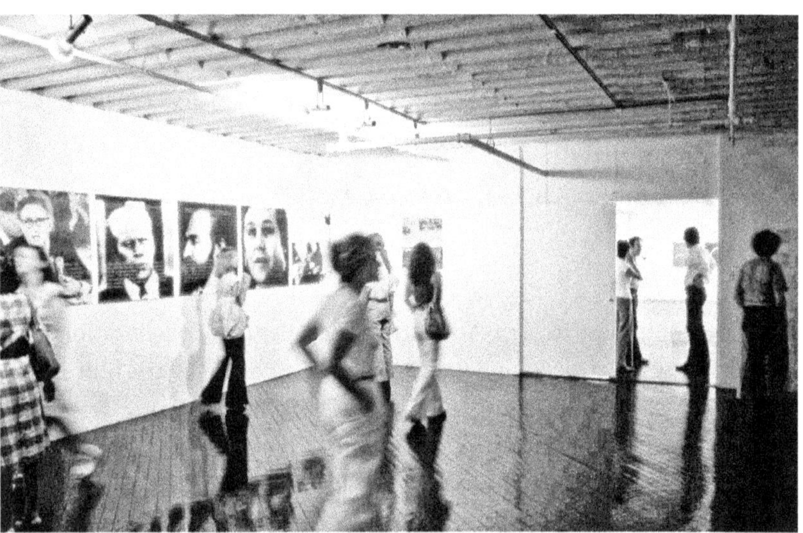

Figure 5.3 Art & Language exhibition at John Weber Gallery, 1976, installation view (left: Art & Language, *The Organization of Culture under Monopoly Capitalism*, 1976; right: Art & Language, *What Would Canada Do without a Flavin?*, 1976).

its participants to comparatively analyze the conditions of artistic production in New York and Belgrade with a focus on institutional factors. For Art & Language, this gave rise to *The Organization of Culture under Self-Management Socialism*, which resulted directly from a brief October 1975 visit to Belgrade by Jill Breakstone, Michael Corris, and Andrew Menard that Popović and Tijardović facilitated during the interval between their two stays in New York.

The Yugoslavia from which Popović and Tijardović arrived was uniquely positioned within the political alliances and hostilities of the Cold War, which made them ideal collaborators for the internationally minded Art & Language. Though an Eastern European socialist state, albeit one with a mixed economy that included a private sector, Yugoslavia was not a signee of the Warsaw Pact and thus remained unaligned with Moscow. László Beke notes, "Yugoslavian artists often considered themselves not eastern but southeastern European. This orientation reflects the country's cultural ties to Italy and Austria, as well as its relative independence from Moscow under the leadership of Marshall Tito."[3] Though more open to the West than other socialist states in Eastern Europe, Yugoslavia was not aligned with the United States or Western Europe either. Aleš Erjavec describes Yugoslavia playing "the Cold War blocs against each other while retaining a shaky equidistance from them."[4] Yugoslavia was also, with India, Egypt, Ghana, and Indonesia, a founder of the Non-Aligned Movement, which provided diplomatic and trade relations for nations not under the sway of Washington or Moscow. International travel played an important role for Yugoslavian artists, and Western publications and visitors from the West, which were not always permitted in certain other socialist states, were allowed. In addition to its diverse set of international connections, Yugoslavia was, as Lutz Becker notes, possessed of "internal internationalism" that consisted of five federal republics: Slovenia, Croatia, Serbia, Bosnia and Herzegovina, and Montenegro.[5] Contacts between artists living in these republics helped to foster a sophisticated art scene in Yugoslavia, including a strong predilection for conceptual art borne out of the many international connections to which Yugoslavian artists had access.[6]

The Yugoslavian variety of conceptual art with which Popović and Tijardović involved themselves had almost no profile in New York when they arrived there. Only a few artists were known and then only in a cursory fashion. In 1970, curator Kynaston McShine included work by the Ljubljana-based OHO group in the exhibition *Information* at the Museum of Modern Art, one of the first major museum surveys of conceptual art.[7] They also appear as one of the few Eastern European inclusions in Lucy R. Lippard's survey of conceptual art, *Six Years*.[8] However, by the time Popović and Tijardović arrived in New York, OHO and other Yugoslavian art groups such as (∃KÔD, whose members translated texts by participants in Art & Language, had abandoned art or ceased to exist owing to their disillusionment with conceptual art, which, according to Popović and Tijardović, many Yugoslavian artists felt to have been, in their final analyses, "just a perpetuation of the Western bourgeois tradition."[9] This feeling stems from visits to Yugoslavia by Western artists including Joseph Beuys and Daniel Buren, which "proved negatively catalytic for many of us, mainly because of the amount of money associated with each artist."[10] Popović and Tijardović cite the specific case of (∃KÔD encountering "'conceptual' works priced in the range of $10,000" at the Biennale de Jeunesse in Paris during 1972 as especially disillusioning.[11]

Popović, Tijardović, and others persevered, however, by reorienting conceptual art in an explicitly political direction and aligning it with the stated goals of the Yugoslavian state, in particular the principle of self-management. Erjavec explains that, in theory, "the aim of self-management was to allow for decision making at the lowest possible level and to make social relations and decisions direct and transparent."[12] This goal was foundational for the Student Cultural Center (SKC) at the University of Belgrade with which Popović and Tijardović were closely involved and which was the main hub for conceptual art activity in Belgrade during the 1970s. Tom Marioni, a conceptual artist who visited Belgrade in 1974, described the SKC as "the main gallery of contemporary art in Belgrade . . . located near the center of town in an old police building that was obtained during a student revolt in 1968. It has a theater, a lounge that serves Turkish coffee and soft drinks, lecture halls, a book store, a library and a gallery."[13] Becker visited Belgrade in 1975 and, with Popović among his assistants, produced a documentary film about the SKC titled *Kino Beleške* (*Film Notes*) that captures its politicized direction. In the film, Dunja Blažević, who directed the SKC gallery at the time, discusses the application of self-management principles to art: "I will talk about the mechanisms for socialising art. In our country there existed so far two ways in which works of art could be financed or bought: publicly or privately. Both are examples of currently dominant property relationships, which reflect clearly the socio-economic basis on which this art come into being, developed, functioned. A third model is being created now; it is the self-management system of free exchange and co-operative work, through work communities, which basically represents a new attitude towards property."[14]

Popović and Tijardović did not necessarily agree with Blažević's optimism about the ideal of self-management as it was actually being practiced at the SKC. In "For Self-Management Art," a text first published in a bulletin called *October 75* brought out by Popović and others in the orbit of the SKC, Popović considers the role of technocracy and bureaucracy in the "world of art," which, he concludes, "finally functions on behalf of the preservation of the hegemony of Western culture over world culture in line with tendencies of late capitalism, and its imperialistic needs and aims."[15] Tijardović develops this insight further in an article for *The Fox* titled "The 'Liquidation' of Art: Self-Management or Self-Protection," and she makes clear her disillusionment with the direction subsequently taken by the SKC relative to its mission statement. In the essay, she discusses how, since its foundation in 1971, "The Gallery wants to be socially justified, which means it is not neutral. It wants to adapt to society, to the aim of this society—self-management."[16] However, she accuses the SKC of failing artists in this regard through its adoption of rhetoric demanding "the 'liquidation' of art" in response to artists' demands for funding, resources, and access to the institution.[17] Tijardović accuses the SKC of hypocrisy because, as an underfunded institution, it has to demand recognition and funding from the state in order to participate in Yugoslavian society, but then, when faced with the same demands from those who help make up its programming and support it in a variety of other ways, it refuses to bestow on them the very things it asks for itself, namely the capacity to manage itself with adequate funding. She is, like Popović, decidedly less assured about the realities of self-management than Blažević. Referring to the principle of self-management, Tijardović concludes, "We have been asked to work independently and to teach others to do so, but in the end it turned out that the institution . . . is only paying lip service to its initial organization, that is, the notion of cooperation."[18]

The similarities between Popović and Tijardović's ideas and Art & Language's own, including a drive to collectivity, a mutual rejection of the conventional art object in favor of conceptual art pursued as a collaborative practice, and a desire to politicize that practice by assuming control over processes of production and distribution, attracted them to one another. Popović contends that, as people who "dropped in from a Communist system," his and Tijardović's relationship with Art & Language was "of direct use to them, for the self-evaluation of their own thinking and knowledge of the social and political role of art."[19] Art & Language attempted to return the favor with its visit to Belgrade, during which Breakstone, Corris, and Menard conducted a series of seminars on the subject of cultural imperialism. Given their estrangement from the English section of Art & Language, Yugoslavia provided Breakstone, Corris, and Menard with the promise of a different kind of international alliance founded on more closely shared political goals and the possibility of refreshing their understanding of art through an encounter with new interlocutors.

Announcements for Art & Language's visit mention four seminars at the SKC on the evenings of October 13–16 and a final seminar on the afternoon of October 17 at the Museum of Modern Art in Belgrade.[20] The events are described as "an occasion for mutual learning," "a (possible) model for an 'international' exhibition(?)," and an attempt to "undermine" cultural imperialism. Corris and Menard, who authored the announcement text, invoke the difficulties of conducting a lecture on this topic as the very reason for meeting to talk about it: "Indeed, cultural imperialism and the psychology of capitalism have been discussed by many artists and critics. But in most cases (at least in the West), artists/critics think of imperialism and capitalism as little more than *topics* for a lecture; that is, they rarely treat the lecture *itself* as problematic, as an activity which, in many ways, recreates all the problems of imperialism." To prevent the lecture from reproducing the very logic that its content would seek to subvert, Corris and Menard propose a format for the discussions that is similar to the Art & Language discussions that Terry Smith moderated in Australia earlier that year. It would involve the collective convening with others with the dual aim of replicating the collaborative discussion-based conditions under which the collective usually worked as well as subjecting that work to the test of its reception in a Yugoslavian context. The aim, however, was different from what

Art & Language had done in Melbourne and Adelaide. Unlike Smith's projects, which sought to give the collective's discourse on provincialism a practical outlet in Australia, Breakstone, Corris, and Menard envisioned thwarting cultural imperialism by redirecting the flow of cultural exchange and instead learning as much as they could about self-management, which appealed to them, so as to apply some version of its principles back in New York. In transcripts of the discussions, Menard speaks directly about what he calls "decentralization," which he defines as "an attempt to take control of our own media as a means of production"—a goal he envisioned for Art & Language's work in the United States.[21]

During the seminars, the picture that Popović offers of the artists at the SKC suggests that the self-management that interests Art & Language so much is not necessarily having its intended effects in Yugoslavia: "The Center was founded in '71, but unfortunately, it never worked out beforehand its sources of finance. So bureaucracy doesn't know who's responsible for financing us, and because it isn't black and white, bureaucracy is trying to avoid its obligations to finance us. Since our activity is in resistance to the existing art, which is a restrictive art in our country, the art bureaucracy wants us to have no power. So I hope you see why the Center is so isolated."[22] Popović concludes his remarks by stating his hope that contact between the SKC and Art & Language would "undermine both imperialism *and* isolation."[23] After the seminars but while still in Belgrade, Corris and Menard wrote about their "gut reaction" to the situation of art and artists there.[24] Characterizing their impressions as "mixed," they lament, "It's a bit sad seeing all the frustration here, at least among the people close to us, the people who invited us here and those we've spoken with most since we've been here."[25] They had visited Belgrade to combat cultural imperialism but came to see how the indigenous contradictions of self-management socialism, such as the isolation Popović described, hampered their Yugoslavian interlocutors as much if not more. Moreover, the SKC was not the promising alternative to the situation facing artists in capitalist New York that they may have hoped to find in Belgrade. About it, they write, "In fact, the Center has become a kind of prisonhouse of dissent, that is, it has become an institutionally (financially) sanctioned means for students, and particularly artists (most of whom are no longer students), to register some kind of dissent, but a means which virtually excludes all other means. . . . The need

HOW MANY YUGOSLAVIAN ARTISTS CAN YOU NAME (NO CHEATING)?

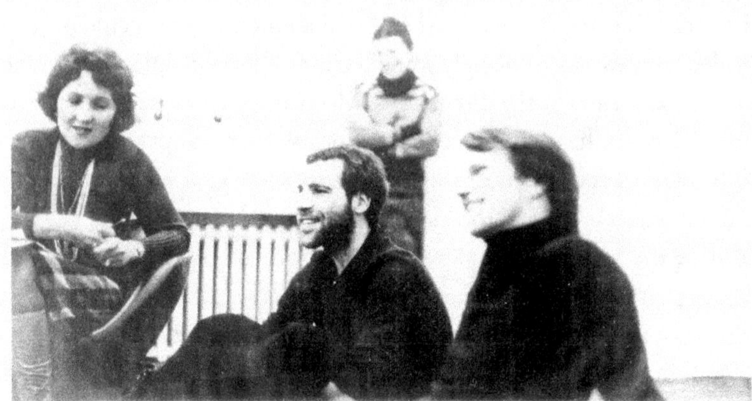

M. Corris Cultural imperialism can come in many forms, but generally the one we're most familiar with is the kind that's in the form of an international exhibit, where the products of one cultural context are embedded in a foreign cultural context. Paradoxically enough, many forms of cultural imperialism, including this one, have been adopted voluntarily. In fact one of the strengths of New York is how well it has been assimilated and accepted as the natural state of affairs for artists in the rest of the world. Obviously there are many ways in which the people in a foreign country can relate to the objects in an international exhibition. And I think the most striking feature of such exhibitions is the fact that your relationship to the objects presented to you is typically that of any consumer to a product. Culture used in this way is oppressive.

Figure 5.4 Panel from Art & Language, *The Organization of Culture under Self-Management Socialism*, 1976. MACBA Collection, MACBA Consortium. Long-term loan of Philippe Méaille.

to work through institutions, the virtual impossibility of independent organization and action, is as overbearing here as it is in the U.S., though for different reasons."[26] In the end, though, Corris and Menard remain hopeful that "future cooperation between New York and Belgrade" might result from the seminars.[27]

The major result of Art & Language's visit to Yugoslavia is a series of panels combining photography and text that appeared at John Weber Gallery as *The Organization of Culture under Self-Management Socialism* (figures 5.4, 5.5). Each of the panels is square and contains three elements in three horizontal registers: first, a question posed by Art & Language; then, an image, usually of the discussions (including one depicting a Yugoslavian

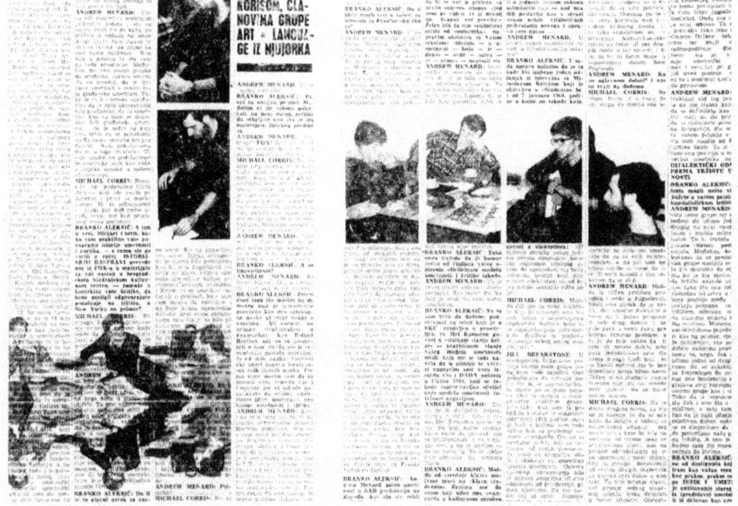

Figure 5.5 Panel from Art & Language, *The Organization of Culture under Self-Management Socialism*, 1976. MACBA Collection, MACBA Consortium. Long-term loan of Philippe Méaille.

student newspaper report on them), taking up the bulk of the panel; and, finally, at the bottom, an excerpt from the seminar transcripts—similar in form and tone to the blurts that Art & Language had previously excerpted from records of its discussions—that can be interpreted as a general address if not a direct answer to the question put forward at the top of that panel. These texts usually criticize some aspect of either of the two art worlds whose meeting prompted the creation of the work. A representative panel features the question "HOW MANY YUGOSLAVIAN ARTISTS CAN YOU NAME (NO CHEATING)?," a photograph of Corris and Menard in Belgrade listening to someone who is not pictured, and a quote from Corris that describes the way international art exhibitions can function as a form of cultural imperialism when "embedded in a foreign cultural context." Panels such as this one are, for Art & Language, an uncharacteristically straightforward way to present ideas, and they are some of its most direct efforts to reach an audience with messages. For those in the collective seeking to do activist work, the juxtaposition of image and text in this manner proved to be an attractive format.

Complementing these panels at John Weber Gallery was a third documentary project: a version of *The Organization of Culture under Monopoly Capitalism*, a work created by Corris, Heller, and Menard that examines the Arts and Artifacts Indemnity Act, which the U.S. Congress enacted on December 20, 1975, "To provide indemnities for exhibitions of artistic and humanistic endeavors, and for other purposes."[28] When shown in galleries, the work consists of some combination of panels with photographs and texts, a video, and a typescript version of the video. A printed version of this material appears in *The Fox*.[29] The chief relevance of *The Organization of Culture under Monopoly Capitalism* lies in its creators' suspicions that alliances between institutions, specifically the state and the museum, were being manipulated to advance American imperialism abroad. To prepare the work, Corris, Heller, and Menard conducted and videotaped interviews with Jack Duncan, counsel to the House Select Subcommittee on Education, and Robert Wade, general counsel to the National Endowment for the Arts, who both played roles in drafting the legislation, as well as man-on-the-street-style interviews with museumgoers at the Metropolitan Museum of Art. Their perplexed comments represent a lack of public awareness concerning the act. Footage of these interviews, plus additional footage of Corris, Heller, and Menard talking to one another and commenting on other parts of the video, forms the basis for the video component of the work. As edited together, the final video jumps back and forth between these sources and builds from a general explanation of the act and the process of its enacting to more pointed questions about how the act serves American interests, especially Cold War interests that pertain to relations between the capitalist United States and the communist Soviet Union and China.

The video is primarily concerned with unpacking what a "national interest" is in the context of the act, and Heller puts this question to Duncan, who answers, "For instance, bringing over the Chinese art, helping the American people to understand and see a sense of history of what those countries have done and vice versa. It would be in the national interest, perhaps, for Russians to see or Chinese to see some of our works of art, so that their people and their leaders could understand . . . rather than just depend on the written word. They could see what the culture is made out of, from its works of art."[30] Later in the video, audio inserts feature Wade discussing his reluctance to allow State Department oversight of indemnification requests, and he acknowledges, "I can see down the road the State Department denying exhibitions because they don't for some reason like it."[31] Menard wagers that Wade's concerns are unfounded, and he says, in conversation with Corris and Heller, "I'll bet you that most of the shows that go out — given the connections between museums and foreign policy anyway — that there is not going to be any problem with the State Department."[32] Menard proposes that the act strengthens relations between the government and "people . . . in the very high echelons of decision-making in the art world," including many who testified in support of the bill, which Heller notes was the recipient of "virtually unanimous agreement" during hearings on it.[33]

When asked whom the act stands to benefit, Duncan cites "the American people," and Wade suggests "the people of the United States."[34] Commenting on this in the follow-up discussion, Heller proposes that, in actuality, the act maintains "the same old relationship to the culture . . . ; people are still going to be in a consumer relationship."[35] Corris laments, "As far as these bureaucrats are concerned, the museums are the best places to administer culture."[36] Menard links these two sentiments by claiming that "concentrating money in the hands of museums . . . means that museums take on a much greater role as cultural institutions; and if they are seen as educational institutions — and they are seen as the salvation of education, in a way — then it means that the salvation of education is once again consumerism."[37] As for how to take more direct responsibility for the means of producing education, Art & Language discusses the possibility of opening a storefront in SoHo that would serve as "a resource center" for the community.[38] (Similar alternative arts spaces, including Franklin Furnace, Artists Space, and Printed Matter, began to appear in New York around this time.) Though such a project never came to fruition, it would have functioned similarly to the self-managed SKC in Belgrade while, at the same time, by occupying the space of a commercial storefront, being adequate to how Art & Language was "embedded in Capitalist society as artists."[39] This project never got beyond the proposal stage, the most developed version of which appears as an article in *Studio International* titled "Now about This Storefront." In it, Breakstone, Corris, Heller, and Menard envision "an integrated network of storefront spaces, a broad, horizontal organization aimed at community self-management, complemented by connections to other Socialist groups."[40] This would serve to decentralize major institutional spaces and their monopolies on the presentation of culture without falling into the isolation in which the SKC became trapped. For Art & Language's contribution to this effort, the authors of this statement consider a storefront "located in New York, in SoHo, and directed mainly at the local art community."[41] Both an architectural edifice and an information center, the storefront would be capable of functioning "as a media alternative to museums."[42] As a decentered space, it would also provide a measure of desired distance from the institutions of the art world and their complicity with the state.

The other direction Art & Language pursued in its John Weber Gallery exhibition was decidedly different. Rather than extending the political activities to which certain of its colleagues were now committed through plain juxtapositions of informative images and text, a separate group within the collective returned to the conceptual interrogation of art world ideology that had long sustained its work, albeit now set to music. At the center of the collective's musical projects is Mayo Thompson, who began playing and recording music with the Red Krayola (originally the Red Crayola) in Houston, Texas, in 1966. Along with drummer Frederick Barthelme and bassist Steve Cunningham, he played guitar and sang in the band's original incarnation, which performed experimental music that drew on psychedelic rock, avant-garde jazz, and contemporary classical music. By 1969, this version of the band had collapsed, and Thompson recorded a solo album titled *Corky's Debt to His Father* for the Texas Revolution label before he and Barthelme relocated to New York, where they became loosely affiliated with conceptual art. (Barthelme published in *Art-Language*.[43]) Not long thereafter, Thompson relocated again, to England, where his own involvement with Art & Language began. When he returned to New York in 1975, he continued to pursue musical projects in collaboration with Art & Language and began formulating a new lineup of the Red Krayola.

Thompson describes the origins of his musical collaboration with Art & Language as stemming from his interest in setting to music language that is not typically lyrical in character:

> When I first met Art & Language, . . . I gave them a copy of my solo album, *Corky's Debt to His Father*, and they said, "It's kind of personal isn't it?" I said, "Something wrong with that? You got another idea?" They said, "Yeah, we could try a whole new thing." I said, "OK, give me some lyrics and I'll put them to music and we'll see what happens." Next thing I know I get four pieces of text through the mail. Sure enough, when I started working on it I thought, this is a new language for me. I was also convinced by that time that you could put anything to music, language-wise, so I thought, Yeah, let's see.[44]

The language put to music on Thompson's first projects with Art & Language, the album *Corrected Slogans* and the video *Nine Gross and Conspicuous Errors*, both of which were included in the John Weber Gallery exhibition, draws equally from the lyrical tropes of socialist workers' songs, the rhetorical strategies of political speeches, and the terminology of Marxist philosophy. From Art & Language's perspective, music provided a new outlet that proved particularly versatile, as it allowed the collective to draw out the satire that was often latent in its work. This manifested both in bitingly clever lyrical content and unrehearsed or even improvised performances that suspended literal meaning and ironized it without sacrificing either rigor or acuity. A turn to music also, at least potentially, came with new audiences, though Art & Language's subversion of the musical tropes it deployed, like its play with political language, denied the populist appeal of popular music as much as it interrupted the traditions of art music with the raucous noise of rock and roll. If one half of Art & Language was doing all that it could to communicate its thinking to the audiences at John

Weber Gallery, this other half was skeptical of any claim for transparent address and preferred to work within the confines of contradictions and ambiguities.

Michael Baldwin wrote most of the lyrics for the twenty-one songs that constitute *Corrected Slogans*. The process of writing, rehearsing, and recording the record stretched from 1973 to 1976 and took place in England, New York, and Captiva, Florida, where Thompson and Christine Kozlov worked as studio assistants to Robert Rauschenberg. Funded in part by a grant from Rauschenberg's Change, Inc. foundation, and released in 1976 as a twelve-inch LP in an initial run of a thousand copies, first pressings feature a blank sleeve with sheets of paper pasted onto both front and back to provide minimal credits (figures 5.6, 5.7). To accord with the provisions Art & Language adopted, the regular participants in the collective go unacknowledged. Instead, the names given are mostly those of the recording engineers, mixers, and the drummer, Jesse Chamberlain, who, apart from musical projects involving the Red Krayola, was otherwise uninvolved with Art & Language. On the album, Thompson plays guitars, keyboards, and synthesizers; Chamberlain plays drums; and the vocalists include, in addition to the instrumentalists, Michael Baldwin; Lynn Lemaster; Charles, Sandra, and Orlando Harrison; Pauline Harrison (no relation); Harold Hurrell; Philip Pilkington; and Mel Ramsden. Much of Thompson's contribution to the record occurred before he began associating with the New York–based participants in Art & Language, and, of them, only Ramsden, who provided the vocal track on the song "Penny Capitalists," contributes.

The individual tracks on *Corrected Slogans* are broadly divisible into two categories. Most are songs, but four other tracks are speeches performed to musical accompaniment, usually a repetitive figure played on either guitar or piano, often with a drum part. Each of these is a relatively clear statement of political position, but the setting of language to music makes a literal reading of the texts difficult. "Harangue," for instance, provides a reading of the current political situation as "a further entrenchment of reaction and the growth of mass repression" without "a conscious socialist transformatory alternative."[45] A voice suggests, "What is needed is an integration of the ideology of socialism . . . socialist . . . transformatory sections . . . with the industrial working class. / Socialist-working class solidarity is historical leadership identity." As a harangue, the aim of the song is to stimulate

MUSIC-LANGUAGE

CORRECTED SLOGANS

Side A (Time: 22:45)
Maharashtra, Keep All Your Friends, Imagination I & II, Coleridge vs Martineau, An Exemplification, Postscript to SDS' Infiltration, War Dance I & II, An Harangue, Ergastulum, The Mistakes of Trotsky. . . Thesmophoriazusae, Louis Napoleon

Side B (Time: 24:06)
Seven Compartments, Petrichenko, Don't Talk to Sociologists . . ., What Are the Inexpensive Things the Panel Most Enjoys? . . . An International, History, Organization, It's an Illusion, Penny Capitalists, Plekhanov, Natura Facit Saltus

Written, performed* and produced by Art & Language(P) 1973—1976

*Drums and

"A contradiction is the norm
For breaking
Dialectically . . ."

(KAYF): Jesse Chamberlain; It's an Illusion sung by Little Tommy Hobbes

Figure 5.6 Music-Language, *Corrected Slogans*, 1976, front cover.

CORRECTED SLOGANS

Recorded by Colin Bateman, Doug Pomeroy, Thomas Duffy
Mixed by Art & Language(P) with Colin Bateman, Doug Pomeroy, Wieslaw Woszczyk
Recorded and mixed at Acorn Records Ltd., Church Road, Stonesfield, Oxford, England (Bateman) and at Basement/Big Apple Studio, 112 Greene Street, New York, N.Y., U.S.A. (Pomeroy, Duffy, Woszczyk)
Mastered by Stu Romain at Frankford/Wayne Mastering Laboratories, 1697 Broadway, New York, N.Y., U.S.A.
Manufactured by North American Music Inc., 300 Brook Street, Scranton, Pennsylvania, U.S.A.
Funded by Music-Language/Art & Language(P), Art & Language Foundation Inc., Change Inc.

The songs which comprise Corrected Slogans are published by Music-Language/Art & Language(P) (BMI), 49 E. 1st Street, New York, N.Y., 10003, U.S.A. and 126, Broughton Road, Banbury, Oxon., England.

Figure 5.7 Music-Language, *Corrected Slogans*, 1976, back cover.

anger and mobilize action, with the driving and heavily distorted guitar track backing the harangue itself serving as an incentive in this general direction. However, its loudness often occludes the incitement to act, so the rousing of sentiment becomes a rousing to something rather vague at best.

The three remaining spoken tracks complicate the conception of solidarity expressed in "Harangue" with warnings about unscrupulous association. "Don't Talk to Sociologists . . ." cautions against alliances with sociologists and anthropologists, who, because of their disciplines' "historical role within bourgeois ideology," are unable to provide "an analysis or even a picture of our conditions of exploitation." Artists, it seems, are no less culpable, as the same track includes a warning not to "unite artists . . . if you or they are made to think that there's a 'rational core' . . . in support of the view that 'society' is maintained harmoniously—rather than by exploitation and force: violence." The track "Organization" issues similar warnings with regard to class: "The organization of activity into social and critical action will be no more than degenerate if it remains in the realm of participatory conflict." The lyrics argue in favor of "transition" before "allegedly progressive smart people" and "the people they feel sorry for" have any mutual class ground on which to collaborate "against the institutional ideology." In the fourth and last of the spoken tracks, "Penny Capitalists," Ramsden provides "the careless purveyors of high culture" with two options: either "to be fixed as the harmless class, the dangerous harmless class" or to "recognise that they are a non-working, not-working class—penny capitalists—and ask themselves what that means: become people in process." All told, it is as if no one—or no one who is middle class, artists included—is a suitable candidate for doing politics, activist or otherwise.

The lyrics to "Penny Capitalists" are excerpted from a small, square, staple-bound pamphlet titled "The Intellectual Life of the Ruling Class Gets Its Apotheosis in a World of Doris Days" authored by Baldwin that, across six pages, excoriates the Venice Biennale as "a necrotic extremity" of the ruling classes (figure 5.8).[46] (Provisional) Art & Language was soon to exhibit in this very exhibition, and its participation would be characteristically antagonistic. Copies of the pamphlet were made available at the John Weber Gallery exhibition as well as in Venice. Deploying particularly fiery rhetoric, Baldwin characterizes artists' "attempts to fix forever their relations with 'the rest of the world,' irrespective of social change" as "the last

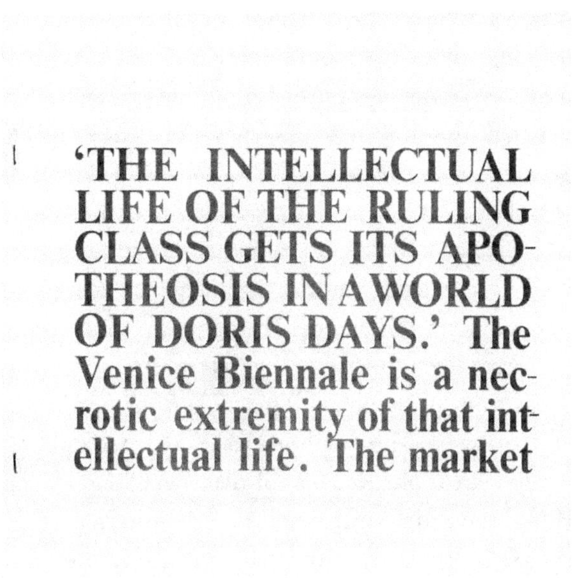

'THE INTELLECTUAL LIFE OF THE RULING CLASS GETS ITS APOTHEOSIS IN A WORLD OF DORIS DAYS.' The Venice Biennale is a necrotic extremity of that intellectual life. The market

Figure 5.8 Art & Language, "The Intellectual Life of the Ruling Class Gets Its Apotheosis in a World of Doris Days," 1976.

defensive gasp of entirely static instruments of capitalism . . . in the effort to be better fed by its masters."[47] If an eternal "fix" is precisely the illusion by which the ruling order is sustained, then the artist, Baldwin suggests, must "learn to function on class lines, recognizing that the requirement for 'realism' includes his own social sectionality. . . . 'Practice' has got to be projective—but artists (given the distribution of function) must earn class activity given a scrutiny of the logic and the phenomenology of class analysis and mediated as a class history of ideology."[48] The task Baldwin here presents for artists is not to join prematurely with the working classes but to carefully and patiently examine their own class position in the belief that alliances with the working classes will ultimately be of no use unless artists first work out their own dependence on and support for the bourgeoisie. The artist's status as "an economic hors concours . . . avails no one of a glimpse of 'freedom.'"[49] Rather than seek a false notion of freedom, "one wants to find intellectual and deontic constraints" that reveal the conditions of social life and make genuine political action possible.[50]

This search for constraints occupies the remainder of the tracks on *Corrected Slogans*. They are songs that draw from romantic lieder, Brechtian singspiel, and the conventions of popular music for both instrumentation and vocalization. Softer than the spoken tracks, they allow the comedic tendency in Art & Language's work to express itself by satirizing naive utopian fantasies besetting political art. These songs provide a lighter counterpoint to the sentiments expressed in Baldwin's pamphlet and in the angrier spoken tracks. "Keep All Your Friends" mocks aspirations of being "fed breakfast in bed and served by a fat millionaire." "Ergastulum" chides those who "want to be free, / Free: like a bird in a tree." The refrain "tio-tio-tio-tio-tinx," appropriated from Aristophanes's play *The Birds*, appears in both "The Mistakes of Trotsky . . . Thesmophoriazusae" ("Thesmophorazusae" is itself a reference to Aristophanes's play of that name) and "What Are the Inexpensive Things the Panel Most Enjoys? . . . An International." References to *The Birds* are appropriate, as the play can be interpreted as an allegory for the kind of fantasy that Art & Language condemns on *Corrected Slogans*. In Aristophanes's play, a pair of disaffected Athenian citizens mobilize the oppressed class of birds to build a city in the sky, appropriately named Νεφελοκοκκυγία (Cloudcoocooland), between the gods and the mortals, allegedly so that the birds can regain their supposed rightful rule over both groups by intervening between them, but throughout the play, Aristophanes hints that the main protagonist, Pisthetaerus, himself transformed into a bird at one point, harbors ulterior motives and is simply using the birds to advance his own ambitions for power. The play ends with a ceremony at which Pisthetaerus is presented Zeus's scepter by Sovereignty, Zeus's mistress, whom he also marries as the birds proclaim him their king. In 1976, this play could have been staged as an allegory about the political ambitions of certain artists.

The comedic direction in Art & Language's work first became more explicit in 1975 with *Nine Gross and Conspicuous Errors*, a video produced entirely in New York using lyrics written by Ramsden (figure 5.9). It was originally intended for classroom use, and Ian Burn showed it to his students in Halifax, though it was not widely adopted in this role. Shot handheld with minimal editing and little camera movement on black-and-white video by the participants, it compiles nine untitled songs performed by Thompson and Chamberlain on combinations of guitar, organ, accordion, and drums,

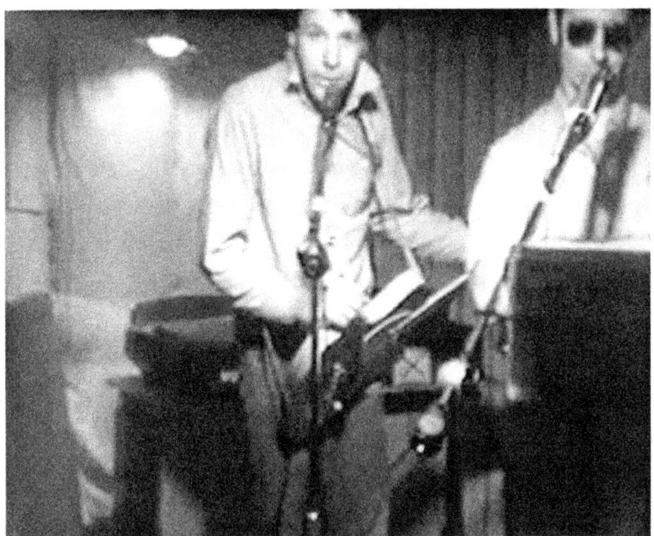

Figure 5.9 Art & Language, *Nine Gross and Conspicuous Errors*, 1975, video still.

mostly in a slapdash rock idiom, while Kathryn Bigelow, Burn, Kozlov, Nigel Lendon, Mel and Paula Ramsden, and Terry Smith, in various combinations, speak or sing, usually in atonal voices, criticisms of "gross and conspicuous errors" of a political nature. "It is a G&CE to desire socialism with capitalist desire," Burn sings at the opening of the first song. "Capitalism," Lendon clarifies, "is in the mode of thought itself." The ham-fisted, fist-raising " . . . together!" that the collective sing in ensemble after Burn singles out, as a G&CE, attempts "to try to realize an activist epistemology by luxurious abstract jesting" rather than in "the day-to-day struggles of all of us" is supreme black comedy made even blacker when performed to Thompson's wordless crooning in the background, which recalls doo-wop, over his own gentle guitar arpeggios and Chamberlain's soft drumming.

The specific political mistakes that Art & Language identifies are less important than the overall tone of its performance, in which it is often difficult to tell whether the performers are chastising mistakes, chastising those who chastise mistakes, or chastising themselves for making the video in the first instance. Suspending such knotty language as "a belief is an approximated correspondence between daft, reified mind and the fetishized social reality of the commodity" in the medium of a song has an inherently disorienting effect, as vocabulary and phrasing that would be difficult enough to follow in writing or plain speech become nearly impossible to assimilate on a single hearing let alone to assimilate with previous lines before another, equally complex line follows and demands assimilation with what came before it. The language dissolves into purely material sound, musically interchangeable with the instrumentation to which it is set, and any rhetorical value that the words possess collapses into the rhetoric of the performance, which is alternately melodic and monotone. By taking on the position of pop stars but doing so in a largely unrehearsed and thoroughly unmusical fashion, Art & Language equates political grandstanding with celebrity, which it deflates by mocking political language within the confines of a jesting sociality that it offers as already more productive politically than pamphleteering, sloganeering, or protesting—a paradoxical redemption. The group is simultaneously enraptured with politics and thoroughly bored with its banality, predictability, and inefficacy. In *Nine Gross and Conspicuous Errors*, as on *Corrected Slogans*, the discourse of the Far Left loses its literal significance until its futility itself becomes productive by clearing the air of bogus ideology and returning to the act of working together as the basis of any politics.

Working together, however, was not going well for (Provisional) Art & Language by this point. Those who continued exploring the complexities of bringing art worlds into contact had lost much of their conceptual rigor in favor of direct messaging, while those developing Art & Language's commitment to examining concepts were growing distanced from the expanding sociality that had in the past rejuvenated those efforts. Learning, so central to Art & Language work, appeared to be at a standstill. Questions about the future direction of the collective came to a head as it mounted its June 1976 exhibition at John Weber Gallery. To discuss the situation, a week of meetings was convened in the basement residence of Beveridge and Condé at 49 East First Street in the East Village. In retrospect, Corris writes, "It became clear to most of us by the end of the week that the true purpose of these meetings was to force the issue of the 'semi-autonomy' of the sub-groups" within Art & Language.[51] "The group was virtually evenly split," Corris adds, "between those who wished to continue to work in and around the art world and its institutions and those who were willing to

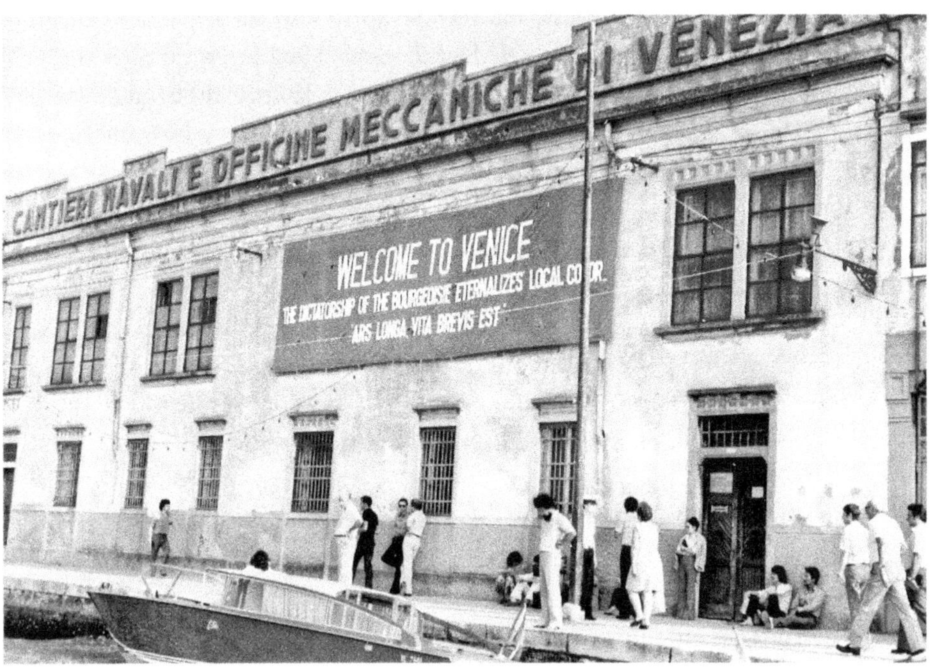

Figure 5.10 Art & Language, banner displayed at the Venice Biennale, 1976.

jettison such a commitment once and for all."[52] Ramsden and Thompson, with support from England, led the former contingent, while Corris, Heller, and Menard advocated for the latter position, and the two groups were unable to reach a compromise either on which direction to take or on whether to permit multiple autonomous groups to operate under the name Art & Language, which would have violated the provisions' strict enforcement of collective agreement on all work made public under the Art & Language name, something Ramsden and Thompson, the authors and chief advocates of the provisions, were unwilling to concede.

The adherents to the provisions managed one further action together before the New York section of Art & Language unraveled irreparably. In August 1976, (Provisional) Art & Language participated in the Venice Biennale with a banner that read "Welcome to Venice / The Dictatorship of the Bourgeoisie 'Eternalizes' Local Color / Ars Longa, Vita Brevis Est" (figure 5.10) — yet another assertion of the collective's awareness of the problems that international cultural exchange creates when undertaken in the interests of a ruling class. Kosuth and Charlesworth also participated in the biennale, and a review in the *New York Times* by Flora Lewis captures the contested state of Art & Language's relations with Kosuth, the breakdown of which occurred between its acceptance of a showing in Venice and his departure from Art & Language:

> Two competing, antagonistic American groups were also permitted to enter contributions.
>
> One, whose leader calls himself Joseph Kossuth [*sic*], brought a batch of huge posters headlined "Where Do You Stand?" Pointing out the importance of knowing one's "social location," it offers a series of multiple-choice prepackaged reactions to the whole Biennale. . . .
>
> The other American group, called "The Fox," protested bitterly against such a leaven of humor. But Mr. di Meana managed to assuage them by allowing them to put up a huge red banner outside the old shipyard at Giudecca, where the "international contemporary" exhibition has been organized.[53]

Lewis also quotes Carlo Ripa di Meana, president of the Venice Biennale, who describes an unproductive meeting between Art & Language and Italian workers very seriously commited to Marxism-Leninism:

> Mr. di Meana said "The Fox" group arranged some open meetings with Italian workers, students and other to explain the depth of their commitment, as artists, to social concerns.
>
> "They were completely sincere," he said, "but to such highly politicized people as Italians you can't be candid in that way. The Italians just didn't trust them, they were so naïve."[54]

For its part, Art & Language argued, "The social practice of the Italian intelligentsia reflects the ideological theories and practices of the Left-leadership and not the direct class conscious history of the rank and file."[55] Regardless, the meetings were unproductive, despite resulting in precisely the sort of misunderstanding that once fueled Art & Language's collectivity, and they were to be the group's final attempt to collaborate internationally.

Art & Language's participation in the Venice Biennale was arranged prior to the June meetings, and it did little if anything to reconcile the fractured group. Of tensions within the collective at this point, Menard wrote that Art & Language "never resolved the principle [*sic*] contradiction . . . between our material base in the glittering bourgeois world of Culture and Highbrow Conversation and our historical projectivity towards (the advanced sectors of) the working class."[56] Characterizing the provisions as "still-born," he suggests, "It's time to get rid of them."[57] Acting on this proposal, Menard, together with Breakstone, Corris, and Heller, who were deepening their relations with Trotskyite, Maoist, and black nationalist collectives in New York, issued a public statement in September 1976 to Artists Meeting for Cultural Change in (Provisional) Art & Language's name, and this use of the collective's name without collective consent drew Ramsden's ire. As Corris describes it, "A confrontation at Ramsden's loft over above-mentioned communiqué" ensued that "resulted in the aforementioned sub-group's disenfranchisement, as Ramsden asserted what he took to be his 'historical' prerogative to the 'name' Art & Language."[58] In actuality, the provisions were finally having their full intended effect: severing the link between Art & Language's two main sections, with Ramsden, now intent on returning to England, preparing to join Baldwin in restarting Art & Language.

Ramsden's anger with Corris in turn inflamed Burn, and Corris claims that Burn "responded incredulously to what he considered to be an absurdly transparent pretext to void the group of its supposedly 'destabilising' elements," leading Burn to side with Corris, Heller, and Menard.[59] Burn, who had been absent for the June meetings while teaching at the University of California, San Diego, had come to hold views irreconcilable with those of his longtime collaborator Ramsden. In a June 1976 interview with Michael Auping conducted in Long Beach, California, during this teaching stint, and coinciding roughly with the June meetings in New York, Burn responded to a question about what the function of art should be by expressing deep concerns about its capacity to function as an instrument of social change and proposing the need for more direct political activity:

"There is no way we can blueprint the future! What we can talk about is the function that art serves in the present society. We can talk about how one might go about transforming the present society. However, the ways of transforming it or changing it are *not* through art. Art plays a very minor role in relation to that kind of change."[60] Following Kosuth's earlier exit, the break between Burn and Ramsden severed the last remaining tie between the earliest New York–based participants in Art & Language, and this ensured that Art & Language had little future remaining there. By early 1977, first Ramsden and later Kozlov and Thompson relocated to England. Breakstone, Corris, Heller, and Menard founded the journal *Red-Herring* in New York, and they edited it until 1978, resulting in two issues. Burn, involved in the first issue of *Red-Herring*, returned to Australia in 1977 to form, with Smith, Lendon, and others, first Media Action Group and then Union Media Services, which were active in Australian union movements of the 1970s and 1980s as providers of pedagogical and publicity work.[61] Beveridge and Condé, also involved in the early stages of *Red-Herring*, similarly allied their artistic practices to the Canadian union movement in Toronto.[62] Bigelow remained in New York to distribute *Art-Language* and *The Fox*, but Art & Language's years as a transnational collective were over, and the group's name came to designate the work of Baldwin and Ramsden, including projects undertaken with either Thompson or Charles Harrison.

As (Provisional) Art & Language fragmented, Popović assembled his film *Struggle in New York* in Belgrade. He initially intended it to be a documentary on radical art practice in New York, but it inadvertently became a portrait of Art & Language's distressed final months there. The struggle to which the film's title refers was so intense that, according to Kristine Stiles, who cites a letter Popović wrote to her, "because of the 'militant radicalism of [those associated with] the Art & Language group,' artists such as Hans Haacke, Vito Acconci, Dennis Oppenheim, Sol LeWitt, Donald Judd, Bernar Venet, Carolee Schneemann, and Robert Mapplethorpe 'refused to take part.'"[63] In its finished form, with a run time of just under an hour, *Struggle in New York* is less a straightforward documentary than a collection of stylistically and thematically diverse short films, each produced, in self-management fashion, by those whose ideas appear in it. By the time Popović assembled his final cut, only Bigelow, Chamberlain, Kozlov, the Ramsdens, and Thompson were participating in Art & Language projects in New York. Many of the group's former participants are included either individually or as members of other groups and collectives, and the film also includes contributions from other people in Popović's extended social circle.

Following an opening credits sequence are the segments that the film's subjects provided, and they, in turn, are followed by a lengthy concluding shot taken from the Staten Island ferry that shows Popović watching Manhattan become gradually smaller, symbolizing his departure for Belgrade, where he edited the film. *Struggle in New York* was shot entirely in black and white, and sound and music are overdubbed throughout most of it, though some segments use synchronous sound. Most feature rudimentary or stationary camera work, and cinematic aesthetics are generally kept to a minimum. The first of the eleven segments, "International Local" by International Local (comprising Charlesworth, Kosuth, and Anthony McCall), consists of seven title cards that display English text in white over a black background as a voice reads them in Serbian. The first sets the scene for the film and provides some insight into its method of production: "New York, November 1976. The proposed topic of this film is 'Art and Society.' This film is itself a social product. The social relations of its production and those of its consumption are the human contexts in which this film, as a product, assumes social meaning. As a vehicle which carries content it is itself the subject of which it speaks."[64] The cards go on to explain that the segments are "individuated products" and that there was "no dialogue" between the various producers, "although at other times and in other contexts we have worked socially and cooperatively with many of these individuals," a testament to the bitter aftermath of Art & Language's fragmentation.[65] The next eight segments — "Whitney Boycott" by Artists Meeting for Cultural Change, "Collective Voice" by Collective Voice (Terry Berkowitz, Corinne Bronfman, and Ruth Rachlin), "Back and Forth" by Beveridge and Condé, "3 Big Reasons" by Adrienne Hamalian and Howard Schamest, "The Bronx" by Klaus Mettig and Katharina Sieverding, "A New Disguise for the Bourgeoisie" by Michael Krugman and Saul Ostrow, "Comment" by Burn, and "The Arts Are a Growth Industry, Alright. If You're Fond of Cancer" by Red Herring (Breakstone, Corris, Heller, and Menard) — tackle themes ranging from feminism to institutional critique to international relations to urban poverty. Some are quite incisive; some deploy the filmic medium creatively; and others are exactly the kind of political art that Art & Language most despised. All told, the segments tackle relevant problems, but they have serious difficulties envisioning ways of transforming the situations they describe, a testament to the impasses that art and politics in New York had reached by this point. Two segments by Art & Language bring the film to a close. The first, attributed to *The Fox* and presented under the title "Art & Language Edition," recaps themes addressed in its recently defunct journal, most of which treat cultural politics from a more skeptical vantage than the assured rhetoric that characterizes certain of the other contributors to *Struggle in New York*. Over images of the covers and contents of the magazine's three issues, a female voice reads aloud the text from the poster that announced the first issue of the magazine, which includes a lengthy list of topics and questions—everything from modernism and the art market to the critique of institutions and the failures of conceptual art—that the magazine had addressed. Returning to this list after the magazine's sudden cessation serves as a reminder that these issues all persist in their irresolution.

This penultimate segment concludes with an image of the cover of the third and final issue of *The Fox*. A cut to the cover of the October 1976 issue of *Art-Language* (figure 5.11), which prominently features a "Fox 4" logo on its cover, serves as a reminder that *The Fox* has ceased publication and that *Art-Language*, based in England, has usurped it. So begins the (Provisional) Art & Language segment created by the few participants in the group remaining in New York. Titled "' . . . And Now for Something Completely Different . . . ,'" this segment is indeed unlike the rest of the film, and the title, borrowed from a phrase popularized by the comedy troupe Monty Python, suggests Art & Language's desire to distance itself from the other contributors (figure 5.12). Its segment replaces the rhetoric of ardent protest manifest throughout the film with the levity of a musical performance that reprises the general format of *Nine Gross and Conspicuous Errors*. It includes songs that shift freely from attacks on one or more persons or tendencies to collections of nuanced inside jokes about Art & Language's history to sarcastic rebukes of hackneyed artistic and political conventions. Thompson plays either electric organ or electric guitar throughout and Chamberlain plays drums while Bigelow, Kozlov, the Ramsdens, and Thompson serve as vocalists who variously sing, speak, sloganeer, and read aloud in vocal tones

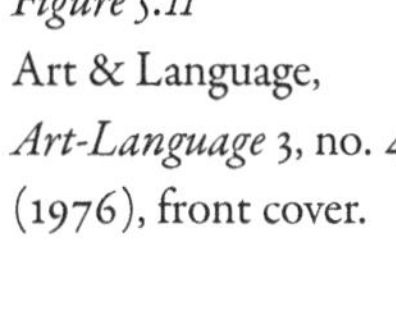

Figure 5.11
Art & Language,
Art-Language 3, no. 4
(1976), front cover.

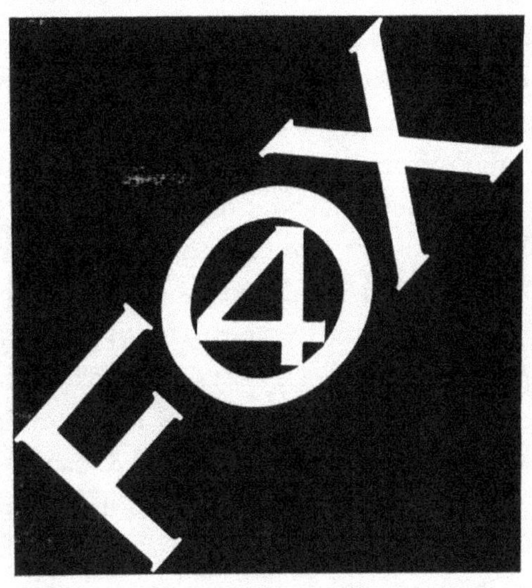

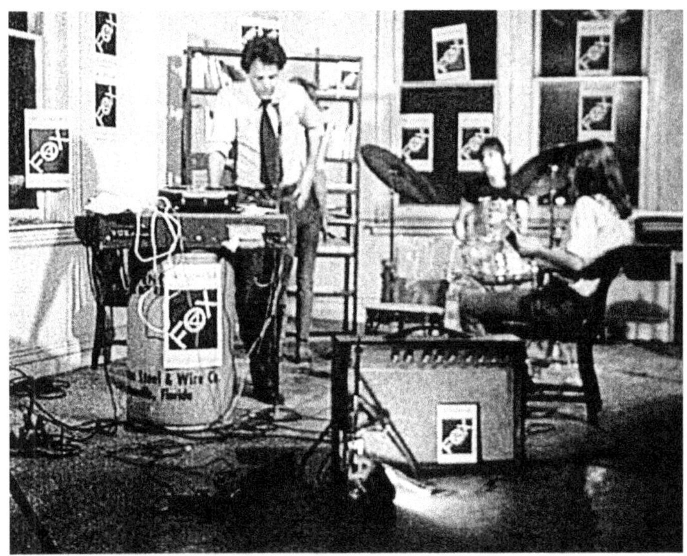

Figure 5.12 Art & Language, " . . . And Now for Something Completely Different . . . ," segment from Zoran Popović, *Struggle in New York*, 1976, film still.

and inflections ranging from plain speech to mad incantation. The band performs in a loft surrounded by copies of the October 1976 issue of *Art-Language* and posters that feature its cover at an enlarged scale. The "Fox 4" logo's resulting ubiquity in the performance space makes clear that the performers' effort to continue its analysis of the art world remained invested in whatever was left of Art & Language's transatlantic alliance.

The first of the songs, "A Lot of Sad Feelings . . . Fan Mail," features Kozlov and Paula Ramsden singing lyrics reminiscent of workers' songs interspersed with Thompson reading excerpts from "fan mail" addressed to Mel Ramsden by Paul Maenz, who is concerned about the distressed state of the group, thus linking workers' concerns to Art & Language's own working conditions and material needs. Disillusioned, Bigelow takes the microphone at the end of the song to read from the October 1976 *Art-Language*. She declares, in an unsettlingly calm tone of voice, "Let's not pretend: most of the power and clout in the art world is in the hands of *Fascists* of one kind or another."[66] This proves to be the final time that Art & Language delivers a verdict on the art world from New York, and it remains as hostile as ever. The second song, "Harangue," shares its title with a track from *Corrected Slogans*. Like that song, it is a rant about political topics, the bite of which is simultaneously suspended and reinforced by the joyous delivery of Bigelow and Ramsden, who together grip a single microphone to attack their erstwhile collaborator Kosuth, who had been the primary instigator behind *The Fox* and objected to its usurpation in the October 1976 issue of *Art-Language*. In the song, Art & Language accuses Kosuth of familiar charges: legislating ownership of meaning by asserting individual control over the collective's efforts.

The third song and the last—apart from a brief coda of sorts featuring the Ramsdens' daughter Anne scat singing over organ and drum accompaniment, which leads into the film's closing credits sequence—is "Plekhanov," which first appeared on *Corrected Slogans*. Kozlov and Thompson perform the song as a duo with Thompson playing organ while Kozlov sings lyrics loosely related to Georgi Plekhanov, the founder of Russian Marxism and, as author of the 1912 book *Art and Social Life*, an early Marxist theorist of art.[67] "Plekhanov" draws to a close with Thompson repeatedly quoting a figure that recurs throughout the finale to Franz Schubert's Trout Quintet, but before this quizzical reassertion of art, Kozlov sings the refrain one last time: "Who's learned the language of the Internationale?"[68] The International Workingmen's Association, which, together with the Paris Commune of 1871, provided lyricist Eugène Pottier with inspiration to write "L'Internationale," the most famous anthem of leftist solidarity, was on Art & Language's mind in 1976. In "The International: England 1 (o.g.) USA 1 (o.g.)," published in *Art-Language* in June 1976, the collective discusses the International's persistence as a valid political option.[69] The title of this essay evokes the scoring line of an international soccer match in which the English and American teams have reached a tie after each scoring own goals, an apt metaphor for Art & Language's fraught state as of late 1976. In October of that year, the collective refers to itself in the pages of *Art-Language* as Art & Language^(i), having abandoned the (Provisional) Art & Language moniker once its purpose was fulfilled. The "^(i)" stands for "international" and emphasizes belated solidarity between England and New York, but within months Art & Language would no longer be international at all. "Who's learned the language of the Internationale?" With these final words, Art & Language's New York section, unable either to maintain the transnational sociality that drove its examinations of art worlds over the preceding eight years or to hold together the incommensurable strands within its work—conceptual art, philosophy, radical politics, pedagogy, and so on—comes to its final impasse with an uncertain gesture toward these words:

> C'est la lutte finale
> Groupons-nous, et demain
> L'Internationale
> Sera le genre humain.

Conclusion

The collapse of Art & Language in 1976 was not exactly a happy event, but it was not a tragic end. Nearly all who had been involved with the collective continued to deploy its animating theoretical and practical concerns through other artistic and intellectual activities that were as dispersed in their impacts on art, art history, politics, and pedagogy as were the places to which people relocated to pursue them. In this respect, the comedic "'. . . And Now for Something Completely Different . . .'" is an appropriate title for the last work that the collective's New York section sent out into the world before disappearing. Its vanishing act is less an ending than another transition in the series of reconfigurations that saw Art & Language move quickly from its earliest work, which involved linguistically interrogating conventions about visual art, through a series of indexing projects focused on knowledge and its acquisition to the more politically conscious and explicitly Marxist work it was doing when it suffered the crisis that jettisoned most of its membership. This process, which also involved many smaller transformations, opened the collective's constituency from a group of four art teachers and art students at a single college in Coventry to an international and eventually transnational cooperative involving dozens of artists and critics working simultaneously on three continents to develop a worldly politics out of conceptual art's internationality. However, after the breakdown of that dynamism, the work Art & Language had done to that point would have "to be lived with," as Charles Harrison wrote, "as forms of history."[1]

With this trajectory in mind, dispersing as Art & Language did in early 1977 can be regarded somewhat paradoxically as a further expansion of the collective's sociality that transcended its identity altogether and opened its project to the participation of anyone who would seek to be involved. The collective's effort to enact through art a cooperatively directed pedagogy or, to use a term that its constituents frequently used, a "community practice" was no longer its own. This is, of course, something that the collective had, in various ways, wanted and even, at times, made into the main goal of its activity as it pursued new collaborators, especially international ones, that would bring vitality to its work by serving as both audiences for it and contributors to it. By giving up exclusive claim to undertaking such a project, others could take it up, and the contemporary art that has followed conceptual art's example proves that Art & Language's project is very much alive, even if the things to which the collective opposed it in the course of its development are also much in evidence, often in new guises but there all the same. Any examination of contemporary art that is more than cursory will reveal an abundance of intellectually sophisticated and socially astute art being made the world over that continues to politicize art's worldliness. Not all of it owes a direct debt to Art & Language, of course, but Art & Language's project was never entirely its own either; it was always, despite its own protestations on this point, part of the broader conceptual art movement and conceptualist tendency by which the radical impulse in art found direction in the aftermath of modern art.

This raises the question of success, which is also the question of failure. In her conclusion to one of the earliest attempts to comprehensively treat conceptual art, Lucy R. Lippard suggests that for a seemingly consequential and transformative movement, it may not have done very much at all, at least in the deepest of senses. She laments in particular conceptual art's easy acquiescence to the market, which blocked the emergence in art of "new critical criteria by which to view and vitalize itself (the function of the Art & Language group and its growing number of adherents)."[2] Lippard wrote these words in 1973. During an Art & Language discussion in 1974, a suggestion was offered to the effect that, were the collective to have a retrospective exhibition, as had apparently been proposed by Lisson Gallery director Nicholas Logsdail, it might best be organized as "a 'history of failures.'"[3] Foremost among these failures would be the failure to bring about a widely followed alternative support structure for art beyond the art world and the institutions, markets, discourses, and attitudes sustaining it. However, failure is not necessarily worse than success. Decades after exiting Art & Language, Terry Atkinson registered this well when he noted that "the failures of Conceptualism were much more intellectually engaging than the achievements of its successes in the museum and the market, such as they were."[4]

Nowhere did Art & Language fail more overwhelmingly and convincingly than in sustaining the international sociality that facilitated its conceptual inquiry into both art and art worlds. This owes something to conceptual art's inherently conflicted relationship to its high degree of internationality. With its prioritization of ephemeral, repeatable, and portable works of art, conceptual art traveled more widely and more quickly than art had previously. Whole exhibitions could be carried in a suitcase and were. Themes such as site, place, mobility, exchange, and communication were among the art's major subjects. Works by conceptual artists abound with maps, snapshots, telegrams, postcards, and other physical manifestations of human movement and messaging between places. Some of its best-known practitioners worked by walking or sending things through the mail. Others recreated work as occasion dictated in one location or another, at one time or another, as they traveled the world continuously like nomads. As a generation, the conceptual artists of the 1960s and 1970s were, moreover, the first artists to be routinely represented by galleries in more than one country at the same time and to find success outside of their home countries as readily as within them. In 1969, Joseph Kosuth's *Second Investigation*, a work composed of thesaurus categories presented piecemeal in newspapers and a variety of other printed media, manifested the extent of conceptual art's internationality to an extreme degree by appearing in about a dozen countries on more than half of the world's continents more or less simultaneously.[5] Enabling this sort of practice was the proliferation of new communications technologies and the reduced cost and increased availability of overseas airfare, both of which permitted art and artists to relocate from anywhere to anywhere else almost instantly and kept all involved with conceptual art in closer contact with one another than any previous art movement of comparable scale.

Early recognition of this new state of affairs appears in one of the first texts to theorize and historicize conceptual art, Kosuth's "Art after Philosophy." In an aside, he registers how little national borders limit artists for whom "nationalism is as out of place in art as it is in any other field."[6] On the other side of the Atlantic Ocean, Charles Harrison, who commissioned Kosuth's essay in 1969 while he was assistant editor of *Studio International* magazine, noted that same year the "extreme internationalism" of recent art.[7] Modernist thinking about "American-Type" painting or the "triumph" of American painting was, by this point, out of touch with what artists in the United States or elsewhere were doing.[8] Already by 1970, curator Kynaston McShine was characterizing *Information*, the most geographically extensive survey of conceptual art yet assembled when it opened at the Museum of Modern Art, as "an international report."[9] By including artists from North and South America, Eastern and Western Europe, Australia, and Asia in this exhibition, McShine configured the nascent movement as art's contribution to developing the "global village" that Marshall McLuhan predicted as the outcome of technologically extending human consciousness in what has come to be called an age of information.[10] Nothing, however, could be further from what Art & Language wanted conceptual art to be and do. From its international collaborations, the collective knew all too well how intellectually and socially debilitating a totalizing representational scheme such as a globe could be. From the internal tendentiousness of its own interdisciplinary collectivity, it knew how small-minded and mean the smaller scale of village life could be. Any transformation in how people think about the world and relate to one another within it would have to come from other lines of inquiry and activity than those on offer in McLuhan's technocratic vision of the future. In other words, conceptual art would have to be put to ends incompatible with its own inherent facility for operating internationally.

To pursue such a politics, Art & Language had to contend not only with the fraught status of an internationality that could easily be put to questionable use. It also had to contend with historically valid models for radicalizing art, which had once drawn much strength from modern art's own internationality, no longer functioning as they had. "It is self-evident that nothing concerning art is self-evident anymore."[11] So begins, in typically exasperating fashion, Theodor Adorno's *Aesthetic Theory*, a book that recognized, as Art & Language also did, the perilous situation that art had to confront at this historical juncture. When it was published in 1970, the artistic strategies that its author and other perspicacious observers of art's historical situation had been supporting were proving impracticable, at least in good faith. Radical approaches to art had taken a variety of tacks, ranging from Adorno's own insistence on art's autonomy from worldly affairs against its incorporation into an everyday life despoiled by capital to Peter Bürger's insistence that art be negated and integrated into worldly life so as to transform capitalist society.[12] By midcentury, however, gains that had been made by following these and other similar directives were no longer forthcoming. Their claims for radicalism were now to be counted among the things concerning art that were no longer self-evident.

Such was the situation that conceptual artists inherited. In a particularly gripping image, T. J. Clark described it well by calling abstract expressionism, which was, for him, the final modernist movement, a "last gasp of oxygen as the plane goes down."[13] To stay with Clark's metaphor, however, is inevitably to acknowledge that modernity's catastrophe was a crash with survivors. Among them were artists who, along with other artists taking after them, would in time retrace routes for travel and exchange forged by their modern predecessors. Some of them would do so by reclaiming the impulse that animated modernist and avant-garde efforts: an impulse to get beyond the falsely self-evident, to get beneath this surface and at more vital things, to get, so to speak, to art's roots and transplant them. When Art & Language set out over the seas those previous generations had traversed, capitalism was establishing itself as a global power through new international alliances and hostilities that would assure the universality of its reign. Art, very much caught up in these developments, played a role in shaping them—and in challenging them. It was, therefore, toward this power and its manifestations in art that the collective began increasingly to direct its efforts. If artistic radicalism, understood as art that pursues political ends such as liberation and justice by contesting in fundamental ways the mental and material conditions mediating its own historical existence, was to thrive in this new world, then the internationalities giving shape to that world had to be on the list of things that it politicized. They had become fundamental. Conceptual art, with its facility for crossing national borders, was in a unique position to politicize them, though doing so turned out to require another counterintuitive form of self-sabotage beyond the development of an approach to internationality at odds with internationalism: conceptual hostility to the concepts that enabled conceptual art.

Art & Language's first efforts to mobilize conceptual art in this direction quickly revealed that, along with a newly consolidated world order, an art world order had also arisen as a key agent ensuring art's global complicity with capital. Henceforth, art worlds would have to be taken into consideration if art was to raise again the actuality or even the possibility of a culture or a sociality not beholden to the commodity form. Since the onset of modernity, art has increasingly been the subject of intellectual discourses (art theory after Alberti, art history after Vasari, art criticism after Diderot, aesthetic philosophy after Kant, and so on) and societal institutions (academies of art, museums, salons, markets, art schools, biennials, and others) that configure its production, distribution, and consumption, often in detrimental ways but not always, in part by bringing concepts to bear upon it. Amid this accrual of discourses and institutions, what Paul Oskar Kristeller called the modern system of the arts emerged to unify the separate arts and the two major mediums comprising the visual arts, painting and sculpture, under a common name with widespread societal legitimacy: "the term 'Art.'"[14] Arthur Danto then coined the term "artworld" to name the outcome and agent of art's, specifically visual art's, persistence across several centuries. His choice of term, which joined, even fused, "art" to "world," implicitly grasped the pervasiveness that this emerging system and its product were attaining.

Kristeller, writing in 1951, and Danto, in 1964, published their respective essays during the beginnings of a historical shift from modern art to contemporary art, a shift in which conceptual art and conceptualism eventually played decisive roles. "Art," the noun that the adjectives "modern" and "contemporary" both modify here, remained firmly in place. Indeed, it was, perhaps for the first time, definitively manifested as a concept. Across what was otherwise a deep and broad transition, the power vested in and produced by art worlds ensured that art is and remains a concept bound up with other concepts that together provide both ways to think about the world and possibilities for acting within it. Concepts, of course, accompany claims for their universality, and this may go some way toward explaining why, in the decades after World War II, amid this shift from modern to contemporary art, conceptualisms that endeavor to reconceive the concept of art emerged globally. Art could no longer be located, as some modernists and avant-gardists had wanted to locate it, outside of worldly events or made, as others had wanted it, to disappear altogether into them. Instead, it had to be dealt with in something like the way that Art & Language dealt with it: as a concept that is distinct from other concepts and possessed of its own worldly presence but also never entirely separated from those concepts and therefore thoroughly enmeshed in the wider world. Art exists between other things, is mediated by them, and mediates them in turn. This is its worldly condition. Whether the theory and practice that its concept facilitates serve entities such as the church, the state, and the market or whether they serve something else, serve themselves, or even, perhaps, do not serve at all remains, as ever, an open question and one that has everything to do with what art and art worlds do. That this is still so owes much to precedents established by conceptual art and legacies that issue from it. For its part, Art & Language scrutinized the concept of art, identified other concepts with which art was regularly clustered, and set to work transforming those conceptual arrangements. Though the concept of art and the art worlds that sustain it survived conceptual art's most intensive and extensive challenges, Art & Language's included, each had to contend with the changes that they brought to bear, and these changes included accommodating contemporary art that is deeply aware of and responsive to the conceptual in art.

"Painting is a *kind* of art," Kosuth chided to make a polemical case for conceptual art over modernism's chief medium. "If you make paintings you are already accepting (not questioning) the nature of art."[15] For Art & Language, this need to question naturalized attitudes about art provided an impetus to develop collaborations involving both international sociality and interdisciplinary inquiry in line with a belief that such things could help it locate the conceptual limits that the art worlds through which it moved imposed. In so doing, it worked to confront these limits and open access to other ways of thinking about and doing art. Although undertaking this continuously shifting interrogation of art and art worlds eventually precipitated the conspiratorial suspicion and hostile infighting that consumed the collective, the history of Art & Language's efforts points to at least two challenges to sustaining a community practice with which artists, whether working individually or collectively, continue to contend—and, by so contending, continue to receive the intellectual and political benefits that such a practice provides. First, the social dynamic in which art always participates, the cacophony of voices always pulling in different directions in and around art, must retain and even intensify its diversity if it is to avoid intellectual complacency. Only a sociality that continuously contests available cognitive approaches can pry art loose from the ways in which it has been conditioned to be. Such contestation may well have been the very thing that led Art & Language to factionalize and centrifugally disperse, but it was also the collective's most trustworthy guide to art and to the world around it. To belong to a world that is tumultuous and conflicted necessitates coming to plain terms with the roiling mess that one and one's cohort inevitably is and then assuming some responsibility for how, to use Art & Language's terms, pandemonium goes on. Lack of clarity is, after all, both the means by which exploitation gets obfuscated and the condition from which learning necessarily transpires. What happens in this zone matters in the utmost.

Harrison retrospectively identified the other impasse facing such an approach when he acknowledged Art & Language's inability to locate an "*actual* alternative public which was not composed of the participants in its own projects and deliberations."[16] Kosuth, however, had foreseen this as a necessary and even an enabling condition for conceptual art as early as 1970, when he claimed that, as is often the case for science and philosophy, which demand an extreme degree of specialization, "an audience separate from the participants doesn't exist" for the sort of intellectual work that conceptual artists do.[17] However, unlike science and philosophy, art does not exclude the nonspecialist so entirely from all forms of participation. As Art & Language's indexing projects, international seminars, and intranational associations amply demonstrate, for learning to transpire in and through art, audiences for that art have to be actively pursued by way of encounters between people who do not necessarily share one another's immediate interests but nevertheless are interested in working together. The alternative to seeking audiences in this way, as Kosuth noted, is that artists "construct, reinforce, and perpetuate a cultural ghetto."[18] Indeed, it is by avoiding such ghettoization through the pursuit of encounters with others that work worth doing can get done. This work is that which transforms the pursuer of an audience into an audience for those it would want to be its own. Pedagogically speaking, such ambiguity concerning who is a teacher and who is a student sustains, for all involved, the effort to learn and, thereby, the opportunity to pursue a community practice by practicing ways of being communal.

The question of who was to be involved in Art & Language's work was thus both a cause of much discrepancy for the collective and the animus behind much of the insight it gleaned from working in the way that it did. Association and education were, as they always are, closely bound to one another. When learning was no longer possible, the grounds for socializing disappeared either temporarily or, at times, permanently. This precipitated changes in the collective's direction or exits from the working group. Ultimately, the inability to identify a common project meant that nearly all involved in Art & Language had to relinquish ties to one another, in some cases definitively and irreparably. This, however, enabled those who had been involved to socialize differently and thus, in most cases, to continue the very work that they had been doing together all along by other means. Only by giving up the internationality through which Art & Language developed its approach to doing conceptual art during the period spanning 1969 to 1977 could the collective's joined efforts to foster intellectuality and sociality find outlets. In the work of those groups and individuals that persisted in this search, theory and practice continued to be related to one another in any number of ways that remained capable of bringing art into the world without its being entirely preconditioned by the prerogatives of an art world.

In a 1981 essay titled "The 'Sixties: Crisis and Aftermath (Or the Memoirs of an Ex-Conceptual Artist)" that serves as his coda to conceptual art, Ian Burn points to the enduring salience of having worked with Art & Language and having endured its many trials and tribulations. Recollecting soberly, Burn methodically tallies the movement's successes and failures. He coins the term "Ex-Conceptual" to explain both his own move beyond conceptual art, which he took to be finished, and also to account for its ongoing importance for him as he continued to negotiate art's ties to the world. "Ex-" is like neither of the favored prefixes that rose to popularity in the 1980s and 1990s to characterize a nascent contemporary art's relationship to its modernist and avant-garde predecessors: "post-" and "neo-."[19] The former claims to break with a past to which it persistently refers to provide it with substance, while the latter is similarly unable to transcend the program of what it revives. By contrast, "ex-" acknowledges a past without prescribing a future. Prefixed to the adjective "conceptual," Burn suggests that "ex-" provides a release from within "the market-dominated avant-garde heritage" out of which conceptual art enabled labor performed in the vicinity of art's concept to reclaim itself.[20] "The real value of Conceptual Art," he writes, bringing his text to a close, "lay in its *transitional* (and thus genuinely historical) character."[21] For Burn, as for Art & Language generally, conceptual art, facilitated by its internationality, enabled artistic thoughts and actions to take place beyond art worlds—yet still within them—and, thereby, to make history not previously familiar to art history.

Notes

Introduction

1. Charles Harrison, *Essays on Art & Language* (Cambridge, MA: MIT Press, 2001), 127. Harrison's first book on Art & Language, which he coauthored with Fred Orton, *A Provisional History of Art & Language* (Paris: Galerie Eric Fabre, 1982), has been supplemented by two more comprehensive volumes: the aforementioned Harrison, *Essays on Art & Language*, and a companion volume, Charles Harrison, *Conceptual Art and Painting: Further Essays on Art & Language* (Cambridge, MA: MIT Press, 2001). In addition to texts too numerous to list scattered throughout other books, exhibition catalogs, magazines, and journals, a volume of interviews Harrison gave late in his life includes yet another comprehensive account. See Charles Harrison, *Looking Back* (London: Ridinghouse, 2011).

2. On Art & Language's New York section, see Michael Corris, "Inside a New York Art Gang: Selected Documents of Art & Language, New York," in *Conceptual Art: A Critical Anthology*, eds. Alexander Alberro and Blake Stimson (Cambridge, MA: MIT Press, 1999), 60–71; Michael Corris, "The Dialogical Imagination: The Conversational Aesthetic of Conceptual Art," in *Neo-Avant-Garde*, ed. David Hopkins (Amsterdam: Rodopi, 2006), 301–310; Alexander Alberro, "One Year under the Mast: Alexander Alberro on *The Fox*," *Artforum*, Summer 2003, 162–164, 206; Christopher Gilbert, "Art & Language, New York, Discusses Its Social Relations in 'The Lumpen-Headache,'" in *Conceptual Art: Theory, Myth, and Practice*, ed. Michael Corris (Cambridge: Cambridge University Press, 2004), 326–341; Chris Gilbert, "Art & Language and the Institutional Form in Anglo-American Collectivism," in *Collectivism after Modernism: The Art of Social Imagination after 1945*, eds. Blake Stimson and Gregory Sholette (Minneapolis: University of Minnesota Press, 2007), 77–93; and Alan W. Moore, *Art Gangs: Protest and Counterculture in New York City* (Brooklyn: Autonomedia, 2011), 65–79. Favoring Art & Language's English section, Harrison treats the collective's transatlantic relations most extensively in Harrison, *Essays on Art & Language*, 82–128. Throughout this small body of lit-

erature, references to the New York section's contact with artists in Australia, Yugoslavia, and other countries are scant when present at all.

3. T. J. Clark, quoted in Benjamin H. D. Buchloh, Serge Guilbaut, and David Solkin, eds., *Modernism and Modernity: The Vancouver Conference Papers* (Halifax: Press of the Nova Scotia College of Art & Design, 2004), 276–277.

4. Clement Greenberg, "Avant-Garde and Kitsch," in *The Collected Essays and Criticism, Vol. 1: Perceptions and Judgments, 1939–1944*, ed. John O'Brian (Chicago: University of Chicago Press, 1986), 11.

5. Mel Ramsden, "On Practice," in *Institutional Critique: An Anthology of Artist's Writings*, ed. Alexander Alberro and Blake Stimson (Cambridge, MA: MIT Press, 2009), 176.

6. On the aftermath of conceptual art and its consequences for contemporary art generally, see Alexander Alberro and Sabeth Buchmann, eds., *Art after Conceptual Art* (Cambridge, MA, and Vienna: MIT Press and Generali Foundation, 2006); Terry Smith, "One and Three Ideas: Conceptualism before, during, and after Conceptual Art," in *Moscow Symposium: Conceptualism Revisited*, ed. Boris Groys (Berlin: Sternberg Press, 2012), 42–72; and Camiel van Winkel, *During the Exhibition the Gallery Will Be Closed: Contemporary Art and the Paradoxes of Conceptualism* (Amsterdam: Valiz, 2012).

7. On dematerialization, see Lucy R. Lippard and John Chandler, "The Dematerialization of Art," *Art International*, February 1968, 31–36; Lucy R. Lippard, ed., *Six Years: The Dematerialization of the Art Object from 1966 to 1972* (New York: Praeger, 1973); as well as Terry Atkinson, "Concerning the Article 'The Dematerialization of Art,'" in Alberro and Stimson, *Conceptual Art*, 52–58, which includes Art & Language's skeptical response to Lippard's thinking.

8. Harrison speaks of conceptual art vis-à-vis a "suppression of the beholder" in the second chapter of Harrison, *Essays on Art & Language*. Buchloh refers to an "elimination of visuality" in Benjamin H. D. Buchloh, "Conceptual Art 1962–1969: From the Aesthetic of Administration to the Critique of Institutions," *October* 55 (winter 1990): 107.

9. Ramsden made the first use of the term "institutional critique" in print, and he dismisses it as insufficient for establishing the sort of communal practice in which Art & Language saw itself engaged. See Ramsden, "On Practice," 176. Alexander Alberro recognized this important first in "Institutions, Critique, and Institutional Critique," in Alberro and Stimson, *Institutional Critique*, 8. For the further development of institutional critique as an art historical concern, see Douglas Crimp, *On the Museum's Ruins* (Cambridge, MA: MIT Press, 1993); John C. Welchmann, ed., *Institutional Critique and After* (Zurich: JRP|Ringier, 2006); Alberro and Stimson, *Institutional Critique*; and Gerald Raunig and Gene Ray, eds., *Art and Contemporary Critical Practice: Reinventing Institutional Critique* (London: MayFly, 2009).

Also relevant are books on artists practicing a version of institutional critique, such as Kirsi Peltomäki, *Situation Aesthetics: The Work of Michael Asher* (Cambridge, MA: MIT Press, 2010); and Rachel Haidu, *The Absence of Work: Marcel Broodthaers, 1964–1976* (Cambridge, MA: MIT Press, 2010).

10. The name "conceptual art" itself was by no means given, as the first three books published on the subject in its epicenter of New York attest by invoking a range of possible names for the new art. See Ursula Meyer, ed., *Conceptual Art* (New York: Dutton, 1972); Gregory Battcock, ed., *Idea Art* (New York: Dutton, 1973); and Lippard, *Six Years*. The last's full title, which includes several subtitles, plays with the issue of naming: *Six Years: The dematerialization of the art object from 1966 to 1972: A cross-reference book of information on some esthetic boundaries: Consisting of a bibliography into which are inserted a fragmented text, art works, documents, interviews, and symposia, arranged chronologically and focused on so-called conceptual or information or idea art with mentions of such vaguely designated areas as minimal, anti-form, systems, earth, or process art, occurring now in the Americas, Europe, England, Australia, and Asia (with occasional political overtones), edited and annotated by Lucy R. Lippard.*

11. Alexander Alberro, "Reconsidering Conceptual Art, 1966–1977," in Alberro and Stimson, *Conceptual Art*, xvii.

12. Peter Osborne, "Conceptual Art and/as Philosophy," in *Rewriting Conceptual Art*, ed. Michael Newman and Jon Bird (London: Reaktion, 1999), 65. Osborne's most sustained discussion of conceptual art can be found in Peter Osborne, *Conceptual Art* (London: Phaidon, 2002).

13. See Peter Osborne, *Anywhere or Not at All: Philosophy of Contemporary Art* (London: Verso, 2013), for a further elaboration of the postconceptual status of contemporary art.

14. For a sampling of these approaches, see Newman and Bird, *Rewriting Conceptual Art*; and Corris, *Conceptual Art*.

15. In addition to Osborne, "Conceptual Art and/as Philosophy," see especially John Roberts's Hegelian approach to conceptual art in "Conceptual Art and Imageless Truth," in Corris, *Conceptual Art*, 305–325. For more on conceptual art and philosophy, see Peter Goldie and Elisabeth Schellekens, eds., *Philosophy and Conceptual Art* (Oxford: Oxford University Press, 2007), which includes a text by Art & Language; and Peter Goldie and Elisabeth Schellekens, *Who's Afraid of Conceptual Art?* (London: Routledge, 2010). Beyond philosophy's predilection for reason and rationalism, there is also a strand of thinking about conceptual art and affect that has shown the extent to which conceptual art is never an entirely rational activity. See, for examples, Eve Meltzer, *Systems We Have Loved: Conceptual Art, Affect, and the Antihumanist Turn* (Chicago: University of Chicago Press, 2013); and Alexander Dumbadze, *Bas Jan Ader: Death Is Elsewhere* (Chicago: University of Chicago

Press, 2013). Similarly, on romantic conceptualism, see Ellen Seifermann and Jörg Heiser, *Romantischer Konzeptualismus/Romantic Conceptualism* (Bielefeld: Kerber Verlag, 2007); and Peter Eleey, *The Quick and the Dead* (Minneapolis: Walker Art Center, 2009). Boris Groys was the first to pair conceptualism and romanticism in "Moscow Romantic Conceptualism," in *History Becomes Form: Moscow Conceptualism* (Cambridge, MA: MIT Press, 2010), 35–56. Osborne also pairs these terms in Peter Osborne, "An Image of Romanticism: Fragment and Project in Friedrich Schlegel's *Athenaeum Fragments* and Sol LeWitt's *Sentences on Conceptual Art*," in *Sol LeWitt's Sentences on Conceptual Art: Manuscript and Draft Materials 1968–69* (Oslo: Office for Contemporary Art Norway, 2009), 5–27. On comedy in conceptual art, with considerable reference to Kosuth's writings and work, see John C. Welchmann, "'Don't Play It for Laughs': John Baldessari and Conceptual Comedy," in *Black Sphinx: The Comedic in Modern Art*, ed. John C. Welchmann (Zurich: JRP|Ringier, 2010), 245–268.

16. On language as material in conceptual art, see Liz Kotz, *Words to Be Looked At: Language in 1960s Art* (Cambridge, MA: MIT Press, 2007). For more recent publications that return to the theme of dematerialization, see Catherine Morris and Vincent Bonin, eds., *Materializing* Six Years*: Lucy Lippard and the Emergence of Conceptual Art* (Cambridge, MA: MIT Press, 2012); and Lucy Lippard, *Lucy Lippard: 4,492,040* (Vancouver: New Documents, 2012). Rosalind Krauss argues that conceptual art (and especially Kosuth's work) brings about a radical transformation in art's relationship to the artistic medium in Rosalind Krauss, *A Voyage on the North Sea: Art in the Age of the Post-Medium Condition* (London: Thames and Hudson, 2000). Craig Dworkin, *No Medium* (Cambridge, MA: MIT Press, 2013), considers the more recent status of artistic mediums and makes extensive reference to conceptual art. The single medium to receive by far the most attention in relation to conceptual art is photography. The initial effort here is found in Jeff Wall, "'Marks of Indifference': Aspects of Photography in, or as, Conceptual Art," in *Reconsidering the Object of Art: 1965–1975*, ed. Ann Goldstein and Anne Rorimer (Cambridge, MA, and Los Angeles: MIT Press and the Museum of Contemporary Art Los Angeles, 1995), 247–258. See also John Roberts, ed., *The Impossible Document: Photography and Conceptual Art in Britain 1966–1976* (London: Cameraworks, 1997); Douglas Fogle, *The Last Picture Show: Artists Using Photography, 1960–1982* (Minneapolis: Walker Art Center, 2003); Diarmuid Costello and Margaret Iversen, eds., *Photography after Conceptual Art* (Chichester: Wiley-Blackwell, 2010); and Matthew S. Witkovsky, *Light Years: Conceptual Art and the Photograph 1964–1977* (Chicago and New Haven, CT: Art Institute of Chicago and Yale University Press, 2011). On the relationship between conceptual art and visual culture more broadly, see Thomas Crow, "Unwritten Histories of Conceptual Art," in Alberro and Buchmann, *Art after Conceptual Art*, 53–64. On conceptual art and media, see Alexander Alberro,

Conceptual Art and the Politics of Publicity (Cambridge, MA: MIT Press, 2004); and Gwen Allen, *Artists' Magazines: An Alternative Space for Art* (Cambridge, MA: MIT Press, 2011).

17. On conceptual art, labor, and work, see Julia Bryan-Wilson, *Art Workers: Art and Radical Politics in the Vietnam War Era* (Berkeley: University of California Press, 2009). On the deskilling of artistic working and technique, see especially John Roberts, *The Intangibilities of Form: Skill and Deskilling in Art after the Readymade* (London: Verso, 2007). Early links between conceptual art and deskilling can be traced to Ian Burn, "The 'Sixties: Crisis and Aftermath (Or the Memoirs of an Ex-Conceptual Artist)," in Alberro and Stimson, *Conceptual Art*, 392–408. Benjamin H. D. Buchloh also touches upon this theme in "Hans Haacke: Memory and Instrumental Reason," *Art in America* 76, no. 2 (February 1988): 97–108, 157–159. On conceptual art and technology, see Edward A. Shanken, "Art in the Information Age: Technology and Conceptual Art," *Leonardo* 35, no. 4 (August 2002): 433–438; Luke Skrebowski, "All Systems Go: Recovering Hans Haacke's Systems Aesthetics," *Grey Room* 30 (August 2008): 54–83; and Charissa N. Terranova, *Automotive Prosthetic: Technological Mediation and the Car in Conceptual Art* (Austin: University of Texas Press, 2014).

18. Peter Wollen, "Global Conceptualism and North American Conceptual Art," in *Global Conceptualism: Points of Origin, 1950s–1980s*, ed. Luis Camnitzer, Jane Farver, and Rachel Weiss (New York: Queens Museum of Art, 1999), 81.

19. Luis Camnitzer, Jane Farver, and Rachel Weiss, "Foreword," in Camnitzer, Farver, and Weiss, *Global Conceptualism*, viii.

20. The essays in Camnitzer, Farver, and Weiss, *Global Conceptualism*, cover much of the world. There are also a number of more geographically specific literatures on different conceptualisms. On African conceptualism, see Salah M. Hassan and Olu Oguibe, eds., *Authentic/Ex-Centric: Conceptualism in Contemporary African Art* (Venice: La Biennale di Venezia, 2001). On Latin America, see Luis Camnitzer, *Conceptualism in Latin American Art: Didactics of Liberation* (Austin: University of Texas Press, 2007). There is a large literature on conceptualism in the Soviet Union. See in particular Groys, *History Becomes Form*; Matthew Jesse Jackson, *The Experimental Group: Ilya Kabakov, Moscow Conceptualism, Soviet Avant-Gardes* (Chicago: University of Chicago Press, 2010); and Alla Rosenfeld, *Moscow Conceptualism in Context* (Munich: Prestel, 2011). On conceptualism in China, see Gao Minglu, "From Elite to Small Man: The Many Faces of a Transitional Avant-Garde in Mainland China," in *Inside Out: New Chinese Art*, ed. Gao Minglu (New York and Berkeley: San Francisco Museum of Modern Art, Asia Society Galleries, and University of California Press, 1998), 158–164; and Gao Minglu, *Total Modernity and the Avant-Garde in Twentieth-Century Chinese Art* (Cambridge, MA: MIT Press, 2011).

21. See, for examples, Terry Smith, "Peripheries in Motion: Conceptualism and

Conceptual Art in Australia and New Zealand," in Camnitzer, Farver, and Weiss, *Global Conceptualism*, 87–98; Suzanna Héman, Jurrie Poot, and Hripsimé Visser, eds., *Conceptual Art in the Netherlands and Belgium 1965–1975: Artists, Collectors, Galleries, Documents, Exhibitions, Events* (Amsterdam and Rotterdam: Stedelijk Museum and NAi, 2002); Christophe Cherix, *In and Out of Amsterdam: Travels in Conceptual Art, 1960–1976* (New York: Museum of Modern Art, 2009); and Sophie Richard, *Unconcealed: The International Network of Conceptual Artists 1967–77. Dealers, Exhibitions and Public Collections* (London: Ridinghouse, 2009).

22. On conceptual art and conceptualism in relation to race in the United States and England, see Valerie Cassel Oliver, ed., *Double Consciousness: Black Conceptual Art since 1970* (Houston: Contemporary Arts Museum, Houston, 2006); Kobena Mercer, "Adrian Piper, 1970–1975: Exiled on Main Street," in *Exiles, Diasporas, and Strangers*, ed. Kobena Mercer (Cambridge, MA, and London: MIT Press and Iniva, 2008), 146–165; Amna Malik, "Conceptualising 'Black' British Art through the Lens of Exile," in Mercer, *Exiles, Diasporas, and Strangers*, 166–189; and John P. Bowles, *Adrian Piper: Race, Gender, and Embodiment* (Durham, NC: Duke University Press, 2011). Many of these texts also deal with gender and feminism. On these latter topics, see also Jayne Wark, "Conceptual Art and Feminism: Martha Rosler, Adrian Piper, Eleanor Antin, and Martha Wilson," *Women's Art Journal* 22, no. 1 (spring–summer 2001): 44–50; and Cornelia Butler and other authors, *From Conceptualism to Feminism: Lucy Lippard's Numbers Shows 1969–74* (London: Afterall, 2012).

23. Desa Philippi, "Matter of Words: Translations in East European Conceptualism," in Newman and Bird, *Rewriting Conceptual Art*, 153. For examples of the extent to which this umbrella has even grown beyond visual art, see "Architecture as Conceptual Art?," *Harvard Design Magazine* 19 (fall 2003/winter 2004); and *Conceptual Architecture* (Hong Kong: Sandu, 2010), on architecture. On poetry and conceptualism, see Vanessa Place and Robert Fitterman, *Notes on Conceptualisms* (New York: Ugly Duckling Press, 2009); Craig Dworkin and Kenneth Goldsmith, eds., *Against Expression: An Anthology of Conceptual Writing* (Evanston, IL: Northwestern University Press, 2011); Caroline Bergvall, Laynie Browne, Teresa Carmody, and Vanessa Place, eds., *I'll Drown My Book: Conceptual Writing by Women* (Los Angeles: Les Figues, 2012); and Triple Canopy, *Corrected Slogans: Reading and Writing Conceptualism* (New York and Denver: Triple Canopy and Museum of Contemporary Art Denver, 2012), which also contains an interview with Michael Corris that touches upon his involvement with Art & Language.

24. Thomas Crow rightly notes that "any persuasive fusing between art and 1960s activism was unlikely from the start. The conceptual demands of advanced practice had become so elevated that anything less than full-time application of one's resources was unlikely to make a mark," in Thomas Crow, *The Rise of the Sixties:*

American and European Art in the Era of Dissent (New York: Abrams, 1996), 179. However, Crow does allow that, in addition to being a staging ground for feminism, conceptual art's engagement with the degraded conditions of urban life in the 1970s, particularly when artists organized artist-run spaces, sustained art's political thrust after the passing of the New Left, and he also speaks, in a way that is instructive for thinking about Art & Language's politics, about how "the *worldly* experience that came with the first building of communities gave artists a vital cognitive grip on the larger environment" (Crow, *The Rise of the Sixties*, 181, emphasis mine). It should also be noted that Art & Language itself made a great many claims about conceptual art's failures and that these and other similar claims, particularly claims about political failures, are well treated in Blake Stimson, "The Promise of Conceptual Art" in Alberro and Stimson, *Conceptual Art*, xxxviii–lii.

25. For a characteristic sampling of this kind of writing, see the essays collected in Charles Harrison, ed., *Art & Language in Practice, Vol. 2: Simposi crític/Critical Symposium* (Barcelona: Fundació Antoni Tàpies, 1999).

26. For one prominent instance of this, see Michael Baldwin, Charles Harrison, and Mel Ramsden, "Art History, Art Criticism and Explanation," *Art History* 4, no. 4 (December 1981): 432–456.

27. Thomas Crow, *Modern Art in the Common Culture* (New Haven: Yale University Press, 1996), viii.

28. Crow explores this methodological point, which occurs when "the object invites and prefigures its analysis," in more detail in Thomas Crow, *The Intelligence of Art* (Chapel Hill: University of North Carolina Press, 1999), 5.

29. From a notebook dated 1974–1975 in Ian Burn private papers, Sydney, Australia, n.p.

30. Clement Greenberg, "After Abstract Expressionism," in *The Collected Essays and Criticism, Vol. 4: Modernism with a Vengeance, 1957–1969*, edited by John O'Brian (Chicago: University of Chicago Press, 1993), 124.

One *A Model of a Possible Art World*

1. [Art & Language,] "Introduction," *Art-Language* 1, no. 1 (May 1969): 10.

2. The back cover of the first issue of *Art-Language* also lists as "contributors" to the journal Adrian Piper and Hanne Darboven, both friends of LeWitt, though whatever efforts Art & Language anticipated from them did not come to pass, as neither published anything there. For Piper's later contributions to Art & Language's journal *The Fox*, see Adrian Piper, "To Art (Reg. intrans. V.)," *The Fox* 1, no. 1 (1975): 60–65; and Adrian Piper, "A Proposal for Pricing Works of Art," *The Fox* 2 (1975): 48–49.

3. Catherine Millet, "Interview with *Art-Language*," in Alberro and Stimson, *Conceptual Art*, 262.

4. Terry Atkinson, "From an Art & Language Point of View," *Art-Language* 1, no. 2 (February 1970): 26. For Art & Language's more recent return to debating the meaning of the term "conceptual art," see Art & Language, "Voices Off: Reflections on Conceptual Art," *Critical Inquiry* 33, no. 1 (autumn 2006): 113–135.

5. [Art & Language,] "Introduction," 10.

6. On Kosuth, Burn, and Ramsden prior to their association with Art & Language, see the first two chapters of Charles Green, *The Third Hand: Collaboration in Art from Conceptualism to Postmodernism* (Minneapolis: University of Minnesota Press, 2001). On Burn and Ramsden's collaborations prior to joining Art & Language, see Ann Stephen, "Soft Talk/*Soft-Tape*: The Early Collaborations of Ian Burn and Mel Ramsden," in Corris, *Conceptual Art*, 80–96. Stephen's text contains numerous valuable excerpts from Burn and Ramsden's otherwise unpublished correspondence. On Burn's early work, see the exhibition catalog, Art Gallery of Western Australia, *Ian Burn: Minimal-Conceptual Work 1965–1970* (Perth: Art Gallery of Western Australia, 1992).

7. A number of these early texts, including several never before published, are reproduced and described in Carles Guerra, *Art & Language Uncompleted: The Philippe Méaille Collection* (Barcelona: Museum of Contemporary Art Barcelona, 2014).

8. On *The Air-Conditioning Show*, see especially Art & Language, "Frameworks," in Van Abbemuseum, *Art & Language* (Eindhoven: Van Abbemuseum, 1980), 1–14.

9. Baldwin's own 1966 visit to New York was the first international activity involving a participant in Art & Language. All of these early visits to New York were prompted largely by Atkinson and Baldwin's interest in minimalism, which they knew from magazines but which was not yet widely exhibited in England. Charles Harrison discusses these visits briefly in Charles Harrison, *Since 1950: Art and Its Criticism* (New Haven, CT: Yale University Press, 2009), 240n80.

10. Michael Baldwin, "Remarks on Air-Conditioning: An Extravaganza of Blandness," *Arts Magazine* 42, no. 2 (November 1967): 22–23.

11. David Bainbridge, "Notes on M1 (1)," Michael Baldwin, "Notes on M1," and David Bainbridge, "Notes on M1 (2)," all in *Art-Language* 1, no. 1 (May 1969): 19–32.

12. See Dan Graham, "Poem-schema," *Art-Language* 1, no. 1 (May 1969): 14–16; and Lawrence Weiner, "Statements," *Art-Language* 1, no. 1 (May 1969): 17–18.

13. Sol LeWitt, "Sentences on Conceptual Art," *Art-Language* 1, no. 1 (May 1969): 13.

14. [Art & Language,] "Introduction," 1.

15. On Atkinson and Kosuth's meeting, see Terry Atkinson, "Rites of Passage," *Art & Design* 34 (1994): 13.

16. On Siegelaub's activities during this period, see Alberro, *Conceptual Art and the Politics of Publicity.*

17. Joseph Kosuth, "Art after Philosophy," in *Art after Philosophy and After: Collected Writings, 1966–1990*, ed. Gabriele Guercio (Cambridge, MA: MIT Press, 1991), 26.

18. On Kosuth's own work during this period, especially his *Investigations* series, see Joseph Kosuth, *Art Investigations and "Problematics" since 1965* (Luzern: Kunstmuseum Luzern, 1973), which remains an unsurpassed and comprehensive reference work. This five-volume catalog also includes texts by many people involved with Art & Language, including Terry Atkinson, Michael Baldwin, Philip Pilkington, David Rushton, Mel Ramsden, and Terry Smith. Kosuth's writings, including but not limited to texts written for Art & Language's publications, are collected in Kosuth, *Art after Philosophy and After*, which covers the years 1966–1990.

19. Ian Burn, "Dialogue," in Alberro and Stimson, *Conceptual Art*, 110.

20. Ursula Meyer, "Introduction," in *Conceptual Art*, ed. Ursula Meyer (New York: Dutton, 1972), xviii.

21. Osborne, "Conceptual Art and/as Philosophy," 49.

22. Alberro, "Reconsidering Conceptual Art, 1966–1977," xvii.

23. Joseph Kosuth, "Introductory Note by the American Editor," *Art-Language* 1, no. 2 (February 1970): 3.

24. See Donald Karshan, *Conceptual Art and Conceptual Aspects* (New York: New York Cultural Center, 1970). At least three exhibitions from the preceding year included some variant of "concept" in their title, but none used "conceptual" or "conceptual art." *When Attitudes Become Form*, which opened on March 22 at the Kunsthalle Bern, used the word "concepts" in its subtitle, *Live in Your Head: Works—Concepts—Processes—Situations—Information*; Eugenia Butler Gallery in Los Angeles presented *Conception-Perception* throughout the month of July; and the Stadtisches Museum in Leverkusen opened the exhibition *Konzeption/Conception* on October 24.

25. The proceedings of the Society for Theoretical Art and Analysis were published on a number of occasions, including the Society for Theoretical Art and Analysis, "Proceedings," in Karshan, *Conceptual Art and Conceptual Aspects*, 21–22; Ian Burn and Mel Ramsden, "Proceedings," in Kynaston McShine, *Information* (New York: Museum of Modern Art, 1970), 32–35; Society for Theoretical Art and Analysis (Ian Burn, Roger Cutforth, and Mel Ramsden), "Proceedings," *Art-Language* 1, no. 3 (June 1970): 1–3; and Society for Theoretical Art and Analysis, "Proceedings," *Art and Australia*, September 1970, 168. Cutforth did not participate in Art & Language.

26. On the Lannis Gallery and the Museum of Normal Art, see Gabriele Guercio, "Introduction," in Kosuth, *Art after Philosophy and After*, xxii–xxiii. For Barthelme's

text, see Frederic [*sic*] Barthelme, "Three from May 23rd, 1969," *Art-Language* 1, no. 2 (February 1970): 8–10. For Kosuth's comment on Kawara, see Kosuth, "Art after Philosophy," 27.

27. Kosuth, "Art after Philosophy," 25.

28. Kosuth, "Art after Philosophy," 27, 29.

29. Ian Burn, "Conceptual Art as Art," in *Dialogue* (Sydney: Allen & Unwin, 1991), 130.

30. On *Conceptual Art and Conceptual Aspects* in general and the controversy its curatorship provoked in particular, see Ann Stephen, *On Looking at Looking: The Art and Politics of Ian Burn* (Melbourne: Miegunyah Press, 2006), 133–143.

31. Joseph Kosuth, quoted in Annette Kuhn, "Culture Shock," *Village Voice*, April 15, 1975, 100. Kosuth further develops this distinction in Joseph Kosuth, "1975," in *Art after Philosophy and After*, 129–143.

32. Buchloh, "Conceptual Art 1962–1969," 126, 134. For the fallout from this essay, see Joseph Kosuth and Seth Siegelaub, "Joseph Kosuth and Seth Siegelaub Reply to Benjamin Buchloh on Conceptual Art," *October* 57 (summer 1991): 152–157; Benjamin Buchloh, "Buchloh Replies to Kosuth and Seth Siegelaub," *October* 57 (summer 1991): 158–161; and Charles Harrison, "Conceptual Art: Myths and Scandals," *Artscribe* 80 (March–April 1990): 15–16. For Buchloh's influence on thinking about conceptual art, see, for instance, the roundtable discussion "Conceptual Art and the Reception of Duchamp," *October* 70 (fall 1994): 127–146.

33. Kosuth, "Art after Philosophy," 19–20.

34. Kosuth, "Introductory Note by the American Editor," 2.

35. Atkinson, "From an Art & Language Point of View," 42.

36. Art & Language, "A Short Introduction on the Work," unpublished manuscript. This brief text is reproduced in Michael Corris, "Introduction: An Invisible College in an Anglo-American World" in Corris, *Conceptual Art*, 3. On the exhibition of lectures, see also Guerra, *Art & Language Uncompleted*, 38.

37. Ian Burn and Mel Ramsden, "Four Wages of Sense," *Art-Language* 2, no. 1 (February 1972): 29. The expression "if someone says it's art, it's art" closely resembles the phrase "if someone calls it art, it's art," which Kosuth attributes to Donald Judd in Kosuth, "Art after Philosophy," 20. See also Philip Pilkington and David Rushton, "Don Judd's Dictum and Its Emptiness," in Van Abbemuseum, *Art & Language*, 44.

38. Ian Burn and Mel Ramsden, "A Question of Epistemic Adequacy," *Studio International* 182, no. 937 (October 1971): 132–135.

39. Arthur Danto, "The Artworld," *Journal of Philosophy* 61, no. 19 (October 15, 1964): 580. The classic study of art worlds is Howard S. Becker, *Artworlds* (Berkeley: University of California Press, 1982). Also relevant is Diana Crane, *The Transformation of the Avant-Garde: The New York Art World, 1940–1985* (Chicago: University of Chicago Press, 1987). For more recent perspectives on art worlds, see Hans Belt-

ing and Andrea Buddensieg, eds., *The Global Art World: Audiences, Markets, and Museums* (Ostfildern: Hatje Kantz Verlag, 2009); Pamela M. Lee, "Boundary Issues: The Art World under the Sign of Globalism," *Artforum* 42, no. 3 (February 2003): 164–167; and Pamela M. Lee, *Forgetting the Art World* (Cambridge, MA: MIT Press, 2012).

40. Buchloh, "Conceptual Art 1962–1969," 133.

41. Buchloh, "Conceptual Art 1962–1969," 143.

42. Ian Burn and Mel Ramsden, "Some Questions on the Characterization of Questions," *Art-Language* 2, no. 2 (summer 1972): 2.

43. Burn and Ramsden, "Some Questions on the Characterization of Questions," 1–2.

44. Burn and Ramsden, "Some Questions on the Characterization of Questions," 5.

45. Burn and Ramsden, "Some Questions on the Characterization of Questions," 9. For the classic formulation of an opposition between modernism and minimalism, see Michael Fried, "Art and Objecthood," *Artforum*, June 1967, 12–23.

46. Burn and Ramsden, "Some Questions on the Characterization of Questions," 10.

47. Burn and Ramsden, "Some Questions on the Characterization of Questions," 7.

48. Burn and Ramsden, "Some Questions on the Characterization of Questions," 10.

49. All citations of this first version of *Comparative Models* are to a manuscript copy in the private papers of Mel Ramsden, Banbury, England. The text is not paginated, so citations indicate the unique titles given at the tops of each page of the manuscript. Multiple copies of this first version exist, and the text varies slightly from copy to copy, as was common with the many texts that Art & Language produced through collective emendation.

50. On *Artforum* during this period, see especially Amy Newman, *Challenging Art: Artforum 1962–1974* (New York: SoHo Press, 2003). Also pertinent are Hal Foster, "Art Critics in Extremis," in *Design and Crime and Other Diatribes* (London: Verso, 2002), 104–122; and Thomas Crow, "Art Criticism in the Age of Incommensurate Values: On the Thirtieth Anniversary of *Artforum*," in *Modern Art and the Common Culture* (New Haven, CT: Yale University Press, 1996), 85–93.

51. Art & Language, *Comparative Models*, "Comparative Models."

52. On the relationship between Danto's thinking on art worlds and Kuhn's thinking on paradigms, see Caroline A. Jones, "The Modernist Paradigm: The Artworld and Thomas Kuhn," *Critical Inquiry* 26, no. 3 (spring 2000): 488–528.

53. Thomas S. Kuhn, *The Structure of Scientific Revolutions*, 3rd ed. (Chicago: University of Chicago Press, 1996). Art & Language read this book in its second edition

of 1970, which is the first edition to contain a postscript Kuhn wrote in 1969 that clarifies the concept of the paradigm. He wrote this postscript in response to various critics, especially Margaret Masterman. See Margaret Masterman, "The Nature of a Paradigm," in *Criticism and the Growth of Knowledge*, ed. Imre Lakatos and Alan Musgrave (Cambridge: Cambridge University Press, 1970), 59–89.

54. See Kuhn, *The Structure of Scientific Revolutions*, 181–191.

55. Kuhn, *The Structure of Scientific Revolutions*, 36. On normal science, see especially chapters 2–4 of this book.

56. Art & Language, *Comparative Models*, "The Priority of Paradigms."

57. Art & Language, *Comparative Models*, "The Priority of Paradigms." Burn and Ramsden invoke H. L. A. Hart's distinction between internal and external. See also Burn and Ramsden, "Four Wages of Sense," 33. For Hart, see H. L. A. Hart, *The Concept of Law* (Oxford: Oxford University Press, 1961).

58. Art & Language, *Comparative Models*, "Paradigm Shifts." The key text on reification is the chapter "Reification and the Consciousness of the Proletariat" in Georg Lukács, *History and Class Consciousness: Studies in Marxist Dialectic* (Cambridge, MA: MIT Press, 1971), 83–222. Lukács's book first appeared in an English translation in May 1971. This was several months before Burn and Ramsden began work on *Comparative Models*. Although they do not cite it, they do make reference to Andrew Higgins, "Clement Greenberg and the Idea of the Avant Garde," *Studio International* 182, no. 937 (October 1971): 144–147, an essay that examines the commodity status of art and considers its implications for Clement Greenberg's various accounts of the avant-garde. Burn and Ramsden's reading of Higgins's essay seems to have prompted an interest in the possibilities of using Marxist concepts in Art & Language's work that would continue to grow in subsequent years.

59. Art & Language, *Comparative Models*, "Paradigm Shifts as Consequences of Anomalies."

60. Art & Language, *Comparative Models*, "Paradigm Shifts."

61. Art & Language, *Comparative Models*, "A Model of Competence."

62. The classic formulation of the relationship between performance and competence, which Burn and Ramsden cite in *Comparative Models*, is found in Noam Chomsky, *Aspects of the Theory of Syntax* (Cambridge, MA: MIT Press, 1965).

63. Art & Language, *Comparative Models*, "Annotation #3."

64. Art & Language, *Comparative Models*, "Annotation #3."

65. *Artforum*, September 1972, 5.

66. Art & Language, "Comparative Models," in Van Abbemuseum, *Art & Language*, 51. All citations from the second version of *Comparative Models* are to a reprint in the catalog for Art & Language's 1980 retrospective at the Van Abbemuseum in Eindhoven.

67. Art & Language, "Comparative Models," 52.

68. Paul Feyerabend, *Against Method*, 3rd ed. (London: Verso, 1993). In the second version of *Comparative Models*, Art & Language adopts the symbols "T" and "T[1]" to refer to the two points of view it will be comparing. This suggests the influence of Feyerabend's 1955 review of Ludwig Wittgenstein's *Philosophical Investigations*, which Feyerabend begins by stating his approach to reviewing Wittgenstein's book as follows: "In discussing this book I shall proceed in the following way: I shall first state a philosophical theory *T*, which is attacked throughout the book. . . . I shall state what seems to be Wittgenstein's own position on the issue. This position will be formulated as a philosophical theory, *T'*, without implying that Wittgenstein intended to develop a philosophical theory (he did not)." See Paul Feyerabend, "Wittgenstein's *Philosophical Investigations*," in *Problems of Empiricism: Philosophical Papers*, vol. 2 (Cambridge: Cambridge University Press, 1981), 99.

69. Feyerabend, *Against Method*, 33. Although *Against Method* did not appear in book form until 1975, three years after the completion of *Comparative Models*, Feyerabend had been developing and publishing his views for some years previously, and Art & Language was familiar with many of these earlier writings. Especially important is an early version of *Against Method* published as Paul Feyerabend, "Against Method: Outline of an Anarchistic Theory of Knowledge," in *Analyses of Theories and Methods of Physics and Psychology*, ed. Michael Radner and Stephen Winokur (Minneapolis: University of Minnesota Press, 1970), 17–130. It is worth noting that Feyerabend was deeply interested in art, especially Dada, on which he drew while formulating his account of epistemological anarchy. See Feyerabend, *Against Method*, 265–266.

70. Michael Corris and Mel Ramsden, "Frameworks and Phantoms," *Art-Language* 2, no. 3 (September 1973): 42.

71. Art & Language, "Comparative Models," 54.

72. Art & Language, "Comparative Models," 54.

73. Art & Language, "Comparative Models," 52.

74. Art & Language, "Comparative Models," 55.

75. Art & Language, "Comparative Models," 55–56.

76. Art & Language, "Comparative Models," 62.

77. Art & Language, "Comparative Models," 56.

Two *A Research Program*

1. The most extensive treatment of *Index 01*, to which I am indebted throughout my discussion of the work, is found in William Wood, "We Are a Cell Aren't We? Art & Language and the Documenta Index" (master's thesis, University of British Columbia, 1992). See also William Wood, "A Fish Ceases to Be a Fish: A Critical History of English Conceptual Art 1966–72" (PhD diss., University of Sus-

sex, 1998). Of additional interest concerning both *Index 01* and *Documenta 5* is Jef Cornelis, *Documenta 5* (Zurich: JRP|Ringier, 2012), a film that Cornelis shot at the exhibition. It includes interviews with several Art & Language participants and a number of other conceptual artists.

2. Harrison and Orton, *A Provisional History of Art & Language*, 32.

3. Carter Ratcliff, "Adversary Spaces," *Artforum*, October 1972, 40.

4. Harrison, *Essays on Art & Language*, 61.

5. Preston Heller and Andrew Menard, "Kozloff: Criticism in Absentia," *Artforum*, February 1973, 32–36.

6. Michael Corris, "The Fine Structure of Collaboration," *Art-Language* 2, no. 3 (September 1973): 35. On the invisible college, see Diana Crane, "Social Structure in a Group of Scientists: A Test of the 'Invisible College' Hypothesis," *American Sociological Review* 34, no. 3 (June 1969): 335–352; and Diana Crane, *Invisible Colleges: Diffusion of Knowledge in Scientific Communities* (Chicago: University of Chicago Press, 1972).

7. Corris, "The Fine Structure of Collaboration," 35.

8. Michael Corris papers of the Art & Language New York group, 1965–2002, Getty Research Institute, Research Library, Accession no. 2003.M.32, Box 1, Folder 14.

9. Imre Lakatos, "Falsification and the Methodology of Scientific Research Programmes," in Lakatos and Musgrave, *Criticism and the Growth of Knowledge*, 132. The mathematician George Pólya wrote the classic treatment of heuristics. See George Pólya, *How to Solve It* (Princeton, NJ: Princeton University Press, 1971). This book, first published in 1945, theorizes the value of heuristic methods and presents a range of examples for students of mathematics. Lakatos translated it into Hungarian. Heuristics is an ancient field of study, and its first major exponent is the third- or fourth-century CE Greek mathematician Pappus. For Pappus's writings, see Ivor Thomas, ed., *Greek Mathematical Works: Aristarchus to Pappus* (Cambridge, MA: Harvard University Press, 1941). Pólya characterizes heuristics as the study of "the methods and rules of discovery and invention" (Pólya, *How to Solve It*, 112). Lakatos uses the term in more or less this way, and he argues for science as an experiential, trial-and-error, ad hoc deployment of heuristic methods. Lakatos depicts this very process in his major work on the philosophy of mathematics, Imre Lakatos, *Proofs and Refutations: The Logic of Mathematical Discovery* (Cambridge: University of Cambridge Press, 1976), which is written in the form of a discussion between a teacher and a group of students. Similarities to Art & Language's own working methods are plentiful, though of course Lakatos did not know the collective's work.

10. Lakatos, "Falsification and the Methodology of Scientific Research Programmes," 133. Lakatos speaks of a research program's negative heuristic as that toward which the *modus tollens*, or the denial of the consequent (which is rendered in symbolic logic "$P \rightarrow Q, \neg Q \therefore \neg P$" or "if P, then Q; not Q; therefore, not P"), is not to

be directed. He gives the example of Isaac Newton's three laws of dynamics and law of gravitation as an example of the negative heuristics of classical physics. If a researcher abandons these, he or she is no longer doing classical physics. This is, of course, precisely what happens when Albert Einstein formulates his theories of relativity.

11. Lakatos, "Falsification and the Methodology of Scientific Research Programmes," 133. Lakatos gives the statement "the planets are essentially gravitating spinning-tops of roughly spherical shape" as an example of a positive heuristic claim in Newton's research program (137). Unlike Newton's negative heuristics, this statement is open to refutation, and, indeed, research eventually shows that, in addition to gravitation, magnetic fields also influence the motion of planets.

12. Lakatos, "Falsification and the Methodology of Scientific Research Programmes," 132. Lakatos cites two examples of research programs that, in spite of false negative heuristics, nevertheless produced progressive problemshifts and made major scientific contributions: William Prout, whose incorrect hypothesis that all atoms are composed of hydrogen atoms led to new discoveries about atomic structure, and Niels Bohr, whose work on light emission proceeded from an inconsistent set of methodological rules but nevertheless led to an improved model of the atom. See 138–154 for Lakatos's comments on Prout and Bohr.

13. Mel Ramsden, "Concerning the Annotations," unpublished manuscript, 1974, n.p., Blurting in A&L Online, http://blurting-in.zkm.de/e/conc_annot.

14. Mel Ramsden, "Concerning the Annotations."

15. Art & Language, typescript of the annotations, MR 18. All citations from this work are to a manuscript copy in the private papers of Terry Smith, Pittsburgh. Because the text is not paginated, citations provide the individual annotations designated by letters and numbers in lieu of conventional page numbers.

16. Art & Language, typescript of the annotations, PH 1.

17. Art & Language, typescript of the annotations, AM 2.

18. Art & Language, typescript of the annotations, AM 2.

19. Art & Language, typescript of the annotations, TS 4.

20. Art & Language, typescript of the annotations, TS 4.

21. Art & Language, typescript of the annotations, TS 4.

22. Art & Language, typescript of the annotations, PH 12.

23. Art & Language, typescript of the annotations, PH 12.

24. Art & Language, typescript of the annotations, MR 10.

25. Art & Language, typescript of the annotations, MR 10.

26. Art & Language, typescript of the annotations, MR 10.

27. Louis Althusser, *For Marx* (London: Verso, 2005), 66. Art & Language's interest in Althusser seems to stem from his status as a key thinker both on science and on relations of theory and practice, but it also demonstrates the collective's increasing awareness of currents in Marxist thought.

28. Art & Language, typescript of the annotations, MR 20.

29. Art & Language, typescript of the annotations, MR 12.

30. Art & Language, *Blurting in A&L* (New York and Halifax: Art & Language Press and Nova Scotia College of Art, 1973). All citations from *Blurting in A&L* preserve the original typography where possible. The full text of *Blurting in A&L* is also available online along with related resources organized by Thomas Dreher at Blurting in A&L Online, http://blurting-in.zkm.de/.

31. Art & Language, *Blurting in A&L*, front cover.

32. On the press of the Nova Scotia College of Art, see Benjamin H. D. Buchloh, "The Press of NSCAD: A Brief Incomplete History and Its Future Books," in *NSCAD: The Nova Scotia College of Art & Design*, ed. Garry N. Kennedy (Halifax: Press of the Nova Scotia College of Art & Design, 1982), 64–75. On the close relations between the Nova Scotia College of Art and conceptual artists, see Bruce Barber, ed., *Conceptual Art: The NSCAD Connection: 1967–1973* (Halifax: Press of the Nova Scotia College of Art & Design, 2001). On the Nova Scotia College of Art & Design generally, including visits by Art & Language, see Garry Neill Kennedy, *The Last Art College, 1968–1978* (Cambridge, MA: MIT Press, 2012). For the transcript of a discussion session with Mel Ramsden and Michael Corris at Nova Scotia College of Art & Design that covers much of Art & Language's work in New York from this period, see Peggy Gale, ed., *Artists Talk: 1969–1977* (Halifax: Press of the Nova Scotia College of Art & Design, 2004), 114–147.

33. Quoted from an untitled transcript of an Art & Language conversation dated April 13, 1973, Terry Smith papers, Pittsburgh, 1.

34. Quoted from an untitled transcript of an Art & Language conversation dated April 13, 1973, Terry Smith papers, Pittsburgh, 1.

35. Quoted from an untitled transcript of an Art & Language conversation dated April 13, 1973, Terry Smith papers, Pittsburgh, 1.

36. Art & Language, *Blurting in A&L*, 2.

37. Art & Language, *Blurting in A&L*, 1–2.

38. Art & Language, *Blurting in A&L*, 2.

39. Art & Language, *Blurting in A&L*, 2.

40. Art & Language, *Blurting in A&L*, 30.

41. Art & Language, *Blurting in A&L*, 37.

42. Art & Language, *Blurting in A&L*, 3.

43. Art & Language, *Blurting in A&L*, front cover.

44. Art & Language, *Blurting in A&L*, 3.

45. Art & Language, *Blurting in A&L*, 1.

46. Art & Language, *Blurting in A&L*, 1.

47. Art & Language, *Blurting in A&L*, 3–4.

48. Art & Language, *Blurting in A&L*, 12.

49. Art & Language, "Handbook(s) to Going-On," *Art-Language* 2, no. 4 (July 1974).

50. Ian Burn and Mel Ramsden, "Problems of Art & Language Space," *Art-Language* 2, no. 3 (September 1973): 53.

51. Burn and Ramsden, "Problems of Art & Language Space," 70–71.

52. The concatenations that comprise *77 Sentences* are reproduced in Christian Schlatter, *Art conceptuel forms conceptuelles* (Paris: Galerie 1900 Δ 2000, 1990), 130–135.

53. From a transcript of an Art & Language conversation dated April 6, 1973, Terry Smith papers, Pittsburgh, 2. The speakers are not indicated in the original transcript, although changes between speakers are notated with a forward slash.

54. Ian Burn, Mel Ramsden, and Terry Smith, "Draft for an Anti-Textbook," *Art-Language* 3, no. 1 (September 1974): 1.

55. Harrison, *Essays on Art & Language*, 115.

56. Art & Language, "Rambling: To Partial Correspondents," *Art-Language* 3, no. 2 (May 1975): 46–51.

57. Burn, Ramsden, and Smith, "Draft for an Anti-Textbook," 42.

58. Burn, Ramsden, and Smith, "Draft for an Anti-Textbook," 5.

59. Burn, Ramsden, and Smith, "Draft for an Anti-Textbook," 13.

60. Burn, Ramsden, and Smith, "Draft for an Anti-Textbook," 3. See Chomsky, *Aspects of the Theory of Syntax*, 3.

61. Burn, Ramsden, and Smith, "Draft for an Anti-Textbook," 25–26.

62. Burn, Ramsden, and Smith, "Draft for an Anti-Textbook," 30.

63. Burn, Ramsden, and Smith, "Draft for an Anti-Textbook," 30.

64. Burn, Ramsden, and Smith, "Draft for an Anti-Textbook," 54.

65. Burn, Ramsden, and Smith, "Draft for an Anti-Textbook," 15.

66. Burn, Ramsden, and Smith, "Draft for an Anti-Textbook," 15.

67. Burn, Ramsden, and Smith, "Draft for an Anti-Textbook," 16.

68. Burn, Ramsden, and Smith, "Draft for an Anti-Textbook," 30.

69. Burn, Ramsden, and Smith, "Draft for an Anti-Textbook," 89.

70. Burn, Ramsden, and Smith, "Draft for an Anti-Textbook," 109.

71. Terry Smith, "Art and Art and Language," *Artforum*, February 1974, 51.

Three *Interplay*

1. Ian Burn, "Art Is What We Do, Culture Is What We Do to Other Artists," in *Dialogue* (Sydney: Allen & Unwin, 1991), 131–139. When republished as part of this anthology of Burn's writings, "Provincialism" was given this new title.

2. A. A. Phillips, "The Cultural Cringe," in *Modernism and Australia: Documents on Art, Design and Architecture 1917–1967*, ed. Ann Stephen, Andrew McNamara, and Philip Goad (Melbourne: Miegunyah Press, 2006), 624.

3. Kenneth Clark, *Provincialism* (Oxford: Oxford University Press, 1962).

4. Bernard Smith with Terry Smith, *Australian Painting, 1788–1990*, 3rd ed. (Melbourne: Oxford University Press, 1991), 333. The first edition of this book appeared in 1962, followed by a second edition in 1971. Bernard Smith asked Terry Smith to write additional chapters to bring the third edition of 1991 up to date.

5. Bernard Smith with Terry Smith, *Australian Painting*, 333.

6. Bernard Smith with Terry Smith, *Australian Painting*, 334.

7. Bernard Smith with Terry Smith, *Australian Painting*, 334.

8. Patrick McCaughey, "Notes on the Centre: New York," *Quadrant*, November 1970, 76–80; Terry Smith, "Provincialism in Art," *Quadrant*, April 1971, 67–71. On these essays, see Heather Barker and Charles Green, "No Place Like Home: Australian Art History and Contemporary Art at the Start of the 1970s," *Journal of Art Historiography* 4 (June 2011): 1–17.

9. Smith, "Provincialism in Art," 67.

10. Smith, "Provincialism in Art," 67.

11. For Brook on post-object art, see Donald Brook, "Flight from the Object," in *Concerning Contemporary Art: The Power Lectures 1968–1973*, ed. Bernard Smith (Sydney: Clarendon, 1975), 16–34. On Brook and his criticism, see Heather Barker and Charles Green, "Flight from the Object: Donald Brook, Inhibodress and the Emergence of Post-Studio Art in Early 1970s Sydney," *Melbourne Art Journal* 4 (2009): 1–23.

12. Terry Smith, "Propositions" in Alberro and Stimson, *Conceptual Art*, 260.

13. For Burn's impressions of the difference between London and Sydney, see Ian Burn, "Situation-Identity," in Stephen, McNamara, and Goad, *Modernism and Australia*, 783–789. See also Art & Language, "Making Art from a Different Place," in Art Gallery of Western Australia, *Ian Burn: Minimal-Conceptual Work 1965–1970* (Perth: Art Gallery of Western Australia, 1992), 7–17, for Mel Ramsden's understanding of his Australian collaborator's cultural difference. Last, see Adrian Piper, "Ian Burn's Conceptualism," in Corris, *Conceptual Art*, 342–358, which Piper delivered as the first Ian Burn Memorial Lecture.

14. Burn, "Art Is What We Do," 132.

15. Burn, "Art Is What We Do," 132.

16. Burn, "Art Is What We Do," 133.

17. Burn, "Art Is What We Do," 133.

18. Burn, "Art Is What We Do," 133. See Carl Andre, quoted in Barbara Rose and Irving Sandler, "Sensibility of the Sixties," *Art in America*, January–February 1967,

49. The full passage from which Andre's remark is excerpted appears in Carl Andre, *CUTS: Texts 1959–2004*, ed. James Meyer (Cambridge, MA: MIT Press, 2004), 30.

19. Burn, "Art Is What We Do," 134.

20. Burn, "Art Is What We Do," 135.

21. Burn, "Art Is What We Do," 136.

22. Burn, "Art Is What We Do," 136.

23. Burn, "Art Is What We Do," 136.

24. Burn, "Art Is What We Do," 138.

25. Burn, "Art Is What We Do," 138.

26. Terry Smith, "The Provincialism Problem," *Artforum*, September 1974, 54–59. On this essay, see Heather Barker and Charles Green, "The Provincialism Problem: Terry Smith and Center-Periphery Art History," *Journal of Art Historiography* 3 (December 2010): 1–17.

27. Smith, "The Provincialism Problem," 54.

28. Smith, "The Provincialism Problem," 54–55.

29. Smith, "The Provincialism Problem," 55.

30. Smith, "The Provincialism Problem," 56.

31. Smith, "The Provincialism Problem," 57.

32. Smith, "The Provincialism Problem," 57.

33. Smith, "The Provincialism Problem," 58.

34. Smith, "The Provincialism Problem," 59.

35. Smith, "The Provincialism Problem," 59.

36. Terry Smith, response to Elwyn Lynn's letter to the editor regarding "The Provincialism Problem," *Artforum*, December 1974, 8.

37. Burn, Ramsden, and Smith, "Draft for an Anti-Textbook," 90.

38. Burn, Ramsden, and Smith, "Draft for an Anti-Textbook," 90.

39. Burn, Ramsden, and Smith, "Draft for an Anti-Textbook," 90.

40. Burn, Ramsden, and Smith, "Draft for an Anti-Textbook," 90.

41. Burn, Ramsden, and Smith, "Draft for an Anti-Textbook," 90.

42. Burn, Ramsden, and Smith, "Draft for an Anti-Textbook," 91.

43. Burn, Ramsden, and Smith, "Draft for an Anti-Textbook," 97.

44. Burn, Ramsden, and Smith, "Draft for an Anti-Textbook," 97.

45. On the International Council, see Max Kozloff, "American Painting during the Cold War," *Artforum*, May 1973, 43–54; and Eva Cockcroft, "Abstract Expressionism, Weapon of the Cold War," *Artforum*, June 1974, 39–41.

46. Jennifer Licht, *Some Recent American Art* (Melbourne: National Gallery of Victoria, 1973). The exhibition traveled to five venues in Australia and New Zealand: National Gallery of Victoria, Melbourne; West Australian Art Gallery, Perth; Art Gallery of New South Wales, Sydney; Art Gallery of South Australia, Adelaide;

and City of Auckland Art Gallery, Auckland. Joseph Kosuth was among the artists selected by Jennifer Licht, and an excerpt of his writing appears in the catalog, the cover of which is literally covered in denim, much like the blue jean–wearing American counterculture in which so many artists at the time partook.

47. Burn, Ramsden, and Smith, "Draft for an Anti-Textbook," 91.

48. Burn, Ramsden, and Smith, "Draft for an Anti-Textbook," 91.

49. Burn, Ramsden, and Smith, "Draft for an Anti-Textbook," 94.

50. Burn, Ramsden, and Smith, "Draft for an Anti-Textbook," 95.

51. Burn, Ramsden, and Smith, "Draft for an Anti-Textbook," 96.

52. Burn, Ramsden, and Smith, "Draft for an Anti-Textbook," 98.

53. Burn, Ramsden, and Smith, "Draft for an Anti-Textbook," 98.

54. Burn, Ramsden, and Smith, "Draft for an Anti-Textbook," 98.

55. Burn, Ramsden, and Smith, "Draft for an Anti-Textbook," 98.

56. Burn, Ramsden, and Smith, "Draft for an Anti-Textbook," 98.

57. Burn, Ramsden, and Smith, "Draft for an Anti-Textbook," 98.

58. Art & Language, "Brainstorming—New York," *Art-Language* 3, no. 2 (May 1975): 36.

59. Art & Language, "Brainstorming," 36.

60. Art & Language, "Brainstorming," 36.

61. Art & Language, "Brainstorming," 38.

62. Art & Language, "Brainstorming," 38.

63. Art & Language, "Brainstorming," 39.

64. Art & Language, "Brainstorming," 38.

65. Art & Language, "Brainstorming," 40.

66. Art & Language, "Brainstorming," 40.

67. Smith, "The Provincialism Problem," 59.

68. Exhibition poster, reprinted in Terry Smith, ed., *Art & Language: Australia 1975* (Banbury: Art & Language Press, 1976), i.

69. Terry Smith, "Introduction: Fighting Modern Masters," in Smith, *Art & Language*, 1. The same text appears in an expanded form as Terry Smith, "Review: Fighting Modern Masters," *The Fox* 2 (1975): 15–21.

70. Peter Coleman, *Obscenity, Blasphemy, Sedition: Censorship in Australia* (Brisbane: Jacaranda Press, 1974).

71. Elwyn Lynn, "Modern Masters of Modern Politics?," *Quadrant*, June 1975, excerpted in Smith, *Art & Language*, 13.

72. Smith, "Introduction," 4.

73. Smith, "Introduction," 4.

74. Annette Kuhn, "Waltz Me Around Again, MoMA," *Village Voice*, August 18, 1975, 42.

75. Smith, *Art & Language*, 24.

76. Smith, *Art & Language*, 24.

77. Smith, *Art & Language*, 26.

78. Smith, *Art & Language*, 109.

79. Smith later published an essay on Art & Language and translation. See Terry Smith, "The Tasks of Translation: Art & Language in Australia and New Zealand 1975–6," in *Now See Hear! Art, Language and Translation*, ed. Ian Wedde and Gregory Burke (Auckland: Victoria University Press, 1990), 250–261. See also Burn's comments about Smith's article on page 209 of the same volume.

80. Smith, *Art & Language*, 72.

81. The letter is reproduced in Smith, *Art & Language*, 149.

82. Smith, *Art & Language*, 138.

83. Smith, *Art & Language*, 148.

84. Smith, *Art & Language*, 198.

85. Smith, *Art & Language*, 183.

86. Smith, *Art & Language*, 180. See also Lucy Lippard, "Notes on Seeing Some Recent American Art in New Zealand," *Auckland City Art Gallery Quarterly* 59 (1975): 2–3.

87. Smith, *Art & Language*, 180.

88. Smith, *Art & Language*, 195–196.

89. Smith, *Art & Language*, 196.

90. Smith, *Art & Language*, 204.

91. Terry Smith, letter to Ian Burn and Mel Ramsden, dated June 7, 1975, Terry Smith private papers, Sydney.

92. Mel Ramsden, letter to Terry Smith, dated June 16, 1975, Terry Smith papers, Sydney.

93. These plans are discussed in Ian Burn, letter to Terry Smith, dated May 1975, Terry Smith papers, Sydney.

94. See Smith, *Art & Language*, 102.

95. Smith, *Art & Language*, 231.

96. "Cur, Piggy Poster Censored," *Auckland Star*, August 5, 1976, 1.

97. Smith, "The Tasks of Translation," 259.

98. Typescript, "SESSION I—Wednesday 4 August '76," Terry Smith papers, Sydney, 1.1. The pagination of the typescript is unorthodox; the first number indicates the session and the second indicates the page of the transcript within that session.

99. Typescript, "SESSION I—Wednesday 4 August '76," 1.4.

Four *Foxes and Hedgehogs*

1. Joseph Kosuth, quoted in Annette Kuhn, "Culture Shock," *Village Voice*, April 14, 1975, 100.

2. For Kosuth's take on his position vis-à-vis Art & Language at this juncture, see Joseph Kosuth, "(Notes) on an 'Anthropologized' Art," in *Art after Philosophy and After*, 95–101.

3. Sarah Charlesworth, "Memo for The Fox," *The Fox* 2 (1975): 37.

4. Harrison, *Essays on Art & Language*, 118.

5. Douglas E. Gerber, ed., *Greek Iambic Poetry: From the Seventh to the Fifth Centuries BC* (Cambridge, MA: Harvard University Press, 1999), 216–217. Gerber's translation does not contain a judgment as to whether the fox or the hedgehog has the right approach. M. L. West's, however, does. He translates the fragment: "The fox knows lots of tricks, / the hedgehog only one—but it's a winner." See M. L. West, ed., *Greek Lyric Poetry* (Oxford: Oxford University Press, 1993), 5.

6. Isaiah Berlin, *The Hedgehog and the Fox: An Essay on Tolstoy's View of History* (New York: Simon and Schuster, 1953), 1–2. For the original essay, see Isaiah Berlin, "Lev Tolstoy's Historical Scepticism," *Oxford Slavonic Papers* 2 (1951): 17–54.

7. Mona da Vinci, "The Fox and Other Fairy Tales," *Soho Weekly News*, December 25, 1975, 17.

8. Da Vinci, "The Fox and Other Fairy Tales," 17.

9. Jenny Holzer, quoted in Michael Auping, *Jenny Holzer* (New York: Universe, 1992), 74.

10. The initial source of their disagreement apparently dates to 1972, when an anthology of writings by Art & Language appeared that included texts by Kosuth and the collective's four English founders but neither Burn nor Ramsden. For the anthology, see Art & Language, *Art & Language: Texte zum Phänomen Kunst und Sprache* (Cologne: DuMont, 1972). For anecdotes about its publication, see Harrison and Orton, *A Provisional History of Art & Language*, 29–30.

11. On the AWC, see Lucy Lippard, "The Art Workers' Coalition," in *Idea Art*, ed. Gregory Battcock (New York: Dutton, 1973), 102–115.

12. Harrison, *Essays on Art & Language*, 122.

13. Sarah Charlesworth, "A Declaration of Dependence," *The Fox* 1, no. 1 (1975): 1.

14. Charlesworth, "A Declaration of Dependence," 1.

15. Charlesworth, "A Declaration of Dependence," 1.

16. Charlesworth, "A Declaration of Dependence," 2.

17. Charlesworth, "A Declaration of Dependence," 2.

18. Charlesworth, "A Declaration of Dependence," 2.

19. Charlesworth, "A Declaration of Dependence," 3.

20. Charlesworth, "A Declaration of Dependence," 3.

21. Charlesworth, "A Declaration of Dependence," 5.
22. Charlesworth, "A Declaration of Dependence," 5.
23. Charlesworth, "A Declaration of Dependence," 5.
24. Charlesworth, "A Declaration of Dependence," 5.
25. Charlesworth, "A Declaration of Dependence," 6.
26. Joseph Kosuth, "The Artist as Anthropologist" in *Art after Philosophy and After*, 117.
27. Kosuth, "The Artist as Anthropologist," 117.
28. Kosuth, "The Artist as Anthropologist," 119, 117.
29. Kosuth, "The Artist as Anthropologist," 119–120.
30. Kosuth, "The Artist as Anthropologist," 120.
31. Ramsden, "On Practice," 171–172.
32. Ramsden, "On Practice," 172–173.
33. Ramsden, "On Practice," 196.
34. Ramsden, "On Practice," 172.
35. Ramsden, "On Practice," 172.
36. Ramsden, "On Practice," 177.
37. Ramsden, "On Practice," 190.
38. Ramsden, "On Practice," 189.
39. Ramsden, "On Practice," 190.
40. Ramsden, "On Practice," 191.
41. Ramsden, "On Practice," 189.
42. Ramsden, "On Practice," 189–190.
43. Michael Baldwin and Philip Pilkington, "For Thomas Hobbes," *The Fox* 1, no. 1 (1975): 8.
44. Art & Language, "Utopian Prayers and Infantile Marxism," *Art-Language* 3, no. 2 (May 1975): 89–92.
45. Art & Language, "Utopian Prayers and Infantile Marxism," 89.
46. Art & Language, "A Note on Pseudo-Debate," *Art-Language* 3, no. 2 (May 1975): 95.
47. Art & Language, "A Note on Pseudo-Debate," 95.
48. Art & Language, "A Note on Pseudo-Debate," 95.
49. Ian Burn, "The Art Market: Affluence and Degradation," in *Dialogue*, 152–166.
50. Burn, "The Art Market," 152–153.
51. Burn, "The Art Market," 154.
52. Burn, "The Art Market," 154, 161.
53. Burn, "The Art Market," 159.
54. Burn, "The Art Market," 158–159.
55. Burn, "The Art Market," 165.

56. Art & Language, "'Mr. Lin Yutang Refers to "Fair Play" . . . ?,'" *Art-Language* 3, no. 2 (May 1975): 68–80.

57. See Art & Language, "Pedagogical Sketchbook (AL)," *Art-Language* 3, no. 2 (May 1975): 31–40.

58. Art & Language, "'Mr. Lin Yutang Refers to "Fair Play" . . . ?,'" 70. "'While We've Been . . .'" refers to the first section heading of Burn, "The Art Market" and is used throughout "'Mr. Lin Yutang'" to refer to Burn's essay, likely because a final title had not been decided upon when Burn sent a draft of the text to England.

59. Art & Language, "'Mr. Lin Yutang Refers to "Fair Play" . . . ?,'" 74.

60. Art & Language, "'Mr. Lin Yutang Refers to "Fair Play" . . . ?,'" 74.

61. Art & Language, "'Mr. Lin Yutang Refers to "Fair Play" . . . ?,'" 76.

62. Art & Language, "'Mr. Lin Yutang Refers to "Fair Play" . . . ?,'" 76.

63. Art & Language, "'Mr. Lin Yutang Refers to "Fair Play" . . . ?,'" 76.

64. Art & Language, "'Mr. Lin Yutang Refers to "Fair Play" . . . ?,'" 79.

65. Art & Language, "Strategy Is Political: Dear M . . . ," *Art-Language* 3, no. 2 (May 1975): 81–86.

66. Art & Language, "Strategy Is Political," 81.

67. Art & Language, "Strategy Is Political," 82.

68. Art & Language, "Strategy Is Political," 81.

69. Art & Language, "Strategy Is Political," 83.

70. Art & Language, "Strategy Is Political," 83.

71. Art & Language, "Strategy Is Political," 85.

72. Art & Language, "Strategy Is Political," 86.

73. Ian Burn, "Art-Language, Volume 3 Number 2," *The Fox* 2 (1975): 53.

74. Art & Language, "Strategy Is Political," 86.

75. Art & Language, "'To Begin With, While I Am Clearly a Marxist Sympathizer . . . ,'" *Art-Language* 3, no. 2 (May 1975): 15.

76. Art & Language, "'To Begin With,'" 15.

77. Art & Language, "Art and Language," *Art-Language* 3, no. 2 (May 1975): 41.

78. Ian Burn, unpublished notebook, dated 1974–1975, Ian Burn private papers, Sydney, n.p.

79. Corris, "Inside a New York Art Gang," 474.

80. On AMCC, see Terry Smith, "Without Revolutionary Theory . . . ," *Studio International*, March–April 1976, 134–137; and Nancy Marner, "Art & Politics '77," *Art in America*, July–August, 1977, 64–66.

81. Artists Meeting for Cultural Change, "To the American Art Community from Artists Meeting for Cultural Change," broadside dated December 14, 1975, n.p.

82. Artists Meeting for Cultural Change, "To the American Art Community," n.p.

83. Artists Meeting for Cultural Change, "To the American Art Community," n.p. When actually exhibited, the exhibition bore the title *American Art: An Exhibition from the Collection of Mr. & Mrs. John D. Rockefeller 3rd*. Documentary footage of the protest appears in Zoran Popović's film *Struggle in New York*. For the exhibition catalog, see E. P. Richardson, *American Art: An Exhibition from the Collection of Mr. and Mrs. John D. Rockefeller 3rd* (San Francisco: Fine Arts Museums of San Francisco, 1976).

84. Catalog Committee of Artists Meeting for Cultural Change, *An Anti-Catalog* (New York: Catalog Committee of Artists Meeting for Cultural Change, 1977).

85. Sarah Charlesworth, "For Artists Meeting," *The Fox* 3 (1976): 40.

86. Charlesworth, "For Artists Meeting," 40.

87. Charlesworth, "For Artists Meeting," 41.

88. Quoted in Charlesworth, "For Artists Meeting," 45.

89. Quoted in Charlesworth, "For Artists Meeting," 45–46.

90. Quoted in Charlesworth, "For Artists Meeting," 46.

91. Quoted in Charlesworth, "For Artists Meeting," 46.

92. Quoted in Charlesworth, "For Artists Meeting," 46.

93. Corris, "Inside a New York Art Gang," 477.

94. Draft of the AICU's "Principles of Unity" submitted by the Congress of Afrikan Peoples, quoted in Corris, "Inside a New York Art Gang," 477. On Baraka's activism, see Komozi Woodard, *A Nation within a Nation: Amiri Baraka (LeRoi Jones) and Black Power Politics* (Chapel Hill: University of North Carolina Press, 1999).

95. Quoted in Corris, "Inside a New York Art Gang," 481.

96. Mel Ramsden, open letter to Art & Language, quoted in Corris, "Inside a New York Art Gang," 474.

97. Mel Ramsden, open letter to Art & Language, quoted in Corris, "Inside a New York Art Gang," 474.

98. For Art & Language's retrospective account of both AMCC and the AICU, see Art & Language, "'Artists Meeting for Cultural Change' and 'Anti-Imperialist Cultural Union': A History of Two Cultural Organizations, as Illustration," *Art-Language* 4, no. 2 (October 1977): 66.

99. Art & Language, "'Artists Meeting for Cultural Change,'" 67.

100. Art & Language, "'Artists Meeting for Cultural Change,'" 71–72.

101. Karl Beveridge and Ian Burn, "Don Judd," *The Fox* 2 (1975): 129.

102. Beveridge and Burn, "Don Judd," 139.

103. Beveridge and Burn, "Don Judd," 139. These passages are taken from Judd's comments in "The Artist and Politics: A Symposium," *Artforum*, September 1970, 37.

104. Beveridge and Burn, "Don Judd," 139.

105. Beveridge and Burn, "Don Judd," 140.

106. Karl Beveridge, quoted in Clive Robertson, "The Art World and Its Other: Forever the Twain Shall Meet?," in *Condé and Beveridge: Class Works*, ed. Bruce Barber (Halifax: Press of the Nova Scotia College of Art & Design, 2008), 42.

107. Peter Benchley, "The Lumpen-Headache," *The Fox* 3 (1976): 3.

108. Benchley, "The Lumpen-Headache," 1.

109. The details concerning this stamp are outlined in Harrison, *Essays on Art & Language*, 276–277n56.

110. Benchley, "The Lumpen-Headache," 4.

111. Benchley, "The Lumpen-Headache," 4.

112. Benchley, "The Lumpen-Headache," 4.

113. Benchley, "The Lumpen-Headache," 3.

114. Benchley, "The Lumpen-Headache," 11.

115. Benchley, "The Lumpen-Headache," 12.

116. Benchley, "The Lumpen-Headache," 12.

117. Benchley, "The Lumpen-Headache," 14.

118. Benchley, "The Lumpen-Headache," 14.

119. Benchley, "The Lumpen-Headache," 20.

120. Benchley, "The Lumpen-Headache," 21.

121. Benchley, "The Lumpen-Headache," 21.

122. Benchley, "The Lumpen-Headache," 22.

123. Benchley, "The Lumpen-Headache," 22.

124. Benchley, "The Lumpen-Headache," 23.

125. Benchley, "The Lumpen-Headache," 35.

126. Benchley, "The Lumpen-Headache," 36–37.

127. Carole Condé and Karl Beveridge, "The Edge of Edge," *The Fox* 3 (1976): 80.

128. Condé and Beveridge, "The Edge of Edge," 80.

129. Condé and Beveridge, "The Edge of Edge," 80.

130. Condé and Beveridge, "The Edge of Edge," 82.

131. Condé and Beveridge, "The Edge of Edge," 82.

132. Condé and Beveridge, "The Edge of Edge," 83.

133. Condé and Beveridge, "The Edge of Edge," 83.

134. Condé and Beveridge, "The Edge of Edge," 84.

Five *Keep All Your Friends*

1. Hilton Kramer, "Yankee Go Home," *New York Times*, June 6, 1976, 1, 27.

2. See Zoran Popović, *Borba u New Yorku* (Zagreb: Centar za fotografiju film

i TV, 1977), which is a booklet version of the film. All citations to the film in this chapter refer to this printed reference.

3. László Beke, "Conceptual Tendencies in Eastern European Art," in Camnitzer, Farver, and Weiss, *Global Conceptualism*, 49.

4. Aleš Erjavec, "Neue Slowenische Kunst—New Slovenian Art: Slovenia, Yugoslavia, Self-Management, and the 1980s," in *Postmodernism and the Postsocialist Condition: Politicized Art under Late Socialism*, ed. Aleš Erjavec (Berkeley: University of California Press, 2003), 136. See also, in the same volume, Miško Šuvaković, "Art as a Political Machine: Fragments on the Late Socialist and Postsocialist Art of Mitteleuropa and the Balkans," 90–134.

5. Lutz Becker, "Art for an Avant-Garde Society: Belgrade in the 1970s," in *East Art Map: Contemporary Art and Eastern Europe*, ed. IRWIN (London: Afterall, 2006), 391.

6. On conceptual art in Yugoslavia, see Miško Šuvaković, "Conceptual Art," in *Impossible Histories: Historical Avant-Gardes, Neo-Avant-Gardes, and Post-Avant-Gardes in Yugoslavia, 1918–1991*, ed. Dubravka Djurić and Miško Šuvaković (Cambridge, MA: MIT Press, 2003), 210–245. See also Miško Šuvaković, *Konceptualna Umetnost* (Novi Sad: Muzej Savremene Umesnosti Vojvodine, 2007), which provides a global account of conceptual art and includes an especially substantial treatment of its Yugoslavian and Eastern European manifestations.

7. McShine, *Information*, 98–102. On OHO, see Igor Zabel, "A Short History of OHO," in IRWIN, *East Art Map*, 410–432. See also Marko Pogačnik and I. G. Plamen, "OHO Manifesto," in *Primary Documents: A Sourcebook for Eastern and Central European Art since the 1950s*, ed. Laura Hoptman and Tomáš Pospiszyl (New York and Cambridge, MA: Museum of Modern Art and MIT Press, 2002), 92–95.

8. Lippard, *Six Years*, 152–153.

9. Zoran Popović and Jasna Tijardović, "A Note on Art in Yugoslavia," *The Fox* 1, no. 1 (1975): 50.

10. Popović and Tijardović, "A Note on Art in Yugoslavia," 49.

11. Popović and Tijardović, "A Note on Art in Yugoslavia," 50.

12. Erjavec, "Neue Slowenische Kunst," 138.

13. Tom Marioni, "Real Social Realism," *Vision* 2 (1976): 9.

14. Dunja Blažević, quoted in Becker, "Art for an Avant-Garde Society," 397.

15. Zoran Popović, "For Self-Management Art," in *Theories and Documents of Contemporary Art: A Sourcebook of Artists' Writings*, ed. Kristine Stiles and Peter Selz (Berkeley: University of California Press, 1996), 847, 848.

16. Jasna Tijardović, "The 'Liquidation' of Art: Self-Management or Self-Protection," *The Fox* 3 (1976): 98.

17. Tijardović, "The 'Liquidation' of Art," 98.

18. Tijardović, "The 'Liquidation' of Art," 99.

19. Zoran Popović, quoted in Kristine Stiles, "Language and Concepts," in Stiles and Selz, *Theories and Documents of Contemporary Art*, 809.

20. For the exhibition announcement, see Michael Corris papers of the Art & Language New York group, 1965–2002, Getty Research Institute, Research Library, Accession no. 2003.M.32, Box 6, Folder 1.

21. Art & Language, "Conversations at the Student Cultural Center," Michael Corris papers of the Art & Language New York group, Box 6, Folder 7, 7. The Yugoslavian newspaper *Student* 23 (November 4, 1975) is dedicated largely to the seminars and contains transcripts in Serbian.

22. Art & Language, "Conversations at the Student Cultural Center," 8.

23. Art & Language, "Conversations at the Student Cultural Center," 9.

24. Michael Corris and Andrew Menard, correspondence to Csaba Polanyi, Michael Corris papers of the Art & Language New York group, Box 6, Folder 5, 3.

25. Corris and Menard, correspondence to Csaba Polanyi, 3.

26. Corris and Menard, correspondence to Csaba Polanyi, 1.

27. Corris and Menard, correspondence to Csaba Polanyi, 4.

28. U.S. Congress, Senate, *The Arts and Artifacts Indemnity Act*, S. 1800, 94th Cong., 1st sess. (December 20, 1975).

29. Michael Corris, Preston Heller, and Andrew Menard, "The Organization of Culture under Monopoly Capitalism, Part I: 'How Do You Feel about the Arts and Artifacts Indemnity Act?' The Organization of Culture under Monopoly Capitalism, Part II: Culture Ain't No Headless Horseman," *The Fox* 3 (1976): 128–154.

30. Corris, Heller, and Menard, "The Organization of Culture under Monopoly Capitalism," 135.

31. Corris, Heller, and Menard, "The Organization of Culture under Monopoly Capitalism," 139.

32. Corris, Heller, and Menard, "The Organization of Culture under Monopoly Capitalism," 139.

33. Corris, Heller, and Menard, "The Organization of Culture under Monopoly Capitalism," 140.

34. Corris, Heller, and Menard, "The Organization of Culture under Monopoly Capitalism," 141.

35. Corris, Heller, and Menard, "The Organization of Culture under Monopoly Capitalism," 141.

36. Corris, Heller, and Menard, "The Organization of Culture under Monopoly Capitalism," 141.

37. Corris, Heller, and Menard, "The Organization of Culture under Monopoly Capitalism," 141.

38. Corris, Heller, and Menard, "The Organization of Culture under Monopoly Capitalism," 143.

39. Corris, Heller, and Menard, "The Organization of Culture under Monopoly Capitalism," 143.

40. Jill Breakstone, Michael Corris, Preston Heller, and Andrew Menard, "Now about This Storefront," *Studio International*, March–April 1976, 108–109.

41. Breakstone, Corris, Heller, and Menard, "Now about This Storefront," 109.

42. Breakstone, Corris, Heller, and Menard, "Now about This Storefront," 109.

43. Barthelme, "Three from May 23rd, 1969."

44. Mayo Thompson, quoted in David Keenan, "The Merry Prankster," *Wire*, August 2005, 37.

45. All lyrics from *Corrected Slogans* are quoted from the liner notes of the 1997 reissue of the album on compact disc, which are without pagination. See Art & Language and the Red Crayola, *Corrected Slogans*, CD (Drag City/Dexter's Cigar, 1997).

46. (Provisional) Art & Language, "The Intellectual Life of the Ruling Class Gets Its Apotheosis in a World of Doris Days" (Banbury: Art & Language Press, 1976), front cover.

47. (Provisional) Art & Language, "The Intellectual Life of the Ruling Class," 1.

48. (Provisional) Art & Language, "The Intellectual Life of the Ruling Class," 5.

49. (Provisional) Art & Language, "The Intellectual Life of the Ruling Class," 1.

50. (Provisional) Art & Language, "The Intellectual Life of the Ruling Class," 3.

51. Corris, "Inside a New York Art Gang," 480.

52. Corris, "Inside a New York Art Gang," 481.

53. Flora Lewis, "Venice Biennale's Revival Offers Vitality," *New York Times*, August 25, 1976, 22.

54. Lewis, "Venice Biennale's Revival Offers Vitality," 22.

55. Art & Language, "Doge City," *Art-Language* 3, no. 4 (October 1976): 49.

56. Andrew Menard, quoted in Corris, "Inside a New York Art Gang," 482.

57. Quoted in Corris, "Inside a New York Art Gang," 482.

58. Corris, "Inside a New York Art Gang," 482.

59. Corris, "Inside a New York Art Gang," 482.

60. Ian Burn, quoted in Michael Auping, "A Fox," in *30 Years: Interviews and Outtakes* (Fort Worth and Munich: Modern Art Museum of Fort Worth and Prestel, 2007), 70–71.

61. On Media Action Group and Union Media Services, see Sandy Kirby, ed., *Ian Burn, Art: Critical, Political* (Sydney: University of Western Sydney, 1996); and Sandy Kirby, *Artists and Unions: A Critical Tradition: A Report on the Art & Working Life Program* (Redfern: Australia Council, 1992).

62. On Beveridge and Condé's work, see Barber, *Condé and Beveridge*.

63. Stiles, "Language and Concepts," 809.

64. Popović, *Borba u New Yorku*, 17.

65. Popović, *Borba u New Yorku*, 18.

66. Popović, *Borba u New Yorku*, 39. This text also appears, with slightly different typography, in Art & Language, "Above Us the Waves (A Fascist Index)," *Art-Language* 3, no. 4 (October 1976): 64.

67. Georgi Plekhanov, *Art and Social Life* (Moscow: Progress, 1977).

68. Popović, *Borba u New Yorku*, 42.

69. Art & Language, "The International: England 1 (o.g.) USA 1 (o.g.)," *Art-Language* 3, no. 3 (June 1976): 66–72.

Conclusion

1. Harrison, *Essays on Art & Language*, 128.

2. Lippard, *Six Years*, 263.

3. Burn, Ramsden, and Smith, "Draft for an Anti-Textbook," 87.

4. Atkinson, "Rites of Passage," 13. On or by Atkinson, see also Terry Atkinson, *Work 1977–1983* (London: Whitechapel Art Gallery, 1983); Terry Atkinson, *Indexing, the World War I Moves, and the Ruins of Conceptualism* (Manchester: Cornhouse, 1992); and Atkinson's introduction to Dave Rushton, *Don Quixote's Art and Television* (Edinburgh: Institute of Local Television, 1998), xi–xv.

5. On Kosuth's *Second Investigation*, see the second volume of Kosuth, *Art Investigations and 'Problematics' Since 1965*.

6. Kosuth, "Art after Philosophy," 29.

7. Charles Harrison, "Against Precedents," in Christian Rattemeyer and other authors, *Exhibiting the New Art: "Op Losse Schroeven" and "When Attitudes Become Form" 1969* (London: Afterall, 2010), 195.

8. On "American-Type" painting, see Clement Greenberg, "'American-Type' Painting," in *The Collected Essays and Criticism, Vol. 3: Affirmations and Refusals, 1950–1956*, ed. John O'Brian (Chicago: University of Chicago Press, 1993), 217–236. See also Irving Sandler, *The Triumph of American Painting: A History of Abstract Expressionism* (New York: Praeger, 1970).

9. McShine, *Information*, 1.

10. On the "global village," see Marshall McLuhan, *The Gutenberg Galaxy* (Toronto: University of Toronto Press, 1962); and Marshall McLuhan, *Understanding Media* (New York: McGraw-Hill, 1964).

11. Theodor Adorno, *Aesthetic Theory* (Minneapolis: University of Minnesota Press, 1997), 1.

12. Theodor Adorno makes a case that "an emphasis on autonomous works is itself socio-political in nature" in "Commitment," *New Left Review* I/87–88 (September–

December 1974): 89. Inversely, Peter Bürger speaks of "the demand that art be reintegrated into the praxis of life" in *Theory of the Avant-Garde* (Minneapolis: University of Minnesota Press, 1984), 109n4.

13. T. J. Clark, *Farewell to an Idea: Episodes from a History of Modernism* (New Haven, CT: Yale University Press, 1999), 403.

14. Paul Oskar Kristeller, "The Modern System of the Arts," in *Renaissance Thought and the Arts* (Princeton, NJ: Princeton University Press, 1990), 164.

15. Kosuth, "Art after Philosophy," 18.

16. Charles Harrison, "Art Object and Artwork," in *L'Art conceptual, une perspective*, 2nd ed., ed. Claude Gintz (Paris: Musée d'Art Moderne de la Ville de Paris, 1989), 63.

17. Kosuth, "Introductory Note from the American Editor," 3.

18. Kosuth, "(Notes) on an 'Anthropologized' Art," 100.

19. On the proliferation of "post-" and "neo-" in contemporary art, see Hal Foster, *The Return of the Real* (Cambridge, MA: MIT Press, 1996), especially the chapters that bookend the volume, which are titled "Who's Afraid of the Neo-Avant-Garde?" and "Whatever Happened to Postmodernism?" See also the more journalistic Calvin Tomkins, *Post- to Neo-: The Art World of the 1980s* (New York: Henry Holt, 1988).

20. Burn, "The 'Sixties," 405.

21. Burn, "The 'Sixties," 405.

Bibliography

Adorno, Theodor. *Aesthetic Theory*. Minneapolis: University of Minnesota Press, 1997.

Adorno, Theodor. "Commitment." *New Left Review* I/87–88 (September-December 1974): 75–89.

Alberro, Alexander. *Conceptual Art and the Politics of Publicity*. Cambridge, MA: MIT Press, 2004.

Alberro, Alexander. "Institutions, Critique, and Institutional Critique." In *Institutional Critique: An Anthology of Artists' Writings*, edited by Alexander Alberro and Blake Stimson, 2–19. Cambridge, MA: MIT Press, 2009.

Alberro, Alexander. "One Year under the Mast: Alexander Alberro on *The Fox*." *Artforum*, summer 2003, 162–164, 206.

Alberro, Alexander. "Reconsidering Conceptual Art, 1966–1977." In *Conceptual Art: A Critical Anthology*, edited by Alexander Alberro and Blake Stimson, xvi–xxxvii. Cambridge, MA: MIT Press, 1999.

Alberro, Alexander, and Sabeth Buchmann, eds. *Art after Conceptual Art*. Cambridge, MA and Vienna: MIT Press and Generali Foundation, 2006.

Alberro, Alexander, and Blake Stimson, eds. *Conceptual Art: A Critical Anthology*. Cambridge, MA: MIT Press, 1999.

Alberro, Alexander, and Blake Stimson, eds. *Institutional Critique: An Anthology of Artists' Writings*. Cambridge, MA: MIT Press, 2009.

Allen, Gwen. *Artists' Magazines: An Alternative Space for Art*. Cambridge, MA: MIT Press, 2011.

Althusser, Louis. *For Marx*. London: Verso, 2005.

Andre, Carl. *CUTS: Texts 1959–2004*, edited by James Meyer. Cambridge, MA: MIT Press, 2004.

"Architecture as Conceptual Art?," *Harvard Design Magazine* 19 (fall 2003/winter 2004).

Art & Language. "Above Us the Waves (A Fascist Index)." *Art-Language* 3, no. 4 (October 1976): 63–71.

Art & Language. "Art and Language." *Art-Language* 3, no. 2 (May 1975): 41–43.
Art & Language. *Art & Language: Texte zum Phänomen Kunst und Sprache.* Cologne: DuMont, 1972.
Art & Language. "'Artists Meeting for Cultural Change' and 'Anti-Imperialist Cultural Union': A History of Two Cultural Organizations, as Illustration." *Art-Language* 4, no. 2 (October 1977): 66–81.
Art & Language. *Blurting in A&L.* New York and Halifax: Art & Language Press and Nova Scotia College of Art, 1973.
Art & Language. "Brainstorming—New York." *Art-Language* 3, no. 2 (May 1975): 31–40.
Art & Language. "Comparative Models." In Van Abbemuseum, *Art & Language,* 51–62. Eindhoven: Van Abbemuseum, 1980.
Art & Language. "Doge City." *Art-Language* 3, no. 4 (October 1976): 49–62.
Art & Language. "Frameworks." In *Art & Language,* 1–14. Eindhoven: Van Abbemuseum, 1980.
Art & Language. "Handbook(s) to Going-On." *Art-Language* 2, no. 4 (July 1974).
Art & Language. "The International: England 1 (o.g.) USA 1 (o.g.)." *Art-Language* 3, no. 3 (June 1976): 66–72.
[Art & Language.] "Introduction." *Art-Language* 1, no. 1 (May 1969): 1–10.
Art & Language. "Making Art from a Different Place." In Art Gallery of Western Australia, *Ian Burn: Minimal-Conceptual Work 1965–1970,* 7–17. Perth: Art Gallery of Western Australia, 1992.
Art & Language. "'Mr. Lin Yutang Refers to "Fair Play" . . . ?'" *Art-Language* 3, no. 2 (May 1975): 68–80.
Art & Language. "A Note on Pseudo-Debate." *Art-Language* 3, no. 2 (May 1975): 95.
Art & Language. "Pedagogical Sketchbook (AL)." *Art-Language* 3, no. 2 (May 1975): 31–40.
Art & Language. "Rambling: To Partial Correspondents." *Art-Language* 3, no. 2 (May 1975): 46–51.
Art & Language. "Strategy Is Political: Dear M. . . ." *Art-Language* 3, no. 2 (May 1975): 81–86.
Art & Language. "'To Begin With, While I Am Clearly a Marxist Sympathizer. . . .'" *Art-Language* 3, no. 2 (May 1975): 13–28.
Art & Language. "Utopian Prayers and Infantile Marxism." *Art-Language* 3, no. 2 (May 1975): 89–92.
Art & Language. "Voices Off: Reflections on Conceptual Art." *Critical Inquiry* 33, no. 1 (autumn 2006): 113–135.
Art & Language and the Red Crayola. *Corrected Slogans.* CD. Drag City/Dexter's Cigar, 1997.

Art Gallery of Western Australia. *Ian Burn: Minimal-Conceptual Work 1965–1970.* Perth: Art Gallery of Western Australia, 1992.

"The Artist and Politics: A Symposium." *Artforum* (September 1970): 35–39.

Atkinson, Terry. "Concerning the Article 'The Dematerialization of Art.'" In *Conceptual Art: A Critical Anthology*, edited by Alexander Alberro and Blake Stimson, 52–58. Cambridge, MA: MIT Press, 1999.

Atkinson, Terry. "From an Art & Language Point of View." *Art-Language* 1, no. 2 (February 1970): 25–60.

Atkinson, Terry. *Indexing, the World War I Moves, and the Ruins of Conceptualism.* Manchester: Cornhouse, 1992.

Atkinson, Terry. "Rites of Passage." *Art & Design* 34 (1994): 12–19.

Atkinson, Terry. *Work 1977–1983.* London: Whitechapel Art Gallery, 1983.

Auping, Michael. "A Fox." In *30 Years: Interviews and Outtakes*, 59–75. Fort Worth and Munich: Modern Art Museum of Fort Worth and Prestel, 2007.

Auping, Michael. *Jenny Holzer.* New York: Universe, 1992.

Bainbridge, David. "Notes on M1 (1)." *Art-Language* 1, no. 1 (May 1969): 19–22.

Bainbridge, David. "Notes on M1 (2)." *Art-Language* 1, no. 1 (May 1969): 30–32.

Baldwin, Michael. "Notes on M1." *Art-Language* 1, no. 1 (May 1969): 23–29.

Baldwin, Michael. "Remarks on Air-Conditioning: An Extravaganza of Blandness." *Arts Magazine* 42, no. 2 (November 1967): 22–23.

Baldwin, Michael, Charles Harrison, and Mel Ramsden. "Art History, Art Criticism and Explanation." *Art History* 4, no. 4 (December 1981): 432–456.

Baldwin, Michael, and Philip Pilkington. "For Thomas Hobbes." *The Fox* 1, no. 1 (1975): 8–17.

Barber, Bruce, ed. *Conceptual Art: The NSCAD Connection: 1967–1973.* Halifax: Press of the Nova Scotia College of Art & Design, 2001.

Barber, Bruce, ed. *Condé and Beveridge: Class Works.* Halifax: Press of the Nova Scotia College of Art & Design, 2008.

Barker, Heather, and Charles Green. "Flight from the Object: Donald Brook, Inhibodress and the Emergence of Post-Studio Art in Early 1970s Sydney." *Melbourne Art Journal* 4 (2009): 1–23.

Barker, Heather, and Charles Green. "No Place Like Home: Australian Art History and Contemporary Art at the Start of the 1970s." *Journal of Art Historiography* 4 (June 2011): 1–17.

Barker, Heather, and Charles Green. "The Provincialism Problem: Terry Smith and Center-Periphery Art History." *Journal of Art Historiography* 3 (December 2010): 1–17.

Barthelme, Frederic [*sic*]. "Three from May 23rd, 1969." *Art-Language* 1, no. 2 (February 1970): 8–10.

Becker, Howard S. *Artworlds.* Berkeley: University of California Press, 1982.

Becker, Lutz. "Art for an Avant-Garde Society: Belgrade in the 1970s." In *East Art Map: Contemporary Art and Eastern Europe*, edited by IRWIN, 390–400. London: Afterall, 2006.

Beke, László. "Conceptual Tendencies in Eastern European Art." In *Global Conceptualism: Points of Origin, 1950s–1980s*, edited by Luis Camnitzer, Jane Farver, and Rachel Weiss, 41–51. New York: Queens Museum of Art, 1999.

Belting, Hans, and Andrea Buddensieg, eds. *The Global Art World: Audiences, Markets, and Museums*. Ostfildern: Hatje Kantz Verlag, 2009.

Benchley, Peter. "The Lumpen-Headache." *The Fox* 3 (1976): 1–37.

Bergvall, Caroline, Laynie Browne, Teresa Carmody, and Vanessa Place, eds. *I'll Drown My Book: Conceptual Writing by Women*. Los Angeles: Les Figues, 2012.

Berlin, Isaiah. *The Hedgehog and the Fox: An Essay on Tolstoy's View of History*. New York: Simon and Schuster, 1953.

Berlin, Isaiah. "Lev Tolstoy's Historical Scepticism." *Oxford Slavonic Papers* 2 (1951): 17–54.

Beveridge, Karl, and Ian Burn. "Don Judd." *The Fox* 2 (1975): 129–143.

Bowles, John P. *Adrian Piper: Race, Gender, and Embodiment*. Durham, NC: Duke University Press, 2011.

Breakstone, Jill, Michael Corris, Preston Heller, and Andrew Menard. "Now about This Storefront." *Studio International*, March–April 1976, 107–109.

Brook, Donald. "Flight from the Object." In *Concerning Contemporary Art: The Power Lectures 1968–1973*, edited by Bernard Smith, 16–34. Sydney: Clarendon, 1975.

Bryan-Wilson, Julia. *Art Workers: Art and Radical Politics in the Vietnam War Era*. Berkeley: University of California Press, 2009.

Buchloh, Benjamin. "Buchloh Replies to Kosuth and Seth Siegelaub." *October* 57 (summer 1991): 158–161.

Buchloh, Benjamin H. D. "Conceptual Art 1962–1969: From the Aesthetic of Administration to the Critique of Institutions." *October* 55 (winter 1990): 105–143.

Buchloh, Benjamin H. D. "Hans Haacke: Memory and Instrumental Reason." *Art in America* 76, no. 2 (February 1988): 97–108, 157–159.

Buchloh, Benjamin H. D. "The Press of NSCAD: A Brief Incomplete History and Its Future Books." In *NSCAD: The Nova Scotia College of Art & Design*, edited by Garry N. Kennedy, 64–75. Halifax: Press of the Nova Scotia College of Art & Design, 1982.

Buchloh, Benjamin H. D., Serge Guilbaut, and David Solkin, eds. *Modernism and Modernity: The Vancouver Conference Papers*. Halifax: Press of the Nova Scotia College of Art & Design, 2004.

Bürger, Peter. *Theory of the Avant-Garde*. Minneapolis: University of Minnesota Press, 1984.

Burn, Ian. "Art Is What We Do, Culture Is What We Do to Other Artists." In *Dialogue*, 131–139. Sydney: Allen & Unwin, 1991.

Burn, Ian. "Art-Language, Volume 3 Number 2." *The Fox* 2 (1975): 52–57.

Burn, Ian. "The Art Market: Affluence and Degradation." In *Dialogue*, 152–166. Sydney: Allen & Unwin, 1991.

Burn, Ian. "Conceptual Art as Art." In *Dialogue*, 125–130. Sydney: Allen & Unwin, 1991.

Burn, Ian. "Dialogue." In *Conceptual Art: A Critical Anthology*, edited by Alexander Alberro and Blake Stimson, 110–111. Cambridge, MA: MIT Press, 1999.

Burn, Ian. *Dialogue*. Sydney: Allen & Unwin, 1991.

Burn, Ian. "Situation-Identity." In *Modernism and Australia: Documents on Art, Design and Architecture 1917–1967*, edited by Ann Stephen, Andrew McNamara, and Philip Goad, 783–789. Melbourne: Miegunyah Press, 2006.

Burn, Ian. "The 'Sixties: Crisis and Aftermath (Or the Memoirs of an Ex-Conceptual Artist)." In *Conceptual Art: A Critical Anthology*, edited by Alexander Alberro and Blake Stimson, 392–408. Cambridge, MA: MIT Press, 1999.

Burn, Ian, and Mel Ramsden. "Four Wages of Sense." *Art-Language* 2, no. 1 (February 1972): 28–37.

Burn, Ian, and Mel Ramsden. "Problems of Art & Language Space." *Art-Language* 2, no. 3 (September 1973): 53–72.

Burn, Ian, and Mel Ramsden. "Proceedings," in Kynaston McShine, *Information*, 32–35. New York: Museum of Modern Art, 1970.

Burn, Ian, and Mel Ramsden. "A Question of Epistemic Adequacy." *Studio International* 182, no. 937 (October 1971): 132–135.

Burn, Ian, and Mel Ramsden. "Some Questions on the Characterization of Questions." *Art-Language* 2, no. 2 (summer 1972): 1 10.

Burn, Ian, Mel Ramsden, and Terry Smith. "Draft for an Anti-Textbook." *Art-Language* 3, no. 1 (September 1974).

Butler, Cornelia, and other authors. *From Conceptualism to Feminism: Lucy Lippard's Numbers Shows 1969–74*. London: Afterall, 2012.

Camnitzer, Luis. *Conceptualism in Latin American Art: Didactics of Liberation*. Austin: University of Texas Press, 2007.

Camnitzer, Luis, Jane Farver, and Rachel Weiss. "Foreword." In *Global Conceptualism: Points of Origin, 1950s–1980s*, edited by Luis Camnitzer, Jane Farver, and Rachel Weiss, vii–xi. New York: Queens Museum of Art, 1999.

Camnitzer, Luis, Jane Farver, and Rachel Weiss, eds. *Global Conceptualism: Points of Origin, 1950s–1980s*. New York: Queens Museum of Art, 1999.

Catalog Committee of Artists Meeting for Cultural Change. *An Anti-Catalog*. New York: Catalog Committee of Artists Meeting for Cultural Change, 1977.

Charlesworth, Sarah. "A Declaration of Dependence." *The Fox* 1, no. 1 (1975): 1–7.

Charlesworth, Sarah. "For Artists Meeting." *The Fox* 3 (1976): 40–59.
Charlesworth, Sarah. "Memo for *The Fox*." *The Fox* 2 (1975): 34–38.
Cherix, Christophe. *In and Out of Amsterdam: Travels in Conceptual Art, 1960–1976*. New York: Museum of Modern Art, 2009.
Chomsky, Noam. *Aspects of the Theory of Syntax*. Cambridge, MA: MIT Press, 1965.
Clark, Kenneth. *Provincialism*. Oxford: Oxford University Press, 1962.
Clark, T. J. *Farewell to an Idea: Episodes from a History of Modernism*. New Haven, CT: Yale University Press, 1999.
Cockcroft, Eva. "Abstract Expressionism, Weapon of the Cold War." *Artforum* (June 1974): 39–41.
Coleman, Peter. *Obscenity, Blasphemy, Sedition: Censorship in Australia*. Brisbane: Jacaranda Press, 1974.
Conceptual Architecture. Hong Kong: Sandu, 2010.
"Conceptual Art and the Reception of Duchamp." *October* 70 (fall 1994): 127–146.
Condé, Carole, and Karl Beveridge. "The Edge of Edge." *The Fox* 3 (1976): 80–84.
Cornelis, Jef. *Documenta 5*. DVD. Zurich: JRP|Ringier, 2012.
Corris, Michael, ed. *Conceptual Art: Theory, Myth, and Practice*. Cambridge: Cambridge University Press, 2004.
Corris, Michael. "The Dialogical Imagination: The Conversational Aesthetic of Conceptual Art." In *Neo-Avant-Garde*, edited by David Hopkins, 301–310. Amsterdam: Rodopi, 2006.
Corris, Michael. "The Fine Structure of Collaboration." *Art-Language* 2, no. 3 (September 1973): 34–37.
Corris, Michael. "Inside a New York Art Gang: Selected Documents of Art & Language, New York." In *Conceptual Art: A Critical Anthology*, edited by Alexander Alberro and Blake Stimson, 60–71. Cambridge, MA: MIT Press, 1999.
Corris, Michael. "Introduction: An Invisible College in an Anglo-American World." In *Conceptual Art: Theory, Myth, and Practice*, edited by Michael Corris, 1–18. Cambridge: Cambridge University Press, 2004.
Corris, Michael, Preston Heller, and Andrew Menard. "The Organization of Culture under Monopoly Capitalism, Part I: 'How Do You Feel about the Arts and Artifacts Indemnity Act?' The Organization of Culture under Monopoly Capitalism, Part II: Culture Ain't No Headless Horseman." *The Fox* 3 (1976): 128–154.
Corris, Michael, and Mel Ramsden. "Frameworks and Phantoms." *Art-Language* 2, no. 3 (September 1973): 38–52.
Costello, Diarmuid, and Margaret Iversen, eds. *Photography after Conceptual Art*. Chichester: Wiley-Blackwell, 2010.
Crane, Diana. *Invisible Colleges: Diffusion of Knowledge in Scientific Communities*. Chicago: University of Chicago Press, 1972.

Crane, Diana. "Social Structure in a Group of Scientists: A Test of the 'Invisible College' Hypothesis." *American Sociological Review* 34, no. 3 (June 1969): 335–352.
Crane, Diana. *The Transformation of the Avant-Garde: The New York Art World, 1940–1985*. Chicago: University of Chicago Press, 1987.
Crimp, Douglas. *On the Museum's Ruins*. Cambridge, MA: MIT Press, 1993.
Crow, Thomas. "Art Criticism in the Age of Incommensurate Values: On the Thirtieth Anniversary of *Artforum*." In *Modern Art and the Common Culture*, 85–93. New Haven, CT: Yale University Press, 1996.
Crow, Thomas. *The Intelligence of Art*. Chapel Hill: University of North Carolina Press, 1999.
Crow, Thomas. *Modern Art in the Common Culture*. New Haven: Yale University Press, 1996.
Crow, Thomas. *The Rise of the Sixties: American and European Art in the Era of Dissent*. New York: Abrams, 1996.
Crow, Thomas. "Unwritten Histories of Conceptual Art." In *Art after Conceptual Art*, edited by Alexander Alberro and Sabeth Buchmann, 53–64. Cambridge, MA, and Vienna: MIT Press and Generali Foundation, 2006.
Danto, Arthur. "The Artworld." *Journal of Philosophy* 61, no. 19 (October 15, 1964): 571–584.
da Vinci, Mona. "The Fox and Other Fairy Tales." *Soho Weekly News*, December 25, 1975, 17.
Dumbadze, Alexander. *Bas Jan Ader: Death Is Elsewhere*. Chicago: University of Chicago Press, 2013.
Dworkin, Craig. *No Medium*. Cambridge, MA: MIT Press, 2013.
Dworkin, Craig, and Kenneth Goldsmith, eds. *Against Expression: An Anthology of Conceptual Writing*. Evanston, IL: Northwestern University Press, 2011.
Eleey, Peter. *The Quick and the Dead*. Minneapolis: Walker Art Center, 2009.
Erjavec, Aleš. "Neue Slowenische Kunst—New Slovenian Art: Slovenia, Yugoslavia, Self-Management, and the 1980s." In *Postmodernism and the Postsocialist Condition: Politicized Art under Late Socialism*, edited by Aleš Erjavec, 135–174. Berkeley: University of California Press, 2003.
Feyerabend, Paul. *Against Method*, 3rd ed. London: Verso, 1993.
Feyerabend, Paul. "Against Method: Outline of an Anarchistic Theory of Knowledge." In *Analyses of Theories and Methods of Physics and Psychology*, edited by Michael Radner and Stephen Winokur, 17–130. Minneapolis: University of Minnesota Press, 1970.
Feyerabend, Paul. "Wittgenstein's *Philosophical Investigations*." In *Problems of Empiricism: Philosophical Papers*, vol. 2, 99–130. Cambridge: Cambridge University Press, 1981.

Fogle, Douglas. *The Last Picture Show: Artists Using Photography, 1960–1982*. Minneapolis: Walker Art Center, 2003.

Foster, Hal. "Art Critics in Extremis." In *Design and Crime and Other Diatribes*, 104–122. London: Verso, 2002.

Foster, Hal. *The Return of the Real*. Cambridge, MA: MIT Press, 1996.

Fried, Michael. "Art and Objecthood." *Artforum*, June 1967, 12–23.

Gale, Peggy, ed. *Artists Talk: 1969–1977*. Halifax: Press of the Nova Scotia College of Art & Design, 2004.

Gao Minglu. "From Elite to Small Man: The Many Faces of a Transitional Avant-Garde in Mainland China." In *Inside Out: New Chinese Art*, edited by Gao Minglu, 149–166. New York and Berkeley: San Francisco Museum of Modern Art, Asia Society Galleries, and University of California Press, 1998.

Gao Minglu. *Total Modernity and the Avant-Garde in Twentieth-Century Chinese Art*. Cambridge, MA: MIT Press, 2011.

Gerber, Douglas E., ed. *Greek Iambic Poetry: From the Seventh to the Fifth Centuries BC*. Cambridge, MA: Harvard University Press, 1999.

Gilbert, Christopher. "Art & Language and the Institutional Form in Anglo-American Collectivism." In *Collectivism after Modernism: The Art of Social Imagination after 1945*, edited by Blake Stimson and Gregory Sholette, 77–93. Minneapolis: University of Minnesota Press, 2007.

Gilbert, Christopher. "Art & Language, New York, Discusses Its Social Relations in 'The Lumpen-Headache.'" In *Conceptual Art: Theory, Myth, and Practice*, edited by Michael Corris, 326–341. Cambridge: Cambridge University Press, 2004.

Goldie, Peter, and Elisabeth Schellekens, eds. *Philosophy and Conceptual Art*. Oxford: Oxford University Press, 2007.

Goldie, Peter, and Elisabeth Schellekens. *Who's Afraid of Conceptual Art?* London: Routledge, 2010.

Green, Charles. *The Third Hand: Collaboration in Art from Conceptualism to Postmodernism*. Minneapolis: University of Minnesota Press, 2001.

Greenberg, Clement. "After Abstract Expressionism." In *The Collected Essays and Criticism, Vol. 4: Modernism with a Vengeance, 1957–1969*, edited by John O'Brian, 121–134. Chicago: University of Chicago Press, 1993.

Greenberg, Clement. "'American-Type' Painting." In *The Collected Essays and Criticism, Vol. 3: Affirmations and Refusals, 1950–1956*, edited by John O'Brian, 217–236. Chicago: University of Chicago Press, 1993.

Greenberg, Clement. "Avant-Garde and Kitsch." In *The Collected Essays and Criticism, Vol. 1: Perceptions and Judgments, 1939–1944*, edited by John O'Brian, 5–22. Chicago: University of Chicago Press, 1986.

Groys, Boris. *History Becomes Form: Moscow Conceptualism*. Cambridge, MA: MIT Press, 2010.

Groys, Boris. "Moscow Romantic Conceptualism." In *History Becomes Form: Moscow Conceptualism*, 35–56. Cambridge, MA: MIT Press, 2010.
Guercio, Gabriele. "Introduction." In Joseph Kosuth, *Art after Philosophy and After: Collected Writings, 1966–1990*, edited by Gabriele Guercio, xxi–xlii. Cambridge, MA: MIT Press, 1991.
Guerra, Carles. *Art & Language Uncompleted: The Philippe Méaille Collection*. Barcelona: Museum of Contemporary Art Barcelona, 2014.
Haidu, Rachel. *The Absence of Work: Marcel Broodthaers, 1964–1976*. Cambridge, MA: MIT Press, 2010.
Harrison, Charles. "Against Precedents." In Christian Rattemeyer and other authors, *Exhibiting the New Art: "Op Losse Schroeven" and "When Attitudes Become Form" 1969*, 194–199. London: Afterall, 2010.
Harrison, Charles, ed. *Art & Language in Practice, Vol. 2: Simposi crític/Critical Symposium*. Barcelona: Fundació Antoni Tàpies, 1999.
Harrison, Charles. "Art Object and Artwork." In *L'Art conceptual, une perspective*, 2nd ed., edited by Claude Gintz, 61–64. Paris: Musée d'Art Moderne de la Ville de Paris, 1989.
Harrison, Charles. *Conceptual Art and Painting: Further Essays on Art & Language*. Cambridge, MA: MIT Press, 2001.
Harrison, Charles. "Conceptual Art: Myths and Scandals." *Artscribe* 80 (March–April 1990): 15–16.
Harrison, Charles. *Essays on Art & Language*. Cambridge, MA: MIT Press, 2001.
Harrison, Charles. *Looking Back*. London: Ridinghouse, 2011.
Harrison, Charles. *Since 1950: Art and Its Criticism*. New Haven, CT: Yale University Press, 2009.
Harrison, Charles, and Fred Orton. *A Provisional History of Art & Language*. Paris: Galerie Eric Fabre, 1982.
Hart, H. L. A. *The Concept of Law*. Oxford: Oxford University Press, 1961.
Hassan, Salah M., and Olu Oguibe, eds. *Authentic/Ex-Centric: Conceptualism in Contemporary African Art*. Venice: La Biennale di Venezia, 2001.
Heller, Preston, and Andrew Menard. "Kozloff: Criticism in Absentia." *Artforum*, February 1973, 32–36.
Héman, Suzanna, Jurrie Poot, and Hripsimé Visser, eds. *Conceptual Art in the Netherlands and Belgium 1965–1975: Artists, Collectors, Galleries, Documents, Exhibitions, Events*. Amsterdam and Rotterdam: Stedelijk Museum and NAi, 2002.
Higgins, Andrew. "Clement Greenberg and the Idea of the Avant Garde." *Studio International* 182, no. 937 (October 1971): 144–147.
Jackson, Matthew Jesse. *The Experimental Group: Ilya Kabakov, Moscow Conceptualism, Soviet Avant-Gardes*. Chicago: University of Chicago Press, 2010.

Jones, Caroline A. "The Modernist Paradigm: The Artworld and Thomas Kuhn." *Critical Inquiry* 26, no. 3 (spring 2000): 488–528.

Karshan, Donald. *Conceptual Art and Conceptual Aspects*. New York: New York Cultural Center, 1970.

Keenan, David. "The Merry Prankster." *The Wire* 258 (August 2005): 34–41.

Kennedy, Garry Neill. *The Last Art College, 1968–1978*. Cambridge, MA: MIT Press, 2012.

Kirby, Sandy. *Artists and Unions: A Critical Tradition: A Report on the Art and Working Life Program*. Redfern: Australia Council, 1992.

Kirby, Sandy, ed. *Ian Burn, Art: Critical, Political*. Sydney: University of Western Sydney, 1996.

Kosuth, Joseph. "Art after Philosophy." In *Art after Philosophy and After: Collected Writings, 1966–1990*, edited by Gabriele Guercio, 13–32. Cambridge, MA: MIT Press, 1991.

Kosuth, Joseph. *Art after Philosophy and After: Collected Writings, 1966–1990*, edited by Gabriele Guercio. Cambridge, MA: MIT Press, 1991.

Kosuth, Joseph. *Art Investigations and "Problematics" since 1965*. Luzern: Kunstmuseum Luzern, 1973.

Kosuth, Joseph. "The Artist as Anthropologist." In *Art after Philosophy and After: Collected Writings, 1966–1990*, edited by Gabriele Guercio, 107–128. Cambridge, MA: MIT Press, 1991.

Kosuth, Joseph. "Introductory Note by the American Editor." *Art-Language* 1, no. 2 (February 1970): 1–4.

Kosuth, Joseph. "1975." In *Art after Philosophy and After: Collected Writings, 1966–1990*, edited by Gabriele Guercio, 129–143. Cambridge, MA: MIT Press, 1991.

Kosuth, Joseph. "(Notes) on an 'Anthropologized' Art." In *Art after Philosophy and After: Collected Writings, 1966–1990*, edited by Gabriele Guercio, 95–101. Cambridge, MA: MIT Press, 1991.

Kosuth, Joseph, and Seth Siegelaub. "Joseph Kosuth and Seth Siegelaub Reply to Benjamin Buchloh on Conceptual Art." *October* 57 (summer 1991): 152–157.

Kotz, Liz. *Words to Be Looked At: Language in 1960s Art*. Cambridge, MA: MIT Press, 2007.

Kozloff, Max. "American Painting during the Cold War." *Artforum*, May 1973, 43–54.

Kozloff, Max. "The Trouble with Art-as-Idea." *Artforum*, September 1972, 33–37.

Kramer, Hilton. "Yankee Go Home." *New York Times*, June 6, 1976, 1, 27.

Krauss, Rosalind. *A Voyage on the North Sea: Art in the Age of the Post-Medium Condition*. London: Thames and Hudson, 2000.

Kristeller, Paul Oskar. "The Modern System of the Arts." In *Renaissance Thought and the Arts*, 163–227. Princeton, NJ: Princeton University Press, 1990.

Kuhn, Annette. "Culture Shock." *Village Voice*, April 15, 1975, 100.

Kuhn, Annette. "Waltz Me Around Again, MoMA." *Village Voice*, August 18, 1975, 42.

Kuhn, Thomas S. *The Structure of Scientific Revolutions*, 3rd ed. Chicago: University of Chicago Press, 1996.

Lakatos, Imre. "Falsification and the Methodology of Scientific Research Programmes." In *Criticism and the Growth of Knowledge*, edited by Imre Lakatos and Alan Musgrave, 91–196. Cambridge: Cambridge University Press, 1970.

Lakatos, Imre. *Proofs and Refutations: The Logic of Mathematical Discovery*. Cambridge: University of Cambridge Press, 1976.

Lee, Pamela M. "Boundary Issues: The Art World under the Sign of Globalism." *Artforum* 42, no. 3 (February 2003): 164–167.

Lee, Pamela M. *Forgetting the Art World*. Cambridge, MA: MIT Press, 2012.

Lewis, Flora. "Venice Biennale's Revival Offers Vitality." *New York Times*, August 25, 1976, 22.

LeWitt, Sol. "Sentences on Conceptual Art." *Art-Language* 1, no. 1 (May 1969): 11–13.

Licht, Jennifer. *Some Recent American Art*. Melbourne: National Gallery of Victoria, 1973.

Lippard, Lucy. "The Art Workers' Coalition." In *Idea Art*, edited by Gregory Battcock, 102–115. New York: Dutton, 1973.

Lippard, Lucy. *Lucy Lippard: 4,492,040*. Vancouver: New Documents, 2012.

Lippard, Lucy. "Notes on Seeing Some Recent American Art in New Zealand." *Auckland City Art Gallery Quarterly* 59 (1975): 2–3.

Lippard, Lucy R. *Six Years: The Dematerialization of the Art Object from 1966 to 1972*. New York: Praeger, 1973.

Lippard, Lucy R., and John Chandler. "The Dematerialization of Art." *Art International*, February 1968, 31–36.

Lukács, Georg. *History and Class Consciousness: Studies in Marxist Dialectics*. Cambridge, MA: MIT Press, 1971.

Malik, Amna. "Conceptualising 'Black' British Art through the Lens of Exile." In *Exiles, Diasporas, and Strangers*, edited by Kobena Mercer, 166–189. Cambridge, MA, and London: MIT Press and Iniva, 2008.

Marioni, Tom. "Real Social Realism." *Vision* 2 (1976): 7–17.

Marner, Nancy. "Art and Politics '77." *Art in America*, July–August 1977, 64–66.

Masterman, Margaret. "The Nature of a Paradigm." In *Criticism and the Growth of Knowledge*, edited by Imre Lakatos and Alan Musgrave, 59–89. Cambridge: Cambridge University Press, 1970.

McCaughey, Patrick. "Notes on the Centre: New York." *Quadrant*, November 1970, 76–80.

McLuhan, Marshall. *The Gutenberg Galaxy*. Toronto: University of Toronto Press, 1962.

McLuhan, Marshall. *Understanding Media*. New York: McGraw-Hill, 1964.

McShine, Kynaston. *Information*. New York: Museum of Modern Art, 1970.

Meltzer, Eve. *Systems We Have Loved: Conceptual Art, Affect, and the Antihumanist Turn*. Chicago: University of Chicago Press, 2013.

Mercer, Kobena. "Adrian Piper, 1970–1975: Exiled on Main Street." In *Exiles, Diasporas, and Strangers*, edited by Kobena Mercer, 146–165. Cambridge, MA, and London: MIT Press and Iniva, 2008.

Meyer, Ursula, ed. *Conceptual Art*. New York: Dutton, 1972.

Meyer, Ursula. "Introduction." In *Conceptual Art*, edited by Ursula Meyer, vii–xx. New York: Dutton, 1972.

Millet, Catherine. "Interview with *Art-Language*." In *Conceptual Art: A Critical Anthology*, edited by Alexander Alberro and Blake Stimson, 262–265. Cambridge, MA: MIT Press, 1999.

Moore, Alan W. *Art Gangs: Protest and Counterculture in New York City*. Brooklyn: Autonomedia, 2011.

Morris, Catherine, and Vincent Bonin, eds. *Materializing* Six Years*: Lucy Lippard and the Emergence of Conceptual Art*. Cambridge, MA: MIT Press, 2012.

Newman, Amy. *Challenging Art: Artforum 1962–1974*. New York: SoHo Press, 2003.

Newman, Michael, and Jon Bird, eds. *Rewriting Conceptual Art*. London: Reaktion, 1999.

Oliver, Valerie Cassel. *Double Consciousness: Black Conceptual Art since 1970*. Houston: Contemporary Arts Museum, Houston, 2006.

Osborne, Peter. *Anywhere or Not at All: Philosophy of Contemporary Art*. London: Verso, 2013.

Osborne, Peter. *Conceptual Art*. London: Phaidon, 2002.

Osborne, Peter. "Conceptual Art and/as Philosophy." In *Rewriting Conceptual Art*, edited by Michael Newman and Jon Bird, 47–65. London: Reaktion, 1999.

Osborne, Peter. "An Image of Romanticism: Fragment and Project in Friedrich Schlegel's *Athenaeum Fragments* and Sol LeWitt's *Sentences on Conceptual Art*." In *Sol LeWitt's Sentences on Conceptual Art: Manuscript and Draft Materials 1968–69*, 5–27. Oslo: Office for Contemporary Art Norway, 2009.

Peltomäki, Kirsi. *Situation Aesthetics: The Work of Michael Asher*. Cambridge, MA: MIT Press, 2010.

Philippi, Desa. "Matter of Words: Translations in East European Conceptualism." In *Rewriting Conceptual Art*, edited by Michael Newman and Jon Bird, 152–168. London: Reaktion, 1999.

Phillips, A. A. "The Cultural Cringe." In *Modernism and Australia: Documents on

Art, Design and Architecture 1917–1967, edited by Ann Stephen, Andrew McNamara, and Philip Goad, 623–627. Melbourne: Miegunyah Press, 2006.
Pilkington, Philip, and David Rushton. "Don Judd's Dictum and Its Emptiness." In Van Abbemuseum, *Art & Language*, 44–47. Eindhoven: Van Abbemuseum, 1980.
Piper, Adrian. "Ian Burn's Conceptualism." In *Conceptual Art: Theory, Myth, and Practice*, edited by Michael Corris, 342–358. Cambridge: Cambridge University Press, 2004.
Piper, Adrian. "A Proposal for Pricing Works of Art." *The Fox* 2 (1975): 48–49.
Piper, Adrian. "To Art (Reg. intrans. V.)." *The Fox* 1, no. 1 (1975): 60–65.
Place, Vanessa, and Robert Fitterman. *Notes on Conceptualisms*. New York: Ugly Duckling Press, 2009.
Plekhanov, Georgi. *Art and Social Life*. Moscow: Progress, 1977.
Pogačnik, Marko, and I. G. Plamen. "OHO Manifesto." In *Primary Documents: A Sourcebook for Eastern and Central European Art since the 1950s*, edited by Laura Hoptman and Tomáš Pospiszyl, 92–95. New York and Cambridge, MA: Museum of Modern Art and MIT Press, 2002.
Pólya, George. *How to Solve It*. Princeton, NJ: Princeton University Press, 1971.
Popović, Zoran. *Borba u New Yorku*. Zagreb: Centar za fotografiju film i TV, 1977.
Popović, Zoran. "For Self-Management Art." In *Theories and Documents of Contemporary Art: A Sourcebook of Artists' Writings*, edited by Kristine Stiles and Peter Selz, 846–849. Berkeley: University of California Press, 1996.
Popović, Zoran, and Jasna Tijardović. "A Note on Art in Yugoslavia." *The Fox* 1, no. 1 (1975): 49–52.
(Provisional) Art & Language. *"The Intellectual Life of the Ruling Class Gets Its Apotheosis in a World of Doris Days."* Banbury: Art & Language Press, 1976.
Ramsden, Mel. "On Practice." In *Institutional Critique: An Anthology of Artists' Writings*, edited by Alexander Alberro and Blake Stimson, 170–199. Cambridge, MA: MIT Press, 2009.
Ratcliff, Carter. "Adversary Spaces." *Artforum*, October 1972, 40–44.
Raunig, Gerald, and Gene Ray, eds. *Art and Contemporary Critical Practice: Reinventing Institutional Critique*. London: MayFly, 2009.
Richard, Sophie. *Unconcealed: The International Network of Conceptual Artists 1967–77. Dealers, Exhibitions and Public Collections*. London: Ridinghouse, 2009.
Richardson, E. P. *American Art: An Exhibition from the Collection of Mr. and Mrs. John D. Rockefeller 3rd*. San Francisco: Fine Arts Museums of San Francisco, 1976.
Roberts, John. "Conceptual Art and Imageless Truth." In *Conceptual Art: Theory, Myth, and Practice*, edited by Michael Corris, 305–325. Cambridge: Cambridge University Press, 2004.

Roberts, John, ed. *The Impossible Document: Photography and Conceptual Art in Britain 1966–1976*. London: Cameraworks, 1997.
Roberts, John. *The Intangibilities of Form: Skill and Deskilling in Art after the Readymade*. London: Verso, 2007.
Robertson, Clive. "The Art World and Its Other: Forever the Twain Shall Meet?" In *Condé and Beveridge: Class Works*, edited by Bruce Barber, 37–44. Halifax: Press of the Nova Scotia College of Art & Design, 2008.
Rose, Barbara, and Irving Sandler. "Sensibility of the Sixties." *Art in America*, January–February 1967, 44–57.
Rosenfeld, Alla. *Moscow Conceptualism in Context*. Munich: Prestel, 2011.
Rushton, Dave. *Don Quixote's Art and Television*. Edinburgh: Institute of Local Television, 1998.
Sandler, Irving. *The Triumph of American Painting: A History of Abstract Expressionism*. New York: Praeger, 1970.
Schlatter, Christian. *Art conceptuel forms conceptuelles*. Paris: Galerie 1900 Δ 2000, 1990.
Seifermann, Ellen, and Jörg Heiser. *Romantischer Konzeptualismus/Romantic Conceptualism*. Bielefeld: Kerber Verlag, 2007.
Shanken, Edward A. "Art in the Information Age: Technology and Conceptual Art." *Leonardo* 35, no. 4 (August 2002): 433–438.
Skrebowski, Luke. "All Systems Go: Recovering Hans Haacke's Systems Aesthetics." *Grey Room* 30 (August 2008): 54–83.
Smith, Bernard, with Terry Smith. *Australian Painting, 1788–1990*, 3rd ed. Melbourne: Oxford University Press, 1991.
Smith, Terry. "Art and Art and Language." *Artforum*, February 1974, 49–52.
Smith, Terry, ed. *Art & Language: Australia 1975*. Banbury: Art & Language Press, 1976.
Smith, Terry. "One and Three Ideas: Conceptualism before, during, and after Conceptual Art." In *Moscow Symposium: Conceptualism Revisited*, edited by Boris Groys, 42–72. Berlin: Sternberg Press, 2012.
Smith, Terry. "Peripheries in Motion: Conceptualism and Conceptual Art in Australia and New Zealand." In *Global Conceptualism: Points of Origin, 1950s–1980s*, edited by Luis Camnitzer, Jane Farver, and Rachel Weiss, 87–98. New York: Queens Museum of Art, 1999.
Smith, Terry. "Propositions." In *Conceptual Art: A Critical Anthology*, edited by Alexander Alberro and Blake Stimson, 258–261. Cambridge, MA: MIT Press, 1999.
Smith, Terry. "Provincialism in Art." *Quadrant*, April 1971, 67–71.
Smith, Terry. "The Provincialism Problem." *Artforum*, September 1974, 54–59.
Smith, Terry. "Review: Fighting Modern Masters." *The Fox* 2 (1975): 15–21.
Smith, Terry. "The Tasks of Translation: Art & Language in Australia and New Zea-

land 1975–6." In *Now See Hear! Art, Language and Translation*, edited by Ian Wedde and Gregory Burke, 250–261. Auckland: Victoria University Press, 1990.
Smith, Terry. "Without Revolutionary Theory. . . ." *Studio International*, March–April 1976, 134–137.
Society for Theoretical Art and Analysis. "Proceedings." *Art and Australia*, September 1970, 168.
Society for Theoretical Art and Analysis. "Proceedings." In Donald Karshan, *Conceptual Art and Conceptual Aspects*, 21–22. New York: New York Cultural Center, 1970.
Society for Theoretical Art and Analysis (Ian Burn, Roger Cutforth, and Mel Ramsden). "Proceedings." *Art-Language* 1, no. 3 (June 1970): 1–3.
Stephen, Ann. *On Looking at Looking: The Art and Politics of Ian Burn*. Melbourne: Miegunyah Press, 2006.
Stephen, Ann. "Soft Talk/*Soft-Tape*: The Early Collaborations of Ian Burn and Mel Ramsden." In *Conceptual Art: Theory, Myth, and Practice*, edited by Michael Corris, 80–96. Cambridge: Cambridge University Press, 2004.
Stiles, Kristine, and Peter Selz, eds. *Theories and Documents of Contemporary Art: A Sourcebook of Artists' Writings*. Berkeley: University of California Press, 1996.
Stimson, Blake. "The Promise of Conceptual Art." In *Conceptual Art: A Critical Anthology*, edited by Alexander Alberro and Blake Stimson, xxxviii–lii. Cambridge, MA: MIT Press, 1999.
Šuvaković, Miško. "Art as a Political Machine: Fragments on the Late Socialist and Postsocialist Art of Mitteleuropa and the Balkans." In *Postmodernism and the Postsocialist Condition: Politicized Art under Late Socialism*, edited by Aleš Erjavec, 90–134. Berkeley: University of California Press, 2003.
Šuvaković, Miško. "Conceptual Art." In *Impossible Histories: Historical Avant-Gardes, Neo-Avant-Gardes, and Post-Avant-Gardes in Yugoslavia, 1918–1991*, edited by Dubravka Djurić and Miško Šuvaković, 210–245. Cambridge, MA: MIT Press, 2003.
Šuvaković, Miško. *Konceptualna Umetnost*. Novi Sad: Muzej Savremene Umesnosti Vojvodine, 2007.
Terranova, Charissa N. *Automotive Prosthetic: Technological Mediation and the Car in Conceptual Art*. Austin: University of Texas Press, 2014.
Thomas, Ivor, ed. *Greek Mathematical Works: Aristarchus to Pappus*. Cambridge, MA: Harvard University Press, 1941.
Tijardović, Jasna. "The 'Liquidation' of Art: Self-Management or Self-Protection." *The Fox* 3 (1976): 97–99.
Tomkins, Calvin. *Post- to Neo-: The Art World of the 1980s*. New York: Henry Holt, 1988.

Triple Canopy. *Corrected Slogans: Reading and Writing Conceptualism*. New York and Denver: Triple Canopy and Museum of Contemporary Art Denver, 2012.

U.S. Congress. *The Arts and Artifacts Indemnity Act*, S. 1800, 94th Cong., 1st sess. (December 20, 1975).

Van Abbemuseum. *Art & Language*. Eindhoven: Van Abbemuseum, 1980.

van Winkel, Camiel. *During the Exhibition the Gallery Will Be Closed: Contemporary Art and the Paradoxes of Conceptualism*. Amsterdam: Valiz, 2012.

Wall, Jeff. "'Marks of Indifference': Aspects of Photography in, or as, Conceptual Art." In *Reconsidering the Object of Art: 1965–1975*, edited by Ann Goldstein and Anne Rorimer, 247–258. Cambridge, MA, and Los Angeles: MIT Press and the Museum of Contemporary Art Los Angeles, 1995.

Wark, Jayne. "Conceptual Art and Feminism: Martha Rosler, Adrian Piper, Eleanor Antin, and Martha Wilson." *Women's Art Journal* 22, no. 1 (spring–summer 2001): 44–50.

Welchmann, John C. "'Don't Play It for Laughs': John Baldessari and Conceptual Comedy." In *Black Sphinx: The Comedic in Modern Art*, edited by John C. Welchmann, 245–268. Zurich: JRP|Ringier, 2010.

Welchmann, John C., ed. *Institutional Critique and After*. Zurich: JRP|Ringier, 2006.

West, M. L., ed. *Greek Lyric Poetry*. Oxford: Oxford University Press, 1993.

Witkovsky, Matthew S. *Light Years: Conceptual Art and the Photograph 1964–1977*. Chicago and New Haven: Art Institute of Chicago and Yale University Press, 2011.

Wollen, Peter. "Global Conceptualism and North American Conceptual Art." In *Global Conceptualism: Points of Origin, 1950s–1980s*, edited by Luis Camnitzer, Jane Farver, and Rachel Weiss, 73–85. New York: Queens Museum of Art, 1999.

Wood, William. "A Fish Ceases to Be a Fish: A Critical History of English Conceptual Art 1966–72." PhD diss., University of Sussex, 1998.

Wood, William. "We Are a Cell Aren't We? Art & Language and the Documenta Index." Master's thesis, University of British Columbia, 1992.

Woodard, Komozi. *A Nation within a Nation: Amiri Baraka (LeRoi Jones) and Black Power Politics*. Chapel Hill: University of North Carolina Press, 1999.

Zabel, Igor. "A Short History of OHO." In *East Art Map: Contemporary Art and Eastern Europe*, edited by IRWIN, 410–432. London: Afterall, 2006.

Index

www.ingramcontent.com/pod-product-compliance
Lightning Source LLC
LaVergne TN
LVHW012340100826
845148LV00018B/2905

* 9 7 8 0 8 2 2 3 6 1 6 8 8 *